concept shops

W0412002

concept shops

Ingrid Wenz-Gahler

Ladendesign
für Erlebnis, Emotion
und Erfolg

Shop design
aimed at experience, emotion
and success

Verlagsanstalt
Alexander Koch

Aknowledgements · Danksagung

Die voranschreitende Technik erforderte einige liebe Helfer, ohne die allein die Recherche und Erarbeitung des Buches nie in dieser Zeit fertiggeworden wäre. Mein besonderer Dank gilt daher meinem Mann Volkmar Wenz, meinem Sohn Ingmar, seinen Computerfreunden Gero Pflüger aus Hannover und Christoph Kahse aus Berlin sowie Bernd Fahl von der Medien-Agentur Von Oertzen in Frankfurt/M.
Und mein Dank geht besonders an die Lektorin des Verlages Annette Galinski und an alle Designer, Architekten, Unternehmer und Agenturvertreter, die mir in einer wundervollen Zusammenarbeit mit Geduld und Kompetenz ihr Fachwissen und Vertrauen zur Verfügung gestellt haben.

Advances in technology have necessitated the assistance of several kind helpers, without whom even the research and preparation for this book could never have been completed within the available time. My special thanks go to my husband, Volkmar Wenz, to my son Ingmar and his computer friends – Gero Pflüger from Hanover and Christoph Kahse from Berlin, as well as to Bernd Fahl from the Von Oertzen media agency in Frankfurt/M.
I would also like to express my gratitude to the editor Annette Galinski and to all of the designers, architects, business people and agency representatives who – with patience and competence – have put their professional knowledge and confidence at my disposal in the course of this wonderful co-operation relationship.

Übersetzung / Translation:
Darlene Waldschmidt-Sematat B.A., Frankfurt am Main

ISBN 3-87422-644-1

© 2002 by
Verlagsanstalt Alexander Koch GmbH
Leinfelden-Echterdingen
Das Werk einschließlich aller seiner Teile ist urheberrechtlich geschützt. Jede Verwertung außerhalb der engen Grenzen des Urhebergesetzes (auch Fotokopien, Mikroverfilmung und Übersetzung) ist ohne Zustimmung des Verlages unzulässig und strafbar. Dies gilt auch ausdrücklich für die Einspeicherung und Verarbeitung in elektronischen Systemen jeder Art und von jedem Betreiber.

Produktion: Verlagsbüro Wais & Partner, Stuttgart
Gesamtherstellung: Karl Weinbrenner & Söhne GmbH & Co.
Leinfelden-Echterdingen

Bestellnummer: 644

Inhaltsverzeichnis · Contents

Einleitung · Introduction

Noch nie hat sich die Einzelhandelswelt so drastisch geändert wie in den vergangenen Jahren. Während die Schere zwischen den hochwertigen Top-Läden und Niedrigpreisstätten immer weiter auseinander klafft, entstehen gleichzeitig Einkaufszentren und Markenwelten, die neben Waren vor allem Erlebnisse und Unterhaltung anbieten. Hinzugekommen sind digitale Einkaufswelten, die weltweit und zu jeder Tageszeit mit Informationen, Beratung und Events zur Verfügung stehen.

Der klassische Einzelhandel ist dringend gefordert, seine Marketingstrategien und gestalterischen Konzepte zu überdenken, wenn er den anspruchsvollen, konsum-verwöhnten Verbraucher erreichen will, der in einem Markt zunehmend ähnlicher Produkte Zusatzwerte wie Erlebnisse, Geschichten und Lebensinhalte sucht, die ihm auch die Markenindustrie und der Handel liefern sollen.

Dass es bereits gute und erfolgreiche Konzepte gibt, zeigt das vorliegende Buch. Über vierzig Fachgeschäfte aus den verschiedensten Ländern unserer Welt zeigen, wie fantasievoll sie ihre Produkte präsentieren und ihre Läden mit Leben füllen, um ihren Kunden eine Flattform für Information, Kommunikation, Erlebnis und Träume zu bieten und dadurch eine neue Form der Geschäftsbeziehung aufbauen.

Einzelhandelslandschaft – Einkaufsstätten

Unsere Einzelhandelslandschaft ist heute geprägt von einer Vielzahl an unterschiedlichen Einkaufsstätten, die je nach Standort und Produktangebot versuchen, ihre Kunden zu erreichen.

Da haben wir die vielen, mitunter auch traditionellen Fachgeschäfte wie Apotheken, Optik- und Blumenläden. Es gibt Bäckereien, Metzgerläden und Feinkostgeschäfte, die heute ihr Angebot zunehmend mit gastronomischen Elementen wie Stehimbiss, Café, Partyservice und Mittagstisch vermischt haben. Daneben finden sich Kosmetikgeschäfte, Papierläden, Dekobedarf, Möbel- und Modegeschäfte und natürlich all die Serviceunternehmen wie Reinigungen, Reisebüros, Foto-, Copyshops und Frisöre, um nur einige zu nennen.

Zu manchen Produktbereichen haben sich Fachkaufhäuser entwickelt z.B. für Textilien, Schuhe, Kosmetik. Und zunehmend entstehen auch Fachmärkte nicht nur für Mode

Never before has the retail world been changing as drastically as it has in recent years. While the gap between high end, top quality shops and bargain price retail outlets is growing larger and larger, simultaneously shopping centres and brand name worlds that focus primarily on pleasurable experiences and entertainment in addition to merchandise are being created. Furthermore, these sales locations are now being supplemented by digital shopping worlds that are accessible at any time of the day world wide – providing information, consulting services and events.

The conventional retail trade sector is confronted with a need for urgent action: it is faced with the challenge of rethinking its marketing strategies and its design concepts if it wants to reach today's demanding consumer, who is spoiled by a plethora of consumer goods and services. In a market full of products which are becoming increasingly more similar, this consumer is looking for additional value, such as interesting experiences, stories and life content – and he expects the brand name industry and the retail trade sector to supply it.

This book demonstrates that good and successful concepts already exist. Over forty specialist retail stores located in the most diverse countries of the world illustrate how imaginatively they present their products and infuse their shops with life, offering their customers a platform for information, communication, memorable experiences and dreams – and thus establishing a new form of business relationship.

The retail trade landscape – shopping locales

The retail trade landscape of today is characterised by a large number of different types of shopping locale, which attempt to reach their customers in various ways depending on the location and the range of products.

First of all there are innumerable – in many cases traditional – specialist retail shops, such as pharmacies, opticians' and florists' shops. There are the butchers and the bakers ... and the delicatessen stores, who have increasingly been supplementing their assortment of products with gastronomic elements such as stand-up snack-bars, cafés, party service and luncheon meals. In addition, there are cosmetics stores, stationery, interior decorating, furniture and fashion shops, as well as all of the service related

und Heimtextilien sondern vor allem für den Bau- und Gartenbedarf, für Elektronikprodukte, Sanitärartikel, Tier- und Babynahrung und natürlich Autos. An Tankstellen und Bahnhöfen beginnen sich Convenience-Stores zu etablieren, die mit langen Öffnungszeiten kurzfristig Ersatzbedarf für Reisen oder Wochenende befriedigen, aber auch Serviceleistungen wie Reinigung, Postdienst und Lottoannahme anbieten.

Viele Produktbereiche unter einem Dach werden von Kaufhäusern angeboten, die sich in den vergangenen Jahren zu einer Ansammlung von Markenshops (Shop-in-Shops) gewandelt haben, um überleben zu können. Lebensmittelabteilungen wurden zu Frischemärkten mit Verzehrtheken und Feinkostangeboten aus verschiedenen Ländern. Erweitert wurden in den letzten Jahren diese Angebote durch die Hinzunahme von immer mehr Serviceeinheiten (z.B. Schuhreparatur, Frisöre, Foto) und einer ausgeprägten Handelsgastronomie.

Als Antwort auf viele Großmärkte auf der grünen Wiese entstehen seit drei Jahrzehnten innerstädtische Einkaufsgalerien mit meist gehobenem Sortiment und einer Mischung aus Handel und Gastronomie, Kunst und Kultur – Flaniermeilen für Lebensstil und Luxusansprüche. Hier leben Marken und Spezialgeschäfte nebeneinander und ergänzen sich in ihrem Angebot.

Die aktuellsten Großformen des Handels sind die Shopping Malls, deren Idee aus Amerika kommt (Mall of America, die berühmteste) – wie bei uns z.B. das *CentrO* Oberhausen. Handelsangebote werden hier mit Gastronomie und Freizeiteinrichtungen, mit Bürokomplexen, Banken, Kinos und Kulturanlagen vermischt (*Sony Center, Blue Water*). In den künstlichen Einkaufswelten mit städtischem Charakter kann sich der Kunde stundenlang aufhalten, seine Kinder versorgen lassen, Einkäufe tätigen, bummeln, ins Kino oder in den Fitnessclub gehen, die Reinigung oder den Schuhservice nutzen. In vielen Malls gibt es Events und Sonderveranstaltungen, um die Attraktivität zu erhöhen.

Auch bei den Herstellern hat sich einiges getan. Waren Marken bisher überwiegend in Fachgeschäften und Kaufhäusern präsent, so treten sie zunehmend mit eigenen Markenstores nach außen, um Produkte und Markenbotschaften durch ein geeignetes räumliches Umfeld zu vermitteln. Das beginnt bei Factoryoutlets bis hin zu Marken-Flagshipstores von Modezaren wie *Calvin Klein, Jil Sander, Strenesse* und *Prada,* für die sich die großen Designer ausschließlich der besten Architekten bedienen, die ihre Modesprache baulich in Szene setzen. Es sind teilweise atemberaubende Erlebnisräume, in der die Marke spürbar erlebt werden kann.

Wo sich Modemacher für ihre Produkte Architekturtempel bauen lassen, entwickelten andere Marken ganze Welten um sich herum, um Markengedanken, Image und die Nähe

businesses such as dry cleaning, travel agencies, photographers, copy shops and hairdressing salons, to mention only a few.

In some product areas, large specialist retail stores have been established, e.g. in the area of textiles, shoes and cosmetics. Increasingly, these specialist stores not only exist for fashion and interior decorating textiles, but also for building supply and gardening needs, for electronics products, bathroom fixtures and accessories, for pet and baby food, and of course for cars.

At gas stations and train stations convenience stores with extended business hours are beginning to establish themselves, supplying urgently required items to travellers at short notice or on the weekend, and also offering services such as dry cleaning, postal services or lottery ticket sales.

Department stores offer many product areas all under one roof, but in the past years in order to be able to survive many department stores have evolved into a collection of brand name shops (shop-in-shops). Grocery departments have been transformed into markets with snack counters and delicatessen options offering fresh foods and specialties from various countries. In recent years, to an increasing extent department store retail offers have been supplemented by more service elements (e.g. shoe repair, hairdresser, photo service) and a restaurant section tailored specifically to this retail context.

As a response to the many mega markets on the outskirts of cities, the past three decades have witnessed the development of inner city shopping galleries, which generally offer a high quality spectrum of merchandise and a mixture of retail trade and gastronomy, art and culture – venues for a city stroll steeped in lifestyle and luxury tastes. These locales house brand names and specialist retail shops side by side, allowing them to complement each other's respective range of products.

The most contemporary large scale form of retail trade is the shopping mall, for example the *CentrO* in Oberhausen in Germany, which took its inspiration from America. (The Mall of America is among the most famous.) In this form, retail trade is combined with gastronomic and leisure facilities, as well as with office complexes, banks, movie theatres and cultural institutes. (*Sony Center, Blue Water*). In these artificial shopping worlds imbued with urban character, customers can spend hours of time: taking advantage of supervision for children, they can opt to make purchases or merely window shop, watch a movie or go to the fitness club, utilise dry cleaning or shoe repair services. Many malls organise events and special happenings in order to increase their attractiveness.

There have also been changes with regard to the manufacturers. Formerly, brand name merchandise was generally only available in department stores or specialised retail stores. Today manufacturers are approaching customers

zum Produkt spürbar werden zu lassen, die Geschichte der Unternehmen nachzuvollziehen, ein Material zu erleben wie z.B. bei den *Swarovski Kristallwelten* in Matt in Tirol, das *Sony Center* in Berlin, *Nike Town* in London und Berlin und die *Autostadt* von Volkswagen in Wolfsburg. Viele der neu entstanden Brand Lands – Markenwelten – bieten ebenfalls ein komplexes Freizeit- und Informationsangebot – kombiniert mit Gastronomie und Geschäften für ihre Produkte (*Legoland, Ravensburger Spieleland, Autostadt, Sonycenter, Niketown*), aber auch Kurse, Konzerte, Workshops – eine Vermischung von Produktangebot und Information mit Erlebnischarakter.

Die Vielfalt all dieser Handelstypen zeigt das Spektrum der Handelslandschaft auf, in der sich die Läden befinden, die ich hier vorstellen möchte. Es sind Fachgeschäfte sehr unterschiedlicher Produktbereiche, Markenläden und auch neu entstandene Markenwelten, die sich in Europa, den USA, Südamerika und Japan befinden. Was überrascht, ist, dass es nur wenige kulturelle Eigenheiten gibt, die hier im Ladenkonzept zum Ausdruck kommen. Alle aber haben eines gemeinsam: Sie wollen in und mit ihren Läden ihren Kunden Geschichten erzählen von ihren Produkten, von ihrem Umfeld, ihrem Unternehmen, von ihrer eigenen Kultur und Philosophie. Sie wollen etwas von ihrer Tradition und der Art deutlich machen, wie sie mit ihren Kunden umgehen. All diese Komplexität an Gedanken und Informationen soll der Laden selbst mitteilen durch seine Gestaltungsidee: durch die Architektur, die Produktpräsentation, das Licht, die Farben – aber natürlich auch durch sinnliche Wahrnehmungen wie Düfte, Geräusche oder Musik. Und nicht zuletzt durch die Art, wie Kunden in einem Laden behandelt werden.

Wie verhält sich der Verbraucher?

Auch wenn es Marketingstrategen nicht gefällt, aber ein genaues Kundenprofil lässt sich heute kaum noch erstellen und selbst die soziodemographischen Daten helfen hier kaum weiter. Wir wissen, dass sich die Verbraucher ständig wandeln, dass die Geburtenzahlen rückläufig sind und die älteren Menschen als Konsumenten immer wichtiger werden. Singles und Doppelverdiener-Haushalte nehmen drastisch zu. Anhaltspunkte, die uns über die Kunden noch am meisten aussagen und für ein Handelskonzept zu verwerten sind, erhalten wir aus den Einkaufseinstellungen. Discountorientiert sind die Kunden, die „vor allem billig" einkaufen wollen. Die „Smart Shopper" suchen nach Markenartikeln zu günstigen Preisen; einkaufen ohne Stress möchten die, die auf „Convenience" Stores setzen. Und für einen Großteil der Bevölkerung ist heutzutage Shoppen gehen ein lustvolles und spontanes Freizeitvergnügen wie Sport oder Kino, bei dem es um „Spaß und Erlebnisse"

directly with their own brand name stores, with the intention of presenting their products and brand name messages in a suitable interior design context. This variant ranges from factory outlets to the brand name temples of the high priests or priestesses of fashion, such as *Calvin Klein, Jil Sander, Strenesse* or *Prada,* for which the great designers commission only the very best of architects to translate their fashion idiom into a fitting setting in a suitable interior. To some extent this results in breathtaking temples in which the essence of the brand can be perceptibly experienced.

Whereas fashion creators have architectural temples constructed for their products, other brand manufacturers have created entire worlds revolving around the brand itself, in order to effectively communicate the brand's theme and image and to make it possible to actually feel an affinity with the product. Some allow customers to experience the history of the company or to experience a specific material, for example at *Swarovski World of Crystal* in Matt in Tirol, the *Sony Center* in Berlin, *Nike Town* in London and Berlin, or *Volkswagen's Auto City* in Wolfsburg. Many of the new "brand lands" also offer a complex array of leisure activities and information – combined with gastronomy and shops for their products (*Legoland, Ravensburger Spieleland, Auto City, Sony Center, Nike Town*), as well as courses, concerts, workshops – a mixture of the products offered and information, packaged as an especially memorable experience.

The great variety of all of these retail types reveals the spectrum of the retail landscape in which the shops that I have chosen for this book can be found. They include specialist retail shops in the most varying product areas, brand name shops and also newly created brand name worlds, which are located in Europe, the USA, South America and Japan. What is surprising is that there are very

geht. Was das Einkaufsverhalten aber besonders prägt und beeinflusst, ist der bessere Bildungs- und Informationsstand der Bevölkerung und die damit verbundene Forderung nach einer höheren Lebensqualität und einem ausgeprägten Verbraucherbewusstsein. Konsumenten sind heute informierter denn je zuvor. Sie sind ressourcen- und gesundheitsbewusst und stellen hohe Ansprüche an die Qualität der Ernährung, der Bekleidung und des Wohnens, aber auch an elektronische Produkte, an Fahrzeuge und Reisen. Hinzu kommt, dass die neuen digitalen Medien die Kommunikationsmöglichkeiten dahingehend verändert haben, dass Kunden weltweit nicht nur Informationen, sondern auch Produkte per Internet abrufen können, die vielfach auch noch in eine spielerische Erlebniswelt eingepackt sind. Die Ansprüche der Konsumenten beziehen sich aber nicht nur auf die Produkte selbst, sondern auch auf die Art und das Umfeld der Präsentation. Es soll übersichtlich sein, aber auch Neugier wecken, Überraschungseffekte und Highlights anbieten, Lifestyleambiente vermitteln, das Zugehörigkeit oder Authentizität verspricht. Und in zunehmendem Maße möchte der emanzipierte Konsument selbst etwas im Laden machen: etwas an- oder ausprobieren, die Musik, die Digitalkamera, das Fitnessgerät, das Musiksinstrument, das Auto. Darüber hinaus erwartet er Anregungen in der Verarbeitung und Anwendung, interessiert sich für Kurse oder Workshops zum Erlernen von Fachkenntnissen oder zum Treffen mit Gleichgesinnten. Das Interesse um ein Produkt zieht immer weitere Kreise, schließt ergänzende Informationen, Bücher oder Reisen mit ein. Und neben all den Produkterlebnissen möchte der Shopper sich natürlich entspannen: in einem Café, beim Frisör, im Kosmetik- oder Fitnessstudio, im Kino oder Internetcafé. Produktwelt und Handel sollen Erlebnisse, Träume, Ideen liefern und dabei vielfältige Emotionen wecken.

Handel im Wandel?

Diese Entwicklungen machen deutlich, dass sich in unserer westlichen Welt diejenigen Kunden stark emanzipiert haben, die Produkte kennen und hinter dem Produkt vielfach nach einem Zusatznutzen, einer Bedeutung, einem Sinn suchen. Doch wie reagiert der Handel auf diese Veränderungen der Verbraucher? Ist diese Sinn-Suche in den Handelskonzepten ablesbar?
Handelskonzepte haben immer Zeiterscheinungen widergespiegelt. In den 80er-Jahren hatten wir Jahre des wirtschaftlichen Aufschwungs und der Übersättigung, in denen mit Architekturträumen im Handel vor allem um Image und Qualität geworben wurde. Die 90er-Jahre hingegen kommunizierten veränderte Wertvorstellungen in Familie und Umwelt und brachten ein starkes Interesse an Ökoerzeugnissen und natürlichen Materialien hervor.

few culturally specific aspects that manifest themselves in the shop concepts. However, they all have one thing in common: in and with their shops, they want to tell their customers stories – about their products, about their context, their company, about their own culture and philosophy. They want to demonstrate a part of their tradition – their manner of dealing with customers. The shop itself is intended to communicate all of this complexity of thought and information – by means of its type of design, architecture, the product presentation, lighting and colours – but of course also by means of sensual perceptions such as fragrances, sounds and music. And last but not least, by means of the manner in which customers are treated in the shop.

How does the consumer behave?

Even if the marketing strategists do not like this fact, today it is almost impossible to compile a precise customer profile: even socio-demographic data are of no particular use in this area. We know that consumers are continually changing, that the birth rate is dropping and that older people are becoming more important as consumers. Singles and two income households are drastically on the rise. Shopping attitudes are the most likely source of clues, in that they provide us with information about customers and can be exploited for a retail concept. Customers whose main priority is making "bargain price" purchases are discount oriented. "Smart shoppers" look for brand name items at a good price. Those who frequent "convenience" stores prefer shopping without stress. Moreover, for a large part of the population, going shopping is a pleasurable and spontaneous leisure activity just like sports or the movies: the focus is on having "fun" and on that "special experience". But what characterises and influences shopping behaviour most particularly is the improved education and information level of the population and the resulting demand for more quality of life and a more fully developed state of consumer consciousness. Today's consumers are better informed than they ever were. They are more health and natural resource conscious, and they have high standards with regard to food, clothing and life products, as well as electronic products, vehicles and travel. Moreover, the new digital media have changed our communication potential to such an extent that customers world wide can not only access information but also products via the internet – products that are also packaged in a playfully entertaining context. However, consumer demands not only apply to the products themselves, but also to the manner and the context in which these products are presented. Product displays should be clearly arranged, but should also arouse curiosity, provide surprise effects, highlights and a lifestyle

In unserer jetzigen Dekade geht es den Menschen offenbar weniger um die Produkte selbst, als um die Kommunikation und Imagination, um die Bedeutung und den Inhalt, den sie vermitteln. Unsere Gesellschaft hat eine Wandlung von der Industrie- über die Informations- hin zur Kommunikationsgesellschaft erfahren und taumelt derzeit ständig von einem Erlebnis in das nächste. Bereits heute erleben wir einen Wettlauf der Erlebniswelten, wenn wir uns Einkaufszentren, Freizeit- oder Erlebnisparks anschauen. Spektakel, Actions und Events sind auch in den visuellen Medien an der Tagesordnung. Längst ist der Händler zum Animator der Freizeitwelt seiner Kunden geworden, ohne dass seine Ladenbühnen diese Veränderungen immer nachvollzogen hätten. Wenn Kunden etwas erleben wollen, kann der Händler nicht nur vorgefertigte Bühnen und Bilder zum Beeindrucken anbieten. Gesucht sind Konzepte, die nicht nur Show oder Spektakel, sondern längerfristige, sinnliche Erfahrungen vermitteln, die auf Dauer zu einer stärkeren Kundenbindung führen und zur Auseinandersetzung, zum Mitdenken und Mitmachen anregen. Und genau das wünscht sich der Verbraucher heute: eine emotionale Beziehung zu den Läden, in denen er einkauft.
Markenanbieter und all die Händler, die sich und ihren Laden ebenfalls als Marke verstehen, haben das schon lange begriffen und demonstrieren mit ihren eigen Shops und Markenwelten, wie eine Kundenbindung aufgebaut werden kann. In ihren Läden geht es nicht mehr nur darum, ein unverwechselbares Gesicht zu zeigen oder eine einzigartige Gestaltung, die das Produkt überhöht und wertvoll erscheinen lässt. Sie wollen mit ihrem Laden etwas über sich und ihre Produkte mitteilen, über ihre Lebenshaltung, ihren Service, ihre Einstellungen zu ihren Kunden, ihre eigenen Wertvorstellungen. Sie erzählen mit ihren Produkten und ihrem Laden eine Story, die den Mehrwert ausmacht. In diesen Storys kann es um Abenteuer gehen, um Liebe und Geborgenheit, um Lifestyle, Pflege und Wohlbehagen, um Sicherheit oder Überzeugung. Langweilig ist nur das Produkt oder das Unternehmen, über das es nichts zu erzählen gibt. Dies gilt erst recht für die Läden, in denen diese Produkte verkauft werden.

In neuen Handelskonzepten geht es z.B. um
– Shopping zur Unterhaltung,
– neue Formen der Technologie,
– eine Bedeutung der Marken,
– eine Bemühung um den Kunden (Service, Wellness),
– eine Einbeziehung der Kunden, um Interaktion.

Bei den in diesem Buch vorgestellten Läden machen Markenläden deutlich, wie sie ihre Produkt- und Unternehmensstory an die Kunden heranbringen. Da gibt es die poetischen Traumwelten des *Blumarine* Shops der italie-

ambiance that promises a feeling of belonging or authenticity. In addition, to an increasing degree the emancipated consumer wants to actively do something himself in a shop: try something on or out – music, a digital camera or fitness equipment – a musical instrument or a car. Furthermore, he expects stimulation through the workmanship and the possible use of the product. He is interested in attending courses or workshops aimed at learning specialised know-how or meeting people of similar interests. Interest in a product tends cause progressively larger ripples, often encompassing supplementary information, books or travel. Finally, besides all of the products that he experiences, the shopper naturally wants to relax: in a café or at the hairdresser's, in a cosmetics or fitness studio, at the movies or in an internet café. The product world and the retail sector are supposed to provide memorable experiences, dreams and ideas, while arousing all manner of emotions.

The retail trade in a state of flux?

These developments make it clear that, to a great degree, customers in our western world have become emancipated: they know the products and in many cases they look for an additional advantage, significance or meaning.
But how is the retail trade sector reacting to these changes in consumers? Has this search for meaning made itself felt recognisably in retailing concepts?
Retailing concepts have always reflected the tendencies of a particular era. In the eighties, we experienced a time characterised by an economic upswing and overabundance, when the retail sector focussed primarily on image and quality by means of architectural dreams. By contrast, the nineties communicated a change in values with regard to the family and the environment, which resulted in great interest in ecological products and natural materials. In the current decade, it is not so much the products themselves that are important to people, but communication and imagination – the meaning and content that the products convey. Our society has transformed itself from an industrial society – by way of an information society – into a communication society, and at present it is staggering from one experience to the next event. Even today we are already experiencing a competition situation between theme worlds, when we look at shopping centres, leisure and theme parks. Theatrical spectacles, action happenings and events are also the rule in the visual media. The retailer has long since become an entertainment MC in the leisure world of his customers, although his shop's stage setting has not always kept pace with these transformations. When customers want to experience something, the retailer cannot merely offer prefabricated stage settings and pictures to impress them, but rather he must develop

nischen Modestylistin Anna Molinari und für die amerikanische Schuhmarke *Via Spiga*. Der japanische Kosmetikhersteller *Shiseido* lässt sich für seine Marke *Qiora* die Produktphilosophie in eine textile Raumwelt übersetzen. Während der holländische Energieanbieter *Nuon* sein Leistungsangebot eher grafisch herüberbringt, geht es dem Telekommunikationsanbieter *Telfort* darum, mit seinen Kunden ins Gespräch zu kommen. *Camper* hingegen möchte in seinen Läden seine kulturelle Tradition der stilvollen Einfachheit, die Produktphilosophie und Lifestyle zugleich vermitteln. Und bei *Mandarina Duck* wird die Ware über den Raum entdeckt. Sensuelle Erlebniswelten mit Lifestylecharakter bieten *Fila* und *Sony* mit ihren Stores an.

Bei den Fachgeschäften werden in „Showrooms und Galerien" Produktgeschichten erzählt, mit denen sich der Kunde identifiziert. In Läden, die wie „Verkaufsmaschinen" funktionieren, kommt man mit Produktangebot und einem Superservice einfach schnell zur Sache. Bei einigen Ladenkonzepte, kamen die Ideen für die Ladenbühnen „aus dem Produkt" heraus: aus dem Material, der Anwendung, der Verarbeitung oder auch dem Ursprung. Eine andere Form des Geschichtenerzählens ist es, einem Laden „ein Thema" zugrunde zu legen, das mit dem Produkt selbst, dem Umfeld oder der Zielgruppe zu tun hat. Und richtig um das Wohl des Kunden geht es in den Läden mit „Wellness-Charakter".

Ladenbühnen für Show, Erlebnis und Emotion

Es überrascht nicht, dass in zunehmendem Maße für Messestände aber auch für Läden Gestalter hinzugezogen werden, die „Bühnenerfahrung" haben. Geht es doch darum, Läden zu schaffen, die in ihrer Art der Produktpräsentation, ihrer räumlichen Atmosphäre eine Stimmung erzeugen sollen, die die Kunden von der Absicht der Händler überzeugt, Produkt- und Unternehmensgeschichten sichtbar zu machen. Es ist wie im Theater oder Film, wo die ganze Story nach einem Drehbuch abläuft, in dem es auch Anweisungen für das Umfeld gibt. Im Ladendesign sind es Architekten, Innenarchitekten, Visual-Merchandise-Gestalter, Dekorateure, Lichtgestalter und zunehmend Bühnengestalter und Filmdramaturgen, die den Ladenbühnen ein Gesicht geben und sie zum Leben erwecken.

Gestalterische Stilmittel für Ladenbühnen

Natürlich ist es spannend zu erfahren, welche gestalterischen Mittel, Materialien und Möglichkeiten die Designer und Architekten der hier vorgestellten Läden entwickelt und eingesetzt haben, um Räume zum Geschichtenerzählen zu erhalten. Ihre Ideen zeigen auch gestalterische Trends auf.

concepts that demand interaction, provoke thought and encourage participation. The concepts that are most sought after are those that not only communicate a show or a theatrical spectacle, but also long term, sensual experiences that result in permanently stronger customer bonding. And that is exactly what today's customer wants: an emotional relationship with the stores where he shops.
Brand name suppliers and all those retailers that regard themselves – as well as their shops – as a "brand" have long since comprehended this fact and, in their own shops and brand name worlds, they have been demonstrating how customer bonding can be established. The focus of their shops is not merely on creating an unmistakably unique appearance or design, which highlights the product and increases its apparent value. In their shops, they want to communicate something about themselves and their products, about their way of life and mentality, their service, their attitudes to their customers and their own values. Using their products and their shop, they tell a story which generates additional value. These stories may be about adventure, about love and feeling secure, about lifestyle, about personal care and well-being, about safety or about convictions. The only thing that is boring is a product or a company with nothing to tell; and this is definitely true of the shops where such products are sold.

For example, the new retail concepts may focus on
– shopping for entertainment,
– news forms of technology,
– the significance of brand names,
– efforts aimed at the customer (service, wellness),
– involving the customer, interaction.

Among the shops included in this book, the brand name shops clearly illustrate how they convey their product and corporate story to the customers. One approach can be seen in the poetic dream worlds of the *Blumarine* shops of the Italian fashion stylist, Anna Molinari, and in the American shoe brand, *Via Spiga*. For its *Qiora* brand, *Shiseido* – the Japanese cosmetics manufacturer – had its product philosophy translated into a textile spatial world. Whereas the Dutch energy utility company – *Nuon* – communicates its range of services primarily by graphic means, the objective of the telecommunications provider – *Telfort* – lies in achieving a dialogue with its customers. *Camper's* focus is its cultural tradition of stylish simplicity, which is simultaneously its product philosophy and a lifestyle in itself. At *Mandarina Duck* the merchandise is supposed to be discovered via the interior. In their stores, *Fila* and *Sony* offer customers an opportunity to experience sensual worlds with a specific lifestyle character.
In the specialist shops, product stories that the customer can identify with are communicated in showrooms and

Eingänge
Fassaden und Eingänge sind fast durchweg offen und geben vollen Einblick in den Laden. Schaufenster gibt es keine. Die Gestaltungen im Eingangsbereich sind reduziert. Ausnahme: Der Friseursalon *Aida* in New York hat eine plastische Einfassung, die sich im Rauminnern fortsetzt. Mit einem auffallenden Logo arbeitet der *Bread Shop* in London (alte Druckstocktypen) und das *Microcenter* in Athen (farbige balkenähnliche Ausleger und farbige Fassadengrafik). Riesige Videobilder über dem Eingang gibt es bei *Fila Sports.Life* in Mailand.

Der architektonische Raum
Es gibt im gehobenen Produktbereich viele weiße oder cremefarbene offene Räume mit spannenden Durchgängen und Durchblicken, Emporen und Treppen und Transparenz. Vielfach sind die Treppen gestalterische Highlights durch Material und Form. Glatte Wände werden durch größere und kleinere beleuchtete Nischen belebt.
Überraschend ist die skulpturale Auffassung mancher Räume: vom Schriftrelief (*Breadshop*) über eine plastische Faltung der Wände (*Aida* und *Harriet Dorn*) bis zu einem Raum im Raum (*Legrand*). Emotional spannende Läden werden durch den Einsatz von Textilien, die totale Auskleidung des Raumes oder textile Wandbildungen geschaffen. Neugiereffekte und Raumillusionen entstehen durch Lichtgestaltungen, aber auch durch realistische Wandmalereien.

Decken
Die schlichten Räume haben durchweg einfache verputzte Decken mit Einbauleuchten. In manchen Fällen sind es dunkelblaue Decken mit Sternenhimmeleffekt. Auch Industrietouch ist durchaus noch anzutreffen bei Läden, die auf Einfachheit oder Loftcharakter setzen. Schwarz an Wand und Decke lässt die Raumgrenzen verschwinden und steht für Immaterialität als Kontrast zu „glowing walls". Wo Showeffekte erwünscht sind, wird auf bühnen- oder

galleries. In shops that function in the manner of "vending machines", the emphasis is on facilitating and accelerating sales by means of product selection and super service. With some of the shop concepts, the inspirational ideas for the stage settings were derived from the "product itself" – its materials, utilisation and workmanship, as well as origin. Another form of story narration consists in basing a shop on a "theme" that has to do with the product itself, the context or the target group. And in shops with "wellness character" a feeling of well-being for customers is the principal aim.

Retail stage settings geared to shows, special experiences and emotions

It is not surprising that, to a growing extent, designers with "stage experience" are being commissioned for trade fair exhibition stands as well as for retail shops. After all, the objective is to create shops that, by means of the type of product presentation and spatial atmosphere, generate a mood that convinces customers of the retailers' intention to make the product and corporate stories visually perceptible. This is comparable to the theatre or film situation, where the entire story proceeds in accordance with a script, which also includes instructions for the setting. In the retail design sector, architects, interior designers, visual merchandise designers, interior decorators, lighting professionals and, to an increasing degree, stage designers and film dramaturges are giving retail stage settings a face and infusing them with life.

Stylistic methods of design for retail stage settings

Naturally, it is quite fascinating to find out what design methods, materials and modus operandi the designers and architects of the shops that are illustrated in this book have developed and utilised in order to create interiors that convey stories. Their ideas are also indicative of current design trends.

Entries
Façades and entries are almost always open so as to offer an unimpeded view of the shop interior. There are no window displays. Design elements in the entry area are reduced to a minimum.
There are some exceptions. The *Aida* hairdressing salon in New York has a enclosing sculptural framework that extends into the interior. The *Bread Shop* in London utilises a conspicuous logo (old printing block characters), as does the *Microcenter* in Athens (a coloured, beam-like suspended sign and coloured façade graphics). At *Fila Sport.Life* in Milan, gigantic video pictures are shown above the entry.

messeähnliche Gitterkonstruktionen zurückgegriffen. Eine Höhenreduktion wird in einem Fall sogar durch einen hinterleuchteten Fallschirm erreicht. Wo Räume weithin sichtbar grafisch markiert werden sollen, helfen Lichtelemente zur Orientierung.

Böden

Hochwertige Läden kokettieren mit Understatement und weisen meistens polierte Betonböden auf. In wenigen Fällen gibt es in Verbindung mit Beton kleine Umrandungen in Mosaikfliesen, häufig in Gold. Auch ganz heller Terrazzoboden findet in Topmodeläden Eingang. Wandnischen werden manchmal auch mit unterleuchteten Glasböden betont. Als topmodisch und wertvoll gilt offenbar der vor Ort gegossene hochglänzende Epoxydharzboden, den es in vielen Farben gibt. Glänzenden Marmor findet man eher bei Läden in den südlichen Ländern. Fliesen werden bewusst und kontrastreich eingesetzt, kombiniert mit Holzboden oder Glitzerfliesen oder mit Metallflächen. Parkettböden können Gebrauchsspuren tragen oder stehen für Natürlichkeit, Einfachheit, Ursprünglichkeit und Wohnlichkeit. Teppiche sind sehr selten in Teilbereichen zu finden oder aber gezielt mit sinngebendem Dekor (Wassermotiv).

Materialkontraste

Hier lässt der Spieltrieb offenbar die Fantasie überborden. Der polierte Betonboden wird mit feinen Putzwänden kombiniert, mit Mosaikfliesen, schließt problemlos an Teppichböden, Metalle oder Plexiglas an und wird in Edelläden ebenso eingesetzt wie in servicebetonten Läden mit viel Publikumsverkehr. Darauf stehen Möbel oder Wandteile aus warmtonigen heimischen Hölzern wie Birnbaum oder Eiche, die gelegentlich durch Metallteile wie Stahl, Loch- oder Riffelbleche an Bau- und Displayteilen verjüngt werden. Goldene Mosaikfliesen und weiße Marmorkiesel sind neben dem ausdrucksvollen Lärchenholz ein bizarrer Kontrast. Auf Betonböden stehen farbig hinterleuchtete Möbel und Produktwände oder schließen an stark farbige Grafikwände an. Zunehmend werden intensive Farben im Raum verwendet, mit denen Raumteile hervorgehoben werden, am Boden als Epoxydharzboden, an den Wänden in Lack- und Spachteltechniken. Retro-Materialien wie Messingkanten der 50er-/60er-Jahre werden eher verfremdet eingesetzt.

Lichteffekte

Sie spielen in den derzeitigen Läden fast die Hauptrolle. Raumformen werden durch Licht nachgezeichnet, hinterleuchtete Wandschirme spenden diffuses Licht und leuchtende Möbel und Wände schaffen eine cineastische Cyberatmosphäre. Regalnischen werden mit Licht eingerahmt oder ändern ihre Lichtqualität und -farbe in bestimmten Intervallen. Grelles Tageslicht wird durch Vorhänge ge-

The architectural space

In the high quality product area, we find numerous white or cream coloured open spaces full of fascinating passages and views through openings, enlivened by balconies and staircases and characterised by transparency. In many cases the staircases are design highlights by reason of their materials and shape. Interest is often added to smooth walls by inserting larger or smaller illuminated alcoves and recesses.
In some interiors, an element of surprise is introduced with sculptural treatments, ranging from relief lettering (*Bread Shop*) to a sculptural wall treatment (*Aida* and *Harriet Dorn*) or the creation of rooms within rooms (*Legrand*). Emotionally exciting shops are formed using textiles – by entirely sheathing the interior in fabric or fashioning wall elements out of textile materials. Effects that arouse curiosity and create spatial illusions can be achieved with lighting effects, as well as with realistic mural paintings.

Ceilings

Without exception, the austere interiors have simple plastered ceilings with recessed spot lights. In some cases dark blue ceilings conjure up a star studded sky effect. The industrial touch can also be found in shops with a particular focus on simplicity or loft character. Black used on the walls and ceilings makes spatial boundaries seem to disappear and is symbolic of immaterialness as a contrast to "glowing walls". Where show effects are desired, stage or trade fair like grid structures are used. In one case, a reduction of ceiling height is achieved by means of a back lit parachute. Where areas are supposed to be marked graphically so they are visible from afar, lighting elements are often used as an orientation aid.

Floors

High end shops flirt with understatement and generally have polished concrete floors. In some few cases, small borders using mosaic tiles – often in gold – are used in combination with concrete. Very light coloured terrazzo flooring is also making an appearance in the top fashion shops. Wall alcoves are sometimes emphasised by glass flooring illuminated from below. Apparently, high gloss epoxy resin floors, which are poured on location and which are available in numerous colours, are regarded as highly fashionable and valuable. Gleaming marble is more likely to be found in shops in southern climes. On the other hand, tiles are often used purposefully and with an aim to contrasts – in combination with wood flooring or glitter tiles, as well as with metal surfaces. Parquet floors are allowed to show evidence of wear, whereby they are an indication of naturalness and simplicity, liveable cosiness and a lack of artifice. Very rarely, carpets may be found in

dimmt oder Tageslichtcharakter durch hinterleuchtete oder leuchtende Wände geschaffen. In den Modetempeln wird viel mit indirektem Licht und beleuchteten Nischen gearbeitet. Auffallende, oft große Decken- oder Hängeleuchten sind CI-prägend.

Produktpräsentation

Soll das Produkt hervortreten, werden häufig kleinteilige Plexiglaselemente als Halterungen eingesetzt oder auch Ideen aus der Automatenwelt in eine elegante Ladensprache übersetzt. Geht es aber darum, das Produkt über den Raum zu entdecken, gibt es spannende Räume und Raumelemente als Ablenkungsmanöver mit raffinierten und verfremdeten Präsentationsideen. Produkte werden in leuchtenden Objekten wie Kostbarkeiten aufbewahrt, die in ihrer Form Produktinhalte transportieren. Es gibt Displays, die aus dem Material, der Form oder dem Entstehungsprozess des Produktes abgeleitet sind. Produkte schweben auf halterlosen Glas-, Metall- und Holzborden, werden hinter- und unterleuchtet und als Stars in Szene gesetzt. Bewusst stehen sie auf kontrastierenden Materialien, um ihre Eigenheiten zu „ent-decken".

Spielerische Effekte, Interaktion

Neben den schon länger eingeführten Touchscreens und Videowalls gibt es immer mehr Technik zum Spielen und

specific areas, or they are used purposely and incorporate a significant decorative motif (e.g. water motif).

Contrast of materials

Apparently in this area, playfully improvisational impulses lead to the exuberant realisation of fantasies. Polished concrete flooring is combined with fine plaster walls or with mosaic tiles. It merges smoothly into carpeting, metal or Plexiglas, and is used in sophisticated shops as well as in service oriented stores with a great deal of customer traffic. Arranged on this flooring we find furnishings or wall elements made of native woods in warm tones, such as pear or oak, and occasionally pepped up with metal elements, such as steel, perforated or corrugated metal sheeting that is used for structural or display elements. Bold mosaic tiles and white marble pebble stones create a bizarre contrast next to expressive larch wood. On concrete floors, we find furnishings or product walls that are colourfully illuminated from behind, or juxtaposed with graphic walls in strong colours. Increasingly, intensive colours are being used for interiors: they serve to highlight room areas and can be found on floors, where they are used in epoxy resin flooring, and on walls, where they are incorporated into painting and plastering techniques. Retro-materials, such as the brass edging typical of the fifties and sixties, are more likely to be used to create an alienation effect.

Lighting effects

In contemporary shops lighting almost always plays a leading role. Spatial shapes are outlined by means of light: backlit wall screens spread diffused light and glowing furniture and walls are used to create a cinema-like cyber atmosphere. Recessed shelving may be framed by light or the lighting used may change its quality and colour at specific intervals. Bright daylight is dimmed by means of draperies, or daylight character is conjured up by using back lit or glowing walls. To a great extent, fashion temples work with indirect lighting and illuminated alcoves. Conspicuous, sometimes over sized ceiling light fixtures or hanging fixtures often set the tone for a particular corporate image.

Product presentation

If the product is supposed to be highlighted, small Plexiglas elements are often used as holding devices and brackets. Alternatively, inspiration for ideas is taken from the world of vending machines and translated into an elegant retail idiom. However, if the intention is to allow the customers to "discover" the product via the interior space itself, this results in exciting rooms and room elements used as a distraction manoeuvre and combined with sophisticated presentation ideas replete with alienation

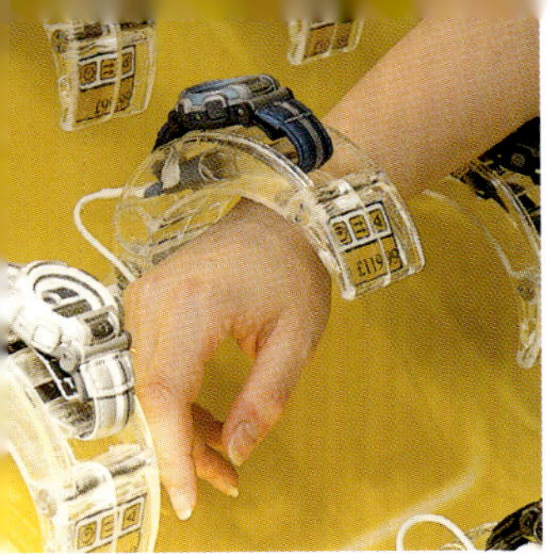

zum Kommunizieren mit Playstations und Internetzugang. Gerade im technischen Bereich können Produkte vielfach ausprobiert werden. Auch ein Automateneffekt für ein Top-Modeprodukt hat etwas Spielerisches an sich, ebenso wie unerwartete Sitzmöglichkeiten zum Herausklappen oder Produkte, die in unerwarteten „Wänden" erst entdeckt werden müssen. Bei einer drehenden Wendeltreppe oder einer Umkleide aus Fiberglasstäben lässt man die Kinder am besten zu Hause. Sie sind im Kinderhaus, an der Rutsche oder in Kuschelecken besser aufgehoben. Die letzten Jahre haben uns Leuchten, Sitzmöbel und auch Tische beschert, die mit ihrer Form die Kunden durchaus zum Schmunzeln reizen. Ein Versuch lohnt sich.

Wellnessideen
Dazu gehören natürlich alle Möglichkeiten, Kunden ein Stück Wohlbehagen zu schenken und dadurch länger im Laden zu behalten: eine Café- oder Saftbar, bequeme Sitzecken und Sofas zum Warten, sanfte Musik, Schatten spendende Hinterhöfe mit Gartencharakter oder ein Verwöhnprogramm von einer Super-Beratung über Musik, Snacks bis hin zu Massagen und Düften. Manchmal ist es schon eine unerwartete Kundentoilette oder der Telefon-, Kopier- oder Faxservice, eine Einpackmöglichkeit für Geschenke oder ganz einfach Einfühlungsvermögen und Freundlichkeit. Verwöhnen kann auch eine gezielte Vorauswahl oder Beschaffungsmöglichkeit für die ganz persönlichen Produkte sein.

Service, Events, E-Commerce
Schon fast selbstverständlich erscheinen Möglichkeiten des Take-aways bei Feinkostläden oder Rezepte vom Lieblingsgebäck beim Bäcker. In Musik- und Sportläden sind

effects. As if they were priceless treasures, products are sometimes displayed in shining objects that convey product content by reason of their shape. Some display methods are derived from the material, the shape or the fabrication process of the product itself. Products float on bracket-less glass, metal and wooden shelves, are backlit or illuminated from below or highlighted like celebrities placed in the spotlight. They are purposefully placed on contrasting materials so that their individual peculiarities can be discovered.

Playful effects and interaction
In addition to the touch screens and video walls that were introduced some time ago, there is increasingly more technology for customers to play and communicate with, including Playstations and internet access. Particularly in the technical area, customers have ample opportunity to try products out. A vending machine effect utilised for a top fashion product also incorporates a playful element, as do unexpected fold-out seating facilities or products that have to be discovered in unexpected "walls". With a revolving spiral staircase or fitting rooms made of fibre glass rods, it is best to leave the children at home. A children's playhouse, slide equipment or cuddly corners are more attuned to a child's needs. Recent years have also seen the advent of humorously designed lamps, seating elements as well as tables that provoke customer smiles simply by reason of their shape. It is worth a try.

Wellness ideas
Naturally, this approach incorporates all those options geared to giving customers a feeling of well-being and thus keeping them in the shop longer. It may include a café or a juice bar, comfortable seating arrangements and sofas for waiting periods, soft strains of music, shady courtyards with a garden-like ambiance or a pampering programme ranging from super consulting service to music, snacks, massages and fragrances. Sometimes, it manifests itself in an unexpected customer restroom facility, telephone, copying or fax service, the option of having a purchase gift wrapped or – quite simply – attentiveness and cordial courtesy. Pampering can also be achieved by means of purposeful product pre-selection or the possibility of procuring very personal products.

Service, events, e-commerce
Nowadays the possibility of take-away service in delicatessen shops and obtaining your favourite cookie recipe from the baker is almost taken for granted. In music and sports shops, visiting celebrities and autograph sessions are particularly popular, as well as mini-concerts or – at the very least – video clips showing the latest stars. Lifestyle products can be infused with life by means of films,

Promibesuche und -signierstunden besonders beliebt, aber auch Mini-Konzerte oder zumindest Videoclips der aktuellen Stars. Lifestyleprodukte können durch Filme, Bücher, Reiseangebote oder gar Speisen belebt werden. Kleine Events und Feste – auch mit Unterstützung durch Nachbarfirmen – schaffen persönliche Kundenbindungen. Viele Kundenkontakte lassen sich heute schon durch das Internet aktivieren und so bieten die Websites Möglichkeiten, etwas über das Unternehmen oder die Produkte mitzuteilen, Produkte zu bestellen, Reklamationen vorzubringen, etwas über den Lieferservice oder Pflegetipps zu erfahren. Viele Unternehmen nutzen die Websites, um über Promis zu berichten, über Top-Veranstaltungen in der Nähe, auf Kurse und Workshops, auf Bücher oder Computer-Software hinzuweisen, Gewinnspiele anzubieten und natürlich für die eigenen Produkte oder eigene Events zu werben.

Design muss glaubwürdig sein

Ein Laden kann ein noch so gutes Konzept und eine fantasievolle Ladenbühne haben, wirklich erfolgreich ist er nur dann, wenn das Gesamtkonzept auch glaubwürdig ist, wenn der Händler und sein Personal mit dem Konzept vertraut sind und dahinter stehen, wenn sie es selbst für ihre Kunden leben. Und das schließt alles ein: das Produktsortiment, das auf die Kunden abgestimmt ist, die Raumgestaltung, die zur Produktidee und zu den Kunden passt, die Servicepalette, die Musik, das Licht und die Dekoration. Dabei spielt es keine Rolle, ob ein Konzept der Einfachheit gefahren wird wie bei *Bergman* oder eines der Tradition wie bei *Perugina*, ob Luxus im Spiel ist wie bei *Via Spiga* oder eine familiäre Vertrautheit aufkommen soll wie bei *Deerberg* oder ob es um eine kunstvolle Art des Versteckens und Entdeckens geht wie bei *Mandarina Duck* oder *Missoni*. Die Geschichte muss glaubwürdig sein und an der richtigen Stelle den richtigen Leuten erzählt werden.

In dem Sinne wünsche ich allen Lesern viel Spaß und viele Anregungen beim Spaziergang durch diese fantasievollen Ladenwelten.

Ingrid Wenz-Gahler

books, travel offers or even food. Small events and festivities – optionally with the support of nearby businesses – can generate personal customer relationships.

Today, many customer contacts in the retail sector can be activated via the internet. Web sites serve to communicate something about the company or its products, to order products, submit complaints or claims, or find information about delivery service or maintenance suggestions. In addition to – naturally – advertising their own products and their own events, many companies use web sites in order to report on celebrities or top events in the vicinity, to draw attention to courses and workshops or to books and computer software, as well as to offer contest participation opportunities.

Design must be credible

It does not matter how good a shop's concept is or how imaginative its retail stage setting. It will only be successful if the overall concept is also credible – if the retailer and his personnel are familiar with the concept and stand behind it – if they truly live it for their customers. This includes everything: an assortment of products which is attuned to the shop's customers and an interior design concept which is suited to the product idea and customers. It includes the range of services offered, the music, lighting and the decorating scheme. In this context it is totally irrelevant whether the concept focuses on simplicity as it does at *Bergman* or on tradition as it does at *Perugina* – whether the element of luxury plays a role as it does at *Via Spiga* or the aim is family oriented familiarity as seen at *Deerberg* – or whether the objective is an artful game of hide and seek as it is at *Mandarina Duck* and *Missoni*. The story itself has to be credible, and it has to be told to the right people in the right place.

Bearing this in mind, I hope that all of my readers will have a great deal of fun and find abundant inspiration during their stroll through these imaginative retail worlds.

Markenläden • Markenwelten

Viele Markenhersteller eröffnen derzeit für ihre Marken und ihre Imagedarstellung eigene Shops bis hin zu Markenwelten. Haben sie doch hier die Möglichkeit, ihre eigene Firmenphilosophie und Firmenkultur bestmöglichst zu präsentieren und mit ihren Kunden zu kommunizieren, ohne jemanden dazwischen zu haben, der die Idee verwässert. Das Spektrum reicht von kleinen Markenshops wie *me Issey Miyake* über Flagshipstores wie die von *Camper* bis hin zu Markenwelten wie *Fila Sport.Life* in Mailand.

In dem kleinen Laden *me*, den *Curiosity* für *Issey Miyak*e entwickelt hat, transportiert das äußerst reduzierte Raumdesign die Modephilosophie: transparent, raffiniert einfach, originell, perfekt, funktionell. Völlig anders sind die *Blumarine* Läden der Italienerin *Anna Molinari*, die so aufregend sind wie ihre Mode: geheimnisvoll, exklusiv, temperamentvoll. Es sind gebaute Emotionen. Und all ihre Läden haben eine eigene Geschichte und ein eigenes Gesicht. Für die hochwertige Schuhmarke *Via Spiga* des amerikanischen Unternehmens *Intershoe* hat der Architekt fast einen Tempel entwickelt, der mit poesievollen Metaphern angereichert ist – eine räumliche Übersetzung von Produktqualitäten, die mehr als nur added values beinhalten. Bei dem Markenladen *Qiora* des japanischen Kosmetikherstellers *Shiseido* trägt der Raum durch seine textile und lichtvolle Gestaltung die Produktphilosophie der Entspannung und des Wohlbehagens. Auch der holländische Energieanbieter *Nuon* lässt seine Kunden die Energien wie Wärme und Kälte spüren durch Farb- und Lichträume, grafisch übersetzt und mit bekannten Endprodukten in Szene gesetzt. Bei *Nuon* geht es aber nicht um eine Marke sondern darum, die Leistungen des Gesamtunternehmens einprägsam darzustellen. Ganz so weit ist *Telfort*, ein britischer Anbieter von Telekommunikationsleistungen, nicht gegangen. Ihm geht es mehr darum, durch eine unkomplizierte kommunikative Atmosphäre die Kunden mit der neuen Technik vertraut und durch Ausprobieren, Beratung und Wohlfühlen seine Unternehmensanliegen deutlich zu machen. Der italienische Schokoladenhersteller *Perugina* hat mit seinem ersten Markenshop versucht, durch vertraute Elemente auf seine langjährige Tradition zu verweisen und zugleich in verführerischer Form das genüssliche Produkt Schokolade im Raum spürbar werden zu lassen. Dass die Unternehmensgeschichte ein wichtiger Teil der Identität ist, macht auch der mallorquinische Schuhhersteller *Camper* mit seinen Läden deutlich, in denen die ländlich-handwerkliche Tradition bildhaft zum Ausdruck kommt durch eine ursprüngliche und stilvolle Einfachheit. Um solche Werte geht es *Mandarina Duck* nicht. Dieses Unternehmen hat schon seit vielen Jahren eigene Läden, die sich mit dem Zeitgeist durchaus änderten. Immer aber ging es um völlig neue Präsentationsideen und um die Auseinandersetzung mit dem Raum.
In Bologna ist es ein skulpturales Präsentationselement, das in den nur mit Licht gestalteten Räumen die Ware in Szene setzt. In Paris hingegen gibt es vielfältige Raumobjekte mit hohem Erlebniswert, über die die Räume und die Ware entdeckt werden. Um ein Erlebnis im Raum geht es auch bei *Missoni* in New York. Hier übernehmen die galerieartig gestalteten Räume die Aufgabe, die Raffinesse der Bekleidung über leuchtende Präsentationsmöbel, Licht- und Farbeffekte in ein Raumerlebnis zu übersetzen.
Bei *Fila Sport.Life* werden leuchtende Möbel und Räume genutzt, eine völlig neue immateriell wirkende Ladenwelt zu gestalten und Sport als Lebensstil sichtbar zu machen durch eine sensuell erlebbare Sportwelt. Und im *Sony Style Store* in Berlin inszeniert *Sony* auf vier Ebenen seine Markenwelt – futuristisch, technisch, verspielt, zum Anfassen und zum Ausprobieren.

Brand shops · brand worlds

Many brand name manufacturers are creating their own shops, or even entire brand worlds, in order to promote their brand and image presentation. In this way they have the opportunity to present their own corporate philosophy and corporate culture in the best possible way and to communicate with their customers without any intermediaries that might dilute the idea. The spectrum ranges from small brand shops such as *me Issey Miyake* to flagship stores such as that of *Camper*, as well as entire brand worlds such as *Fila Sport. Life* in Milan.

In the diminutive *me* shop, which Curiosity developed for *Issey Miyake*, the extremely minimalist interior design conveys the fashion philosophy: sophisticated simplicity that is transparent, original, perfect and functional. The *Blumarine* shops of the Italian fashion designer *Anna Molinari* are completely different and just as exciting as her fashions: mysterious, exclusive, vivacious. Emotions in structural form. Furthermore, each of her shops has its own history and a uniquely individual look. For the high quality shoe brand name *Via Spiga* by the American *Intershoe* company, the architect has designed a veritable temple filled with poetic metaphors – a spatial interpretation of the products' qualities which consist in more than merely added value. In the *Qiora* brand name shop of the Japanese cosmetics manufacturer, *Shiseido*, the interior communicates the product philosophy of relaxation and well-being by means of its textile and light filled design. The Dutch energy utility company, *Nuon* gives its customers the opportunity to feel energy forms such as heat and cold in the interior through colour and light rooms, interpreted by means of graphics and theatrically presented in the form of well-known end products. At *Nuon* the focus is not on the brand name in itself, but on effectively presenting the services of the company as a whole. *Telfort*, a British supplier of telecommunication services, does not go that far. Its focus is more on familiarising its customers with the new technology in an uncomplicated, communicative atmosphere where they can try things out, take advantage of consulting services and simply feel good, and thus on clearly illustrating the company's intentions. In its first brand name shop, the Italian chocolate manufacturer, *Perugina*, attempted to create associations with its venerable tradition by means of familiar elements and at the same time to allow patrons to literally feel the delectable product chocolate in seductive form through the interior itself. The shops of the Majorcan shoe manufacturer, *Camper*, where the rural tradition of craftsmanship is graphically expressed by means of down-to-earth and stylish simplicity, also demonstrates that a company's history is an important part if its identity. This type of value is not the focus at *Mandarina Duck*. For many years, this company has had its own shops, which have definitely changed in accordance with the spirit of the times. But the principal objective has always been developing entirely new presentation ideas and working with spatial interiors. In Bologna a sculpture-like display element directs attention to the merchandise in rooms that are exclusively decorated with light. By contrast, in Paris there are all manner of spatial objects with a high degree of experiential value which allow the patrons to discover the interiors and the merchandise. At *Missoni* in New York the focus is also on how customers experience the interior. Rooms designed like galleries serve to translate the sophistication of the apparel into a spatial experience by means of glowing display furnishings, lighting and colour effects. At *Fila Sport.Life* glowing furnishings and rooms are used to create a completely new, seemingly immaterial retail world and to make sports manifestly visible through a sports world that can experienced sensually. Finally, at the *Sony Style Store* in Berlin, *Sony* has staged a theatrical presentation of its brand name world on four levels – futuristic, technical, tongue-in-cheek – everything just asking to be touched and tried out.

me ISSEY MIYAKE · Tokyo

DESIGN
Curiosity Inc.
Gwenael Nicolas & Hisaaki Hirawata,
Tokyo

me ISSEY MIYAKE ist ein kleiner, transparenter Laden im Ginza-District von Tokyo, einem traditionellen Geschäftsviertel mit Banken und eleganten Läden. Teure Designerläden wie die von *Chanel, Fendi* oder *Celine* befinden sich in der Nachbarschaft. Das Konzept für die neue Marke *me* stammt von *Curiosity*, einer Design-Allianz der Japanerin Reiko Miyamoto und dem Franzosen Gwenael Nicolas. Bei me gibt es nur ein Produkt: Tops – in einer Größe und einem dehnbaren Material, das für alle Größen passt; eine Idee, die auch die gesamte Ladengestaltung beeinflusste. Bereits in der Fabrik wird das Kleidungsstück in einer transparenten PET-Rolle verpackt und in dieser Form in eine gläserne Verkaufsmaschine integriert, die wie ein Automat funktioniert. Wird die vorderste Rolle im Glaskasten entnommen, rutscht sofort eine neue nach. Musterstücke der Tops hängen an einem transparenten Kleiderständer. Die Kundin wählt ein Stück nach Farbe und Struktur und entnimmt ihre Rolle. Auch die ist von den Designern entwickelt worden. Sie lässt sich mit einer großen Schraube an der Seite öffnen und ist dann wie eine Mineralwasserflasche: Transparent mit dem Logo vorn drauf. Ganz Verkaufsmaschine ist auch fast der Laden: schmucklos und einfach in weiß gehalten mit hellgrauem Betonboden. Glas und Acrylglas sind die einzigen Materialien für die Herausstellung der farbigen Top-Stars. *me* ist nicht nur eine Marke sondern auch eine brilliante Designidee, die Verpackung und Display in einem ist.

me ISSEY MIYAKE is a small, transparent shop in the Ginza district of Tokyo, a business district full of banks and elegant shops that is rich in tradition. Expensive designer shops such as *Chanel, Fendi* or *Celine* are located in the vicinity. The concept for the new *me* brand name was developed by *Curiosity*, a designer alliance between the Japanese designer Reiko Miyamoto and the Frenchman Gwenael Nicolas. At me there is only one product: tops – in one size and a stretch fabric that fits all sizes. This idea has influenced the design of the entire shop. The items of clothing are already packed in a transparent PET cylinder at the factory and in this form they are integrated into a glass sales machine that function like an automatic vending machine. If the front cylinder is removed from the glass case, the next one slides into place immediately. Samples of the tops hang on a transparent clothes rack. The customer selects the colour and style she wants and then picks the appropriate cylinder package. This packaging form was also devised by the designers. It can be opened by means of a large screw on the side and resembles a transparent mineral water bottle with the logo on the front. The shop itself is also almost like a vending machine: austere, simple and finished entirely in white with light grey concrete flooring. Glass and acrylic glass are the only materials that have been used to display the exclusive coloured tops. *me* is no merely a brand name: it is also a brilliant design concept which incorporates packaging and display all in one.

Project:
me ISSEY MIYAKE,
Tokyo/Japan

Design:
Curiosity Inc.
Gwenael Nicolas &
Hisaaki Hirawata,
Tokyo

Area:
ca. 25 sqm

Photographer:
Yasuaki Yoshinaga,
Tokyo

Blumarine, Anna Molinari · London

DESIGN
Fabio Novembre, Mailand

Blumarine ist eine der größten italienischen Modemarken und eng mit der Person von Anna Molinari verbunden, die vom kristallblauen Meer ihrer Heimatstadt Capri beeinflusst, nun seit über zwanzig Jahren aufregende Mode für die romantische und glamouröse Frau kreiert, aber auch Lederwaren, Taschen, Brillen, Düfte. Eigene *Blumarine* Boutiquen hat sie in Mailand, London und Asien. Für die Londoner Boutique ließ sich der Architekt von den Farben der englischen Union Jack-Flagge inspirieren und verknüpfte diese mit Ideen von Künstlern vergangener Zeiten. Die viktorianische Eingangstreppe verwandelte sich in eine Glastreppe für die Präsentation und als Einstieg in eine märchenhafte Welt. So wurden aus dem Rot und Blau der Flagge zwei höhlenartige Räume gänzlich in Mosaik ausgekleidet in der Stimmung orientalischer Moscheen. Und fast märchenhaft wachsen im blauen Raum zwei Stiele aus dem Boden und enden in weißen Blüten aus Murano-Glas. Weiß wird sparsam verwendet und taucht nur noch im Kronleuchter aus gebrochenem Kristall im roten Raum auf. Ein Weiß, wie es Malewitsch, ein Künstler der russischen Avantgarde, verwendete. In den roten Raum gelangt man durch zwei lange goldene Mosaikbeine hindurch, erotisch, abstrakt – an die Grafiken des Franzosen Matisse erinnernd. Mittendrin ein tief rotes spiralförmiges Sofa von Edra. Darüber der etwas ungewohnte Anblick dreier tanzender Mädchen als Deckenmosaik. In den Wandnischen trifft man wie zufällig auf die ausgestellte Mode und die Accessoires. Selbst die Umkleidekabinen im ersten Stock wurden in diese Ideen einbezogen: Wände und Decken wurden in dunkelrotem Velour und silbrig glänzendem Material ausgekleidet und gesteppt. Geheimnisvoll, lasziv, exklusiv, revolutionär. *Blumarine* ist ein Austragungsort ungewöhnlicher glamouröser Mode, eine blaue Grotte und ein rotes Boudoir, poetisch, literarisch, grotesk.

Blumarine is one of the major Italian fashion brand names and closely linked to the person and personality of Anna Molinari. Influenced by the crystal blue sea of her home town of Capri, for over twenty years she has been creating exciting fashion for the romantic and glamorous woman, including leather goods, handbags, eyeglasses and fragrances. She has established her own *Blumarine* Boutiques in Milan, London and Asia. For her London boutique, the architect drew his inspiration from the colours of the Union Jack flag and linked them with ideas by artists of previous ages. The Victorian entry stairway has been transformed into a glass staircase which is geared to display presentations and open the way into a fairy tale world. Two cave-like rooms have been sheathed entirely in mosaic tile using the red and blue colours of the flag, thus conjuring up the atmosphere of an oriental mosque. Another fairy tale element has been incorporated into the blue room: two stems crowned by white blossoms made of Murano glass magically sprout from the floor. White has been used sparingly: in the red room it only makes an appearance in a chandelier made of broken crystal. This is a white such as the Russian avant-garde artist Malewitsch would have used. To enter the red room, patrons must pass through two long golden mosaic legs that radiate an erotic, abstract effect reminiscent of the graphic art of the French artist Matisse. A deep red, spiral shaped Edra sofa thrones right in the middle. The ceiling overhead displays an unusual view of three dancing girls in the form of a mosaic ceiling. In the wall alcoves, fashion and accessories are displayed in a seemingly accidental manner. Even the changing rooms on the upper level have been incorporated into the scheme: the walls and ceilings have been sheathed and quilted in dark red velour and shiny silver fabric. Mysterious, lascivious, exclusive, revolutionary – *Blumarine* is a highly theatrical setting for unusual, glamorous fashion – a blue grotto and a red boudoir suffused with the poetic, the literary and the grotesque.

Gepolsterte Umkleideräume in Rot und Silber –
geheimnisvoll und lasziv

Upholstered changing rooms in red and silver – mysterious and lascivious

Project:
Blumarine, Anna Molinari, London/UK

Design:
Fabio Novembre, Milan/Italy

Area:
70 sqm

Photographer:
Alberto Ferrero, Milan

Via Spiga · Mailand

DESIGN
Fabio Novembre, Mailand

Mitten in der City Mailands, ganz in der Nähe mondäner Einkaufsstraßen, gibt es ein Schuhgeschäft ganz anderer Art. Für die Schuhe und Accessoires der Marke *Via Spiga* des amerikanischen Unternehmens *Intershoe* entwickelte der Architekt Fabio Novembre eine sehr ungewöhnliche Präsentation. Es gibt kein Schaufenster, sondern nur eine Klingel, um in die Boutique im Hinterhof zu gelangen, die sich in einem alten Gebäude aus dem 19. Jahrhundert mit kleinen Fenstern befindet. Hier öffnen sich einfache alte Holztüren, an denen offenbar nur die Farbe entfernt wurde, zu einem Laufsteg aus massivem, japanischen Zedernholz. Er führt in zwei kleine Räume ganz in Gold, wie in einem Märchen oder einem Traum. Fast hat man den Eindruck sich in zwei Zeitzonen zu bewegen – auf dem Laufsteg und im sanften, meditativen Raum. Der Laufsteg grenzt an einen Boden aus goldenen Mosaikfliesen und auch auf den gerundeten Wänden setzt sich das Gold fort, vor denen auf Glasplatten die farbigen Schuhe präsentiert sind. Hinter den Wänden fließt weiches Licht empor und lässt die Decke schweben, die Raumgrenzen verschwimmen.
Einziges Möbel im Raum ist eine massive Zedernholztreppe, die in einen Tisch übergeht. Sein einziges Bein ist ein Stamm, der in einem weißen Kiesbett endet. Ist er Laufsteg oder Tisch? Lediglich die S-Chairs von *Cappellini* geben dem meditativen Raum Proportion und menschliche Nähe. Es ist ein ganz poetischer Raum, der hier den Rahmen für die hochwertigen Produkte bildet, ein Raum voller Geschichten von Menschen, die wie in einem Tempel ihre Schuhe draußen abgestellt haben und all denen, die einmal die neuen Besitzer der ausgestellten Schuhe und Taschen werden könnten. Das sanfte Schimmern des Goldenen Raumes scheint Gedanken zu brechen, einzuhüllen – „so wie die Noten einer Barockmusik auf dem Pentagramm eines Zen Gartens", sagt Fabio.

Right in the middle of the city of Milan, in the immediate vicinity of fashionable shopping streets, there is an entirely different kind of shoe shop. The architect – Fabio Novembre – designed a very unusual form of presentation for the shoes and accessories of the *Via Spiga* brand name, which is manufactured by the American *Intershoe* company. There are no display windows, but only a door bell that you must ring to gain entry to the boutique, which can be reached via a rear courtyard and is housed in an old 19th century building with small windows. Simple old wooden doors, from which apparently only the paint has been removed, open to give access to a catwalk made of solid Japanese cedar wood. This leads to two small rooms done entirely in gold, just like in a fairy tale or a dream. The visitor almost has the impression that he is simultaneously in two time zones – on the catwalk and in the softly meditative room. The catwalk merges into a floor consisting of golden mosaic tiles and the gold has also been continued up the curved walls on which the colourful shoes are displayed on sheets of glass. Soft light flows upward behind the walls and makes the ceiling seem to float, thus erasing spatial boundaries. The only object of furniture in the interior is a massive cedar wood staircase that merges into a table. Its leg is a tree trunk that ends in a bed of white gravel. Is this a ramp or a table? Only the S chairs by *Cappellini* give the meditative room proportion and human scale. It is an entirely poetic interior which provides a suitable setting for the high quality products – a room full of stories about the people who leave their shoes outside as in a temple and all those who might well become the new owners of the shoes and handbags on display. According to Fabio, the soft shimmering of the golden room seems to fracture thought and envelope it – like notes of baroque music on the pentagram of a Zen garden.

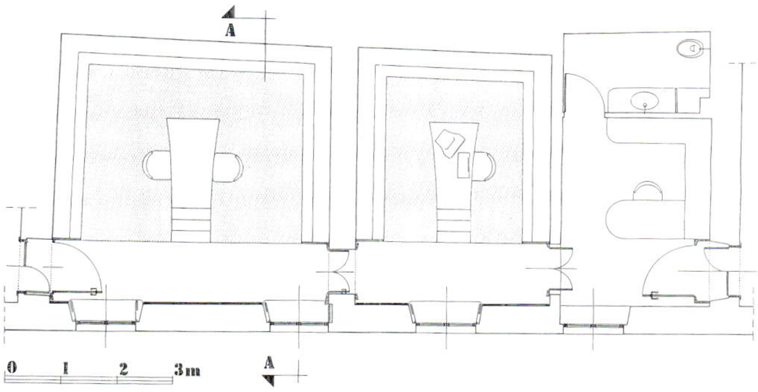

Project:
Via Spiga, Milan/Italy

Design:
Fabio Novembre, Milan
+ Lorenzo de Nicola,
Serena Novembre

Area:
58 sqm

Photographer:
Alberto Ferrero, Milan

Qiora Store and Spa · New York

DESIGN
ARO Architecture Research Office, New York

Qiora ist eine neue Hautpflege-Produktlinie des größten japanischen Kosmetikherstellers *Shiseido*, die in Nordamerika durch einen eigenen Laden eingeführt werden soll. In einer der vornehmsten Gegenden New Yorks, in der Madison Avenue, haben die Kunden nun die Möglichkeit, die Produkte zu kaufen, ihre Wirkung in einem Anwendungsbereich an sich selbst zu erleben und zugleich die Philosophie der Pflegeprodukte durch ein ungewöhnliches Raumerlebnis zu erfahren. Die Wirkung der Pflegeserie basiert auf einer asiatisch-meditativen Lebensform, mit der ganz allmählich durch Entspannung, Einatmen der Düfte und Spüren der Pflegewirkung neue Energie und Wohlbefinden erlangt werden soll, um Körper und Seele von Stress zu befreien. Im *Qiora Store and Spa* wird der Kunde durch den Raum auf diese Produktwirkung vorbereitet. Geschwungene Wände aus lichtblauem leichten Organza-Gewebe formen eine bewegte Raum-Landschaft, die durch fluoreszierende Leuchten mit Warm- und Kaltlicht Tageslichtcharakter erhält. In vornehmer Zurückhaltung werden die Produkte auf kleinen Glastischen vor der Wand und dezent auf Glasborden präsentiert, die durch die Gazevorhänge hindurchscheinen und mit Fieberglastechnik von oben beleuchtet werden – tagsüber weiß und nachts blau. Der Besucher, der hier durch den Raum schreitet, erlebt in den Wänden die geschweifte Form der extravaganten Flakons und Karaffen, unter den Klängen der Musik von *Qiora* (auch zu hören auf der Website unter www.qiora.com) und damit einen wichtigen Teil der Markenphilosophie. Im Hintergrund des Ladens sind drei zylindrische Kabinen für den Anwendungsbereich (Spa) hinter Gaze und etwas dichteren Chintz-Stoffen verborgen. Auch die übrigen Raummaterialien unterstützen das Thema Kosmetik: ein hochglänzender Boden aus weißem Epoxidharz, Glastische mit Edelstahl, weißes Leder. Es ist ein Raum, der die beruhigende Wirkung der Produkte spürbar werden lässt.

Qiora is a new line of skin care products which *Shiseido*, the largest Japanese cosmetics manufacturer, intends to launch in North America in special stores exclusively devoted to the product. In one of the most elegant districts of New York – Madison Avenue – customers now have the opportunity to purchase the products and experience their effect "live" in a spa treatment area. At the same time, the philosophy of the skin care products is underscored by means of an extraordinary spatial experience. The effect of the skin care product line is based on a meditative Asian way of life, which makes it possible to gradually attain new energy and a feeling of well-being through relaxation, breathing in fragrances and experiencing the skin care effect, thus liberating the body as well as the soul from stress. In the *Qiora Store and Spa*, the customer is prepared for the effect of the product by the interior itself. Curved walls fashioned out of light blue, gossamer organza fabric create an animated spatial scene that is suffused with a pseudo day light effect by means of fluorescent lamps with warm and cold light tones. Elegantly inconspicuous, diminutive glass tables arranged in front of the wall and glass shelving elements that shimmer through the gauze draperies and are illuminated from above with fibre glass technology serve to discreetly display the products. White throughout the day, and blue at night. As the visitor progresses through the interior, the walls call to mind the curved shapes of the extravagant flacons and carafes. Together with the strains of *Qiora's* theme music (which can also be heard on the website at www.qiora.com), they constitute an important part of the brand name philosophy. In the rear portion of the store, three cylindrical spa cabins are concealed behind gauze and somewhat more opaque chintz fabric. The other materials used for the interior also underline the cosmetics theme: white epoxy resin for the high gloss floor, glass and stainless steel for the tables and white leather. This is an interior that perceptibly and effectively incorporates the calming effect of the products.

qiora
X63
X64

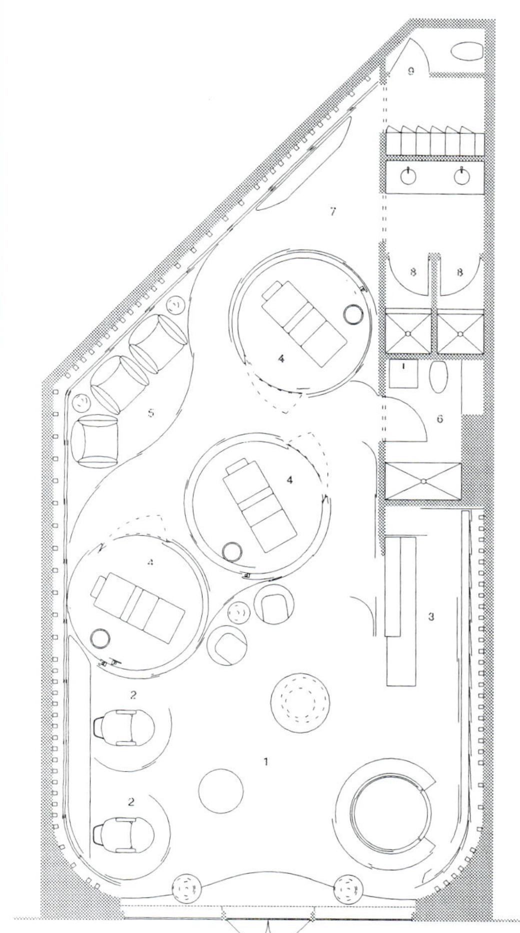

1 Verkaufsbereich
2 Beratungsbereich
3 Kasse
4 Spa Kabine
5 Lounge
6 Herren-Badezimmer
7 Damen-Ankleide
8 Dusche
9 Toilette

1 Retail Area
2 Consultation Area
3 Cash/Wrap Area
4 Spa Cabin
5 Lounge
6 Men's Bathroom
7 Women's dressingroom
8 Shower
9 lavatory

Project:
Qiora Store and Spa,
New York/USA

Design:
ARO Architecture Research
Office, New York

Aoshi Kudo, Designer and
Art Director,
Shiseido Cosmetics, Tokyo

Area:
ca. 140 sqm

Photographer:
Reid Freemann, New York,
David Joseph, Shiseido,
Tokyo

Nuon, Baarn · London

DESIGN
20/20 Design Limited, London

Nuon ist ein großer holländischer Energieanbieter, der seine Erfahrungen weltweit einbringt – von Aktienbeteiligungen in England bis hin zu Wasserprojekten in China und Rumänien. Im Kaufhaus *Nijhof* in Baarn erhielt *Nuon* die Möglichkeit, auf einer Fläche von 200 Quadratmetern Endverbraucher über seine Energieangebote Gas, Heizung und Wasser sowie damit verbundene Produkte und Leistungen zu informieren, zugleich aber auch einer Marke eine lebendige Plattform zu geben. Das Londoner Designunternehmen *20/20 Limited* entwickelte hierfür eine Präsentation, in der Produkte und Inhalte mit Grafik, Licht und Farbe verständlich und erlebbar gemacht werden. Vom Kaufhaus aus öffnet sich ein breiter Durchgang mit Grafikwänden, auf denen *Nuon* seine Kunden willkommen heißt und mit ihnen Kontakt aufnimmt. Im Inneren des Geschäftes geht es eher um die Markenbotschaft und konkrete Angebote wie Heiz-Lösungen zur Verbesserung und Erhaltung des Hauses. Jeder Bereich ist durch eine Farbe und durch ein großes Deckenlicht-Objekt gekennzeichnet. Statt einem unverständlichen Schilderwald gibt es lebendig gestaltete Produkte mit stilvoller Grafik, Lichtwänden und Sachinformationen, die durch Computerterminals und ein Beratungsteam erweitert werden können. Über Energie wird hier nicht nur gesprochen, Energie wird vom Kunden in atmosphärischen Lichträumen erlebt, um für sich selbst die richtigen Lösungen zu finden.

Nuon is a major Dutch utilities provider, which makes use of its expertise world wide – from shareholdings in England to water projects in China and Romania. At the *Nijhof* department store in Baarn on an floor area of 200 square metres, *Nuon* was given the opportunity of informing end consumers about its range of services. This includes gas, heating, water and related products and services. At the same time this was a chance to create an exciting platform for the brand name. To this end the London *20/20 design company* developed a presentation concept which makes products and content comprehensible and makes it possible to experience them first hand by means of graphics, lighting and colour. From the department store a wide passage with walls covered in graphic illustrations opens up, allowing *Nuon* to present information about its relationship to its customers. In the interior of the shop the focus is more on the brand name message and specific products and services, such as heating solutions aimed at the improvement and maintenance of houses. Each area is characterised by colour and a large ceiling mounted beacon. Instead of an incomprehensible forest of signs, the products have been brought to life with stylish graphic illustrations, illuminated walls and factual information which can be supplemented by computer terminals and a team of consultants. The concept does not merely provide a context for talk about energy: the customer can actually experience energy in atmospherically effective rooms delineated by light, and thus find the right solutions himself.

Warmwasser-Bereich in warmen, intensiven Farben

Warmwater area in warm and intensive colours

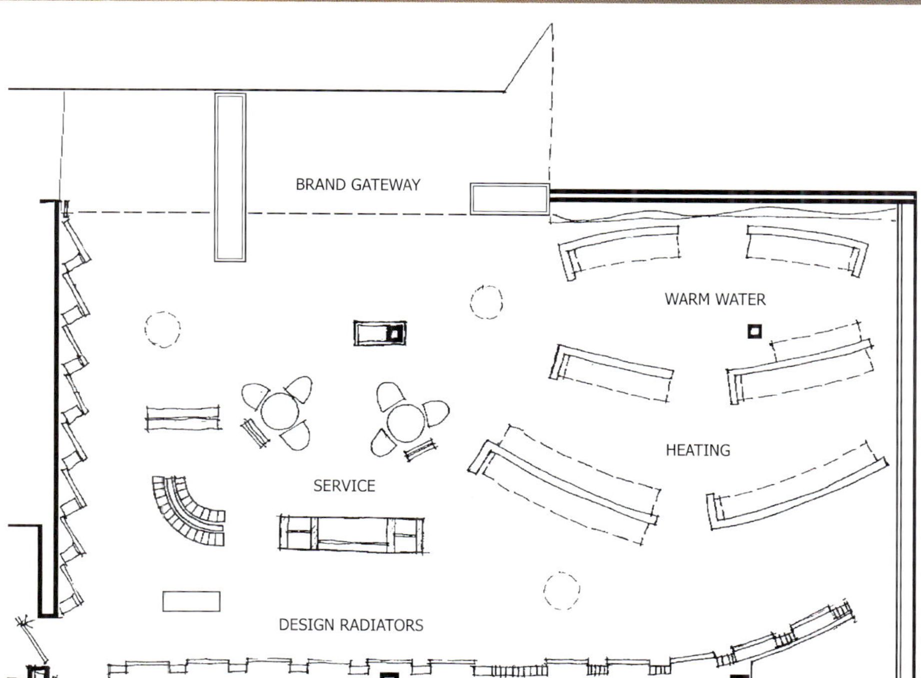

sfeer
design
tijdloos
warmte
modern
stijlvol
wonen
sfeerkachels
Tornado

Close-in boiler

NUON
helderheid
kracht
gemak
rm wonen
ing en warm water
ol wonen
els en designradiatoren
eloos wonen
nderhoud
kennis
ssingen
Energie
Prestatie
Advies
of bel 0800-2021
NUON
helderheid
...zorgt nu
ook voor de
warmte
in huis
sfeer
warmte
oplossingen
doordenken

Heizlösungen werden durch Objekte und Grafik erlebbar gemacht, unterstützt durch Computer-Terminals

Heating solutions can be experienced by objects and graphic-design, supported by computer terminals

◀ Eingangsbereich mit Markenbotschaft

Brand Gateway as a welcoming area for the customers

Project:
Nuon, Baarn/Nederlande

Design:
20/20 Design Limited,
Simon Stacey
and Sarah Page, London

Realisation:
Vizona BV, NL-Diemen

Area:
ca. 200 sqm

Photographer:
Adriano Biondo, Amsterdam,
Robert Howard, London

Telfort Plaza · Den Haag

DESIGN
Jos de Vries,
The Retail Company,
Maarssen

Mit der *Telfort Plaza* eröffnete das niederländische Tochterunternehmen der britischen Telecom in Den Haag direkt neben dem Kaufhaus *De Bijenkorf* seinen ersten Image-Store, um ein breites Publikum mit den neuen Telekommunikations-Techniken vertraut zu machen. An sieben Tagen in der Woche können Jung und Alt alle Möglichkeiten der mobilen, persönlichen Kommunikation und die des Internets kennen lernen und ausprobieren. Gleich am Eingang informiert ein Touch-Screen über das Angebot. Direkt daneben kann an Surf-Plätzen, in der Form angelehnt an Surf-Segel aus dem Sport, im Internet gesurft, können E-mails geschrieben und abgeschickt werden und auch Chatten ist möglich. Über eine Web-Cam lassen sich digitale Fotos erstellen und an Freunde verschicken. Internet-Jockeys informieren und helfen bei der Suche nach Informationen und Websites, z.B. über die Region Den Haag oder das *North Sea Jazz Festival* oder der Erstellung einer eigenen Website. Ansonsten weisen Touch Screens den Weg, unterstützt durch Informations- und Serviceschalter. Alle Technikplätze und die hinterleuchteten Produktwände gruppieren sich um die runde Kassen- und Infotheke im Zentrum, dessen Mittelpunkt eine gläsernen Weltkugel bildet. Die im Raum eingesetzten Firmenfarben Blau und Orange sind die Basis für ein helles und kommunikatives Farbkonzept, das die Angst vor der Technik nehmen soll, materialmäßig übersetzt durch gebürstetes Aluminium und sandgestrahltes Glas. An die Kommunikation per Satellit erinnern die riesigen Glasleuchten unter der Decke in Form von Satellitenschüsseln. Und fast schon Weltraumatmosphäre können die Kids in ihrer Ecke schnuppern. Hier gibt es für sie spezielle Bildschirme im Pilzformat und an einigen Internetplätzen können sie sich mit der Datenautobahn vertraut machen. In der *Telfort Plaza* ist Kommunikations-Technik ein unkompliziertes Alltagsereignis.

With the *Telfort Plaza* directly adjacent to the *De Bijenkorf* department store, the Dutch subsidiary of British Telecom has opened its first image store in order to familiarise a large portion of the public with the new telecommunications technologies. Seven days a week young and old can acquaint themselves with all of the potential uses of mobile, personal communication and the internet and try them out. Right at the entrance there is a touch screen that provides information about the range of products. Directly next to it customers can surf the web at internet surfing places which are reminiscent of wind surfing sails used in the sports activity: they can write and send e-mails, or chat if they wish. A web cam makes it possible to take digital photographs and send them to friends. Internet jockeys provide information and help patrons in their search for information and web sites, e.g. about the region surrounding The Hague or the *North Sea Jazz Festival*, or about how to set up your own website. In addition, touch screens supplemented by information and service counters help visitors navigate through the world of technology. All of the technology areas and the backlit product display walls are grouped around the circular cash register and information counter at the centre, where the focus is a glass globe. Blue and orange – the corporate colours that have been utilised for the interior – serve as the basis for a bright and communicative colour concept that is aimed at reducing people's fear of technology. The materials used to interpret the concept are brushed aluminium and sand blasted glass. On the ceiling, gigantic glass lighting fixtures shaped like satellite dishes evoke thoughts of satellite communication. The kids' corner exudes an almost futuristically space age atmosphere. There are special mushroom shaped monitors and several internet places where young customers can familiarise themselves with the wonders of the data highway. The *Telfort Plaza* demonstrates communication technology for every day life in an uncomplicated manner.

Telfort

Telfort
PLAZA

Telfort

DINSDAG 25 JULI
11.30 UUR MONDELING ENGELS
Telfort

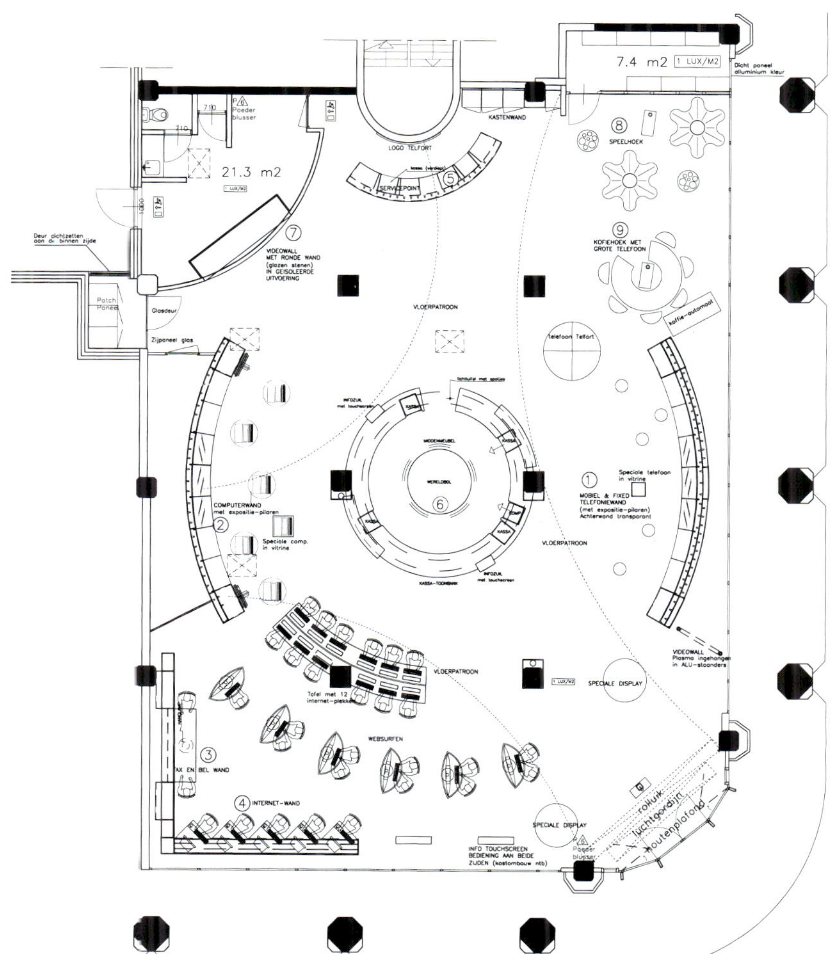

Project:
Telfort Plaza,
Den Haag/Nederlande

Design:
Jos de Vries,
The Retail Company,
Maarssen

Area:
ca. 320 sqm

Photographer:
Victor van Leeuwen,
Waddinxveen

Perugina Showroom · Perugia

DESIGN
Studio D'Architettura
Simone Micheli, Florenz

Wer kennt sie nicht, die süßen verführerischen Bacis des italienischen Schokoladenherstellers *Perugina* aus Perugia in Umbrien. Hier hat Schokolade seit 90 Jahren Tradition, es gibt ein Schokoladen-Museum und sogar eine Messe ausschließlich für Schokolade. Und nun hat *Perugina* im historischen Zentrum der Stadt auch einen eigenen Showroom, der nicht nur die kleinen köstlichen Schokoladenteilchen anbietet sondern zugleich ermöglicht, die ganze Tradition und Wertigkeit der Marke im Raum zu erleben. Die gläserne Fassade des alten Gebäudes ist mit einer goldfarbenen Decke überwölbt, die auf das eigens für diesen Showroom entwickelte Logo strahlt.
Der Raum selbst interpretiert die Firmenfarben Blau und Gold in völlig neuer moderner Weise. So zieht sich erhaben ein dunkelblauer, glänzender Harzboden mit eingelegten goldfarbenen Pegasuspferdchen (dem Firmenzeichen von *Perugina*) durch den ganzen Ladenraum und setzt sich in der ebenfalls dunkelblauen Decke des Raumes fort, nur unterbrochen durch strahlende Lichtpunkte. Eher traditionell muten die gläsernen Wandvitrinen mit dicken Kirschholzrahmen an, in denen die Besonderheiten und Verpackungen ausgestellt sind. Ein Glasregal für lose Ware befindet sich in der verspiegelten Rückwand, die die Raumgrenzen auflöst und die dunkle blaue Höhle endlos erscheinen lässt. Wie eine übergroße Konfektschachtel erscheint die Wandnische in der Spiegelwand, ein Rahmen für das Besondere. Die eigentliche Präsentation der Ware vor den Kunden aber erfolgt auf großen ovalen Tischen aus Kirschholz mit Messingbeinen. Irgendwie erinnern selbst diese an dicke, süße Schokoladenteile.
Während der vordere Teil der Präsentation und dem Verkauf dient, werden im hinteren Ladenteil Schokoladenteile vorbereitet und in spezielle Schachteln und Keramikbehälter versenkt. *Perugina* erhielt mit diesem Showroom einen weichen, einschmeichelnden Raum, der die Tradition der Marke atmet und in dem der Kunde den intensiven Geschmack der Schokolade fast räumlich spüren kann.

Who has not heard of the sweetly tempting bacis of *Perugina* – the Italian chocolate manufacturer of Perugia in Umbria, where chocolate is a tradition that began 90 years ago. There is a chocolate museum and even a trade fair devoted exclusively to chocolate. In the historical city centre, *Perugina* now has its own showroom, which not only offers delicious small chocolate delicacies, but simultaneously provides an opportunity to experience the entire tradition and quality of the brand name, which permeates the entire interior. The glass façade of the venerable building is crowned by a gold coloured arching portico where the logo that was designed specifically for this showroom is displayed. The interior itself interprets the blue and gold corporate colours in a entirely new and modern way. A dark blue, sublimely gleaming resin floor inlaid with gold coloured Pegasus horses – the corporate image of *Perugina* – has been used throughout the interior of the shop. The same dark blue has also been incorporated into ceiling, where it is interspersed with glowing spots of light. The glass wall cabinets with wide cherry wood frames, in which special items and packaging are displayed, are in a more traditional vein. A glass shelf for unpackaged merchandise is mounted on the mirror sheathed rear wall, which seems to dissolve the boundaries of the room and makes the dark blue cavern seem limitless. The wall niche in the mirrored wall resembles a gigantic box of chocolates, a fitting display area for particularly special items. The actual presentation of the merchandise for customers is focused on large oval, cherry wood tables with brass legs. Even these elements are reminiscent of thick, sweet slabs of chocolate.
The front section of the interior is reserved for display purposes and sales, while the rear portion of the shop is devoted to the preparation of the chocolates, which are nestled in special boxes or ceramic containers. This showroom has provided *Perugina* with a soft, temptingly inviting room which exudes the tradition of the brand name. The design of the interior almost allows customers to physically experience the intensive taste of chocolate.

Speziell für diesen Showroom entwickeltes Firmenlogo

Logo – specifically developed for this showroom

Die Firmenfarben Gold und Blau neu interpretiert in glänzend blauem Harz-Boden mit goldenem Firmenzeichen

A gleaming blue raison floor inlaid with gold coloured metal horses interprets the Coporate Colours blue and gold

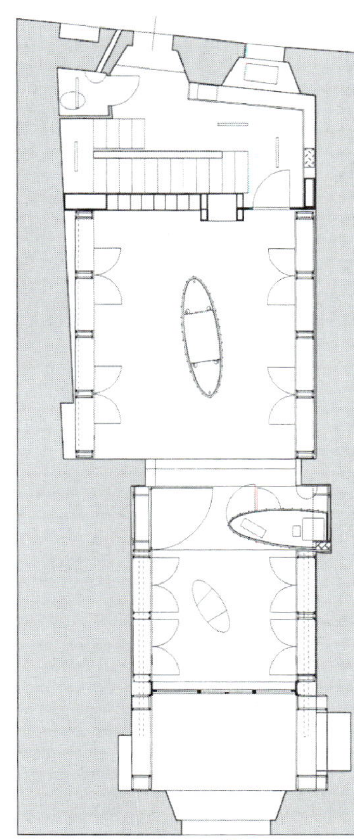

Project:
Perugina Showroom, Perugia/Italy

Design:
Studio D'Architettura Simone Michelli, Florence

Area:
ca. 65 sqm

Photographer:
Graziano Villa, Milan

Camper · Mailand

DESIGN
Shiro Miura, Kyoto, Japan

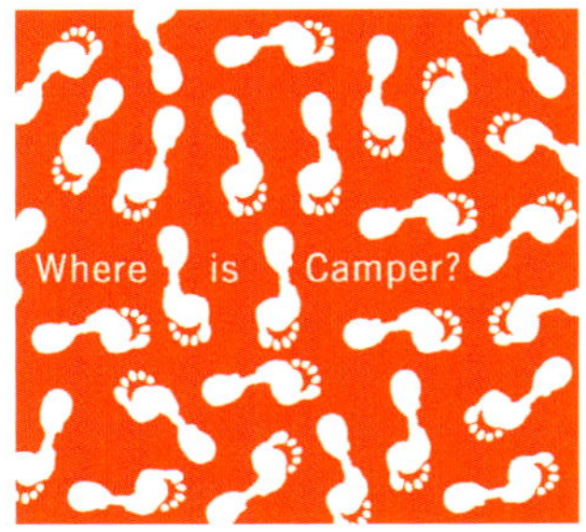

Ländlich einfach mit städtischem Know How – so könnte man die Schuhe von *Camper* beschreiben, ein Unternehmen, das seinen Ursprung im Ideenreichtum des Schuhhandwerkers Antonio Fluxá hat, der aus den bequemen, schlichten und gut genähten Schuhen der Bauern (Camper) Mallorcas eigene Kreationen entwickelte. Vor über 20 Jahren knüpfte der Urenkel Lorenzo Fluxá an diese Ideen an und schuf mit der Marke *Camper* „Schuhe der Landbevölkerung für den urbanen Individualisten“: Bequem, designed, kreativ und qualitätsvoll. Leicht ironisch bewegt er sich damit zwischen authentischem Landleben und Urbanität. Seine neuesten Läden entstanden in Mailand und New York und spiegeln diese Philosophie wider.

Mailand war der erste Laden, der in Anlehnung an den Slogan „Walk-in-Progress“ nach dem Work-in-Progress-Konzept gebaut wurde, das ermöglicht, den Laden zu eröffnen, während die letzten Arbeiten fertig gestellt werden und die Kunden auf diese Weise an dem Baugeschehen teilhaben können. Für seine Gestaltung wurde nicht nur Shiro Miura aus Japan geholt sondern auch viele Materialien und Accessoires. So sind z.B. die Wände mit Paneelen aus japanischem Reispapier verkleidet, nur unterbrochen durch einige Großfotos mit dem mallorquinischen Pferdewagen als Symbol für die Veränderung der Zeit. An beiden Seiten des Raumes ziehen sich niedrige, geschwungene Ausstellungsbänke entlang. Ihre Holzverkleidung und auch die weiße Porzellanplatte darauf stammen aus Japan. Ebenfalls aus japanischen Blättern sind die runden flachen Sitzkissen, in der Form typischer mallorquinischer Ensaimadas (rundes Gebäck) geflochten. Ländlich einfach und bedeutungsvoll ist auch die große Vase aus Lehm. Das leichte Rinnen des herunterlaufenden Wassers ist über Lautsprecher im ganzen Raum zu hören – ein Raum der Ruhe und des Friedens in der Hektik dieser eleganten Mailänder Geschäftsstraße.

The essence of *Camper* shoes can be described as country simplicity combined with big city know-how: The idea is over one hundred years old and is based on the comfortable, simple and well made shoes worn by Majorcan farmers (Campers). In Majorca for over 20 years, *Camper* has been creating the shoes of the rural inhabitants for urban individualists – comfortable, specially designed, creative and high quality. Thus, in a slightly ironic vein it oscillates between authentic country life and urbanity. Its newest shops, which also reflect this philosophy, have been established in Milan and New York.

Milan was the first shop to be built. In tune with the "walk in progress" slogan, it was constructed according to a work in progress concept, thus making it possible to open the shop while the last construction work was being completed. That way customers had the opportunity to experience the construction process first hand. Shiro Miura from Japan was commissioned with the design, and many materials and accessories also originated in Japan. For example, the walls are covered in panels of Japanese rice paper, occasionally interrupted by several large scale photographs of the Majorcan horse drawn carriage as a symbol of the changes effected by time. Low, curved display surfaces line both sides of the room. The wood sheathing on them and the china slab are also originally from Japan. The flat round seating cushions in the shape of the typical Majorcan round pastries called ensaimadas are filled with Japanese leaves. The large vase made of mud is similarly simple and meaningful. The soft splash of trickling water is transmitted throughout the interior via loudspeakers – conjuring up a place imbued with tranquillity and peace amidst the hectic hubbub of this elegant Milan shopping street.

Project:
Camper, Milan/Italy

Design:
Shiro Miura, Kyoto/Japan

Photographer:
Camper, Inca (Mallorca)/
Spain

Camper · New York

DESIGN
**Marti Guixé,
Barcelona/Spanien**

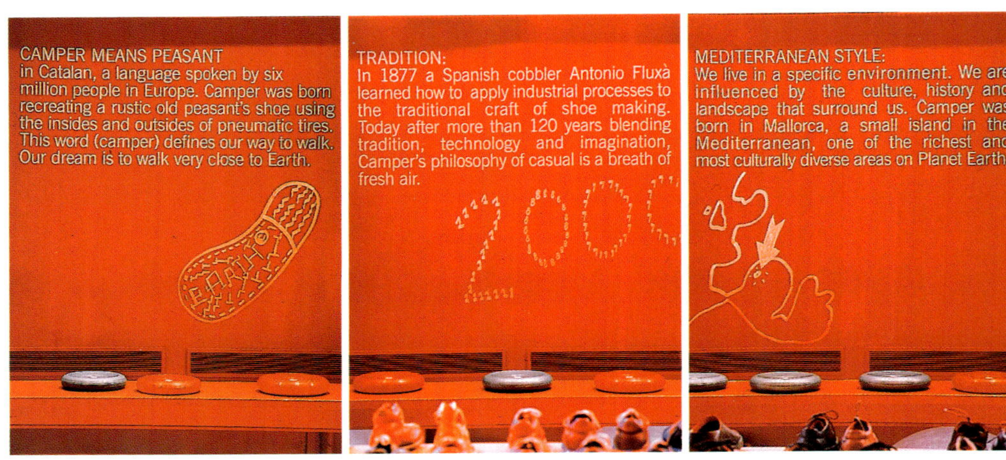

Für den Laden in **New York** suchte der Katalane Marti Guixé eine Parallele zwischen Mallorca und Manhattan. Er fand sie: Beides sind Inseln und beide holen ihre Kraft aus dem Stein. Der Raum für dieses Kräftespiel befindet sich in einem denkmalgeschützten Gebäude aus dem frühen 20. Jahrhundert mit einer schmalen Straßenfront. Als Ausgleich dafür gibt es im Innern eine lange Plattform, einen Laufsteg, der an beiden Schmalseiten in Treppen übergeht, auf dem die ganze Schuhparade ausgebreitet ist, darauf wartend, anprobiert und mitgenommen zu werden. Über den Schuhen die riesigen *XXL Dome-Leuchten* von Ingo Maurer. Gegenüber dem Laufsteg stehen Bänke mit runden Ledersitzkissen. Ganz nach Feng Shui-Philosophie sind die Spiegel zum Anschauen der Schuhe unter der Sitzfläche angebracht, um den Raum nicht zu stören. Über den Bänken wird auf den Wänden in warmem Rot die Geschichte des Unternehmens erzählt, die auf der Rückwand des Raumes in einem Großfoto eines Trockenmauerwerks in Mallorca endet. Es ist ein lichtvoller Raum, der das Herz Mallorcas mitten in Soho widerspiegelt, natürlich, spartanisch, voll von Kultur und Fantasie.

For the **New York** shop, Catalonian native Marti Guixé looked for a parallel between Majorca and Manhattan. He found it: both are islands and both derive their strength from stone. The setting for this contest of strength is located in an early twentieth century building with a narrow façade, which is listed as an historic monument. In the interior this is balanced by a long platform – a catwalk which merges into stairs at both of the narrow ends. This is where the entire parade of shoes is spread out – waiting to be tried on and taken home. Above the shoes hang gigantic *XXL dome lights* by Ingo Maurer. Opposite the catwalk there are benches with round leather cushions. In accordance with the Feng Shui philosophy, the mirrors are mounted below the seats. Above the benches, the story of the company is related on a warm red background, merging into a blow up photograph of a dry stone wall in Majorca on the rear wall of the room. This is an interior filled with light that reflects the heart of Majorca in the middle of Soho – natural, Spartan, full of culture and fantasy.

Project:
Camper, New York/USA

Design:
Marti Guixé,
Barcelona/Spain

Photographer:
Camper, Inca (Mallorca)/
Spain

Mandarina Duck · Bologna

DESIGN
Studio AMDL, Mailand

Es ist bereits die vierte Ladengeneration, die Michele de Lucchi für das italienische Unternehmen *Mandarina Duck* entwickelt, das seit über zwanzig Jahren ungewöhnlich kreative Lederwaren, Bekleidung und Accessoires herstellt. Angefangen von beigefarbenen Steinläden über Aluminium-Läden mit ergänzbaren Wänden bis zu den heutigen durch Harmonie und Persönlichkeit geprägten, wurden immer Visionen und Emotionen umgesetzt – Eckpfeiler der Unternehmensidentität.
Im zweigeschossigen Laden in Bologna schieben sich skelettartige Skulpturen mit gewundenen überlappenden Ablagen für liegende und hängende Ware durch den Raum. Prähistorisch, sinnlich, üppig – mit einer weißen Pfirsichhaut überzogen, völliger Kontrast zu den kargen weißen Wänden, deren Grenzen zum Boden nur durch eine beleuchtete opale Plexiglasform definiert werden. Nichts behindert den Blick und den umherschreitenden Kunden, der immer wieder Neues entdecken kann. Im Schaufenster hängt nur das neue Logo – ein gelbes Quadrat mit Firmenschriftzug. Das Licht aber begrenzt und führt den Kunden durch die Räume, dringt aus horizontalen Lichtspalten, den „Tagliatellen", aus der Decke, schickt Lichtpunkte nach unten auf die Ware. Selbst die Umkleidekabinen sind Lichtobjekte aus weißem, weichem filmähnlichem Material. Die Lichtfarben im Raum wechseln ständig, um metaphorisch den Wechsel der Modesaisons aufzuzeigen – und mit ihnen auch die Stimmungen, wenn sich die sanften Düfte der Heilkräuter im ganzen Laden ausbreiten. *Mandarina Duck* ist nicht nur einfach ein Laden – sondern eine neue Sinneswelt.

This is already the fourth generation of shops that Michele de Lucchi has designed for *Mandarina Duck*, an Italian company which has been manufacturing unusually creative leather goods, clothing and accessories for over twenty years. He started with a beige coloured shop rendered in stone, tried out aluminium shops with continual walls and progressed to today's shops, which are full of harmony and personality. He has always converted key concepts into visions and emotions, thereby establishing the cornerstones of the firm's corporate identity. In the small two storey shop in Bologna, skeleton-like sculptural objects with curvilinear, overlapping shelves for folded and hanging merchandise thrust upward throughout the room. Covered in a white peach-like skin they appear prehistoric, sensual and voluptuous – and create a complete contrast to the austere white walls, whose demarcation area with the floor is only defined by an illuminated opal Plexiglas shape. Nothing obstructs views or impedes the customers who stroll through the interior, repeatedly discovering something new. The window display only contains the new logo – a yellow square lettered with the company's name. However, lighting serves to delineate the perimeter and guide customers through the interior: it radiates from horizontal light cracks – so-called tagliatelli – on the ceiling and focuses points of light downwards onto the merchandise. Even the fitting rooms are light objects made of soft white, film-like material. The colours used for the lighting of the interior change constantly, so as to metaphorically illustrate the change of the fashion seasons as well as the associated respective moods, when the gentle fragrance of medicinal herbs permeates the entire shop. *Mandarina Duck* is not merely a shop – but a new world of the senses.

Skelettartige Skulpturen für die Produktpräsentation und Raumgestaltung

Skeleton-like sculptural objects for product presentation and interior design

Erdgeschoss / Ground floor

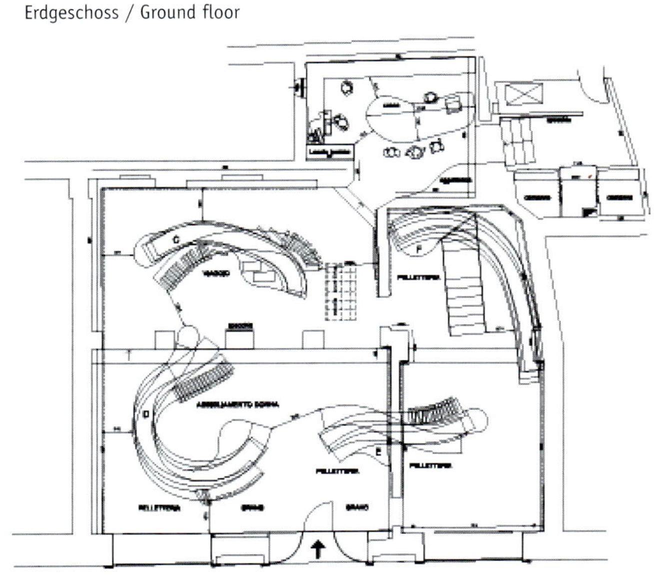

Obergeschoss / First floor

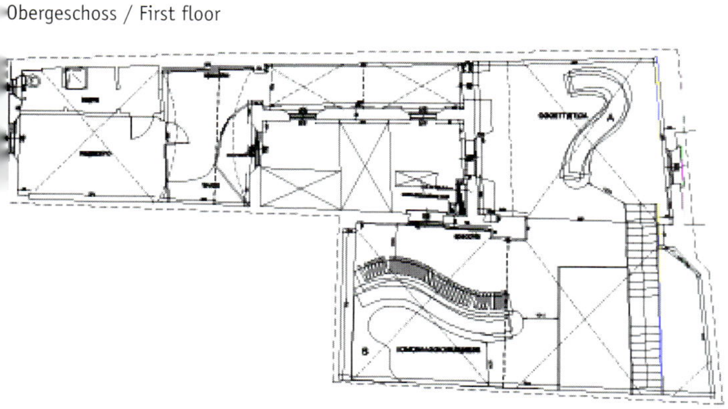

Project:
Mandarina Duck, Bologna/Italy

Design:
Studio AMDL, Michele de Lucchi + Angelo Micheli, Silvia Suardi, Milan

Area:
270 sqm, 2 floors

Photographer:
Santi Caleca, Milan

Mandarina Duck · Paris

DESIGN
Droog Design und NL Architects, Amsterdem

Bisher eher in kleineren Läden angesiedelt, wagte der italienische Hersteller hochwertiger Lederwaren und Damen- und Herrenmode, *Mandarina Duck*, mit seinem Pariser Flagship-Store den Sprung in die Haute Couture. Die Entscheidung, *Droog Design* und *NL Architects* auszuwählen hieß für sie, kein Standard- oder Minimaldesign zu erhalten sondern einen Raum ohne Architektur, einen Überraschungseffekt, etwas zum Gefallen. Entstanden sind leere weiße Räume mit freistehenden Elementen, sogenannten „Cocoons", die Container und Objekt zugleich sind, Räume zum Entdecken von immer wieder Neuem. Da ist die beidseitig nutzbare Pinwand am Eingang, an der Taschen auf Metallspitzen zu schweben scheinen. An der Wand neben der Treppe stecken Taschen zwischen farbigen Gummibändern, wie sie beim Fahrrad verwendet werden. Ein Tunnel besteht aus riesigen Paletten für Accessoires und gleich dahinter überrascht eine flache begehbare Metallkugel auf drei dünnen Beinen, einem Ufo gleich, mit einen Innenleben aus Damen- und Herrenbekleidung. Erlebnis pur bietet die rotierende Wendeltreppe, die die Kunden nach oben zu beamen scheint. Hier im ersten Stock gibt es fast noch mehr zu sehen: Eine organisch gebogene Wand aus Metallketten schwingt sich um leicht rotierende Taschenetageren und die Blister Wall stößt kurze Atemgeräusche aus, um die Kleidung mittels Vakuum auf Acrylplatten zu halten. Besonders aufregend aber sind die Umkleidekabiner, wo man hinter raschelnden hellgrünen Fiberglasstäben wie hinter hohen Grashalmen verschwindet. Was sich hier den Kunden bietet ist eine Entdeckungsreise ohne Hast und Eile in eine ganz neue Raum- und Produktwelt.

Up until now *Mandarina Duck* has been located in smaller shops, but now the Italian manufacturer of high quality leather goods and ladies' and men's fashion has taken the plunge into haute couture with its Paris flagship store. The decision to select *Droog Design* and *NL Architects* meant that the result would be neither standard nor minimal design, but rather an interior without architecture, a surprise effect, a pleasurable experience. The resulting interior consists of empty white rooms with free-standing elements, so-called cocoons that simultaneously serve as containers and art objects – rooms where there is always something new to be discovered. At the entrance, a bulletin board where handbags seem to float on metal spikes can be utilised from both sides. On the wall next to the stairway handbags are held by colourful elastic straps similar to those used for bicycle racks. A tunnel has been fashioned out of gigantic palettes displaying accessories. Right behind it, customers can enter a surprising flat metal sphere on three spindly legs that resembles a UFO. The rotating spiral staircase which appears to beam customers heavenwards is a truly unique experience. On the upper level there is almost more to see: an organically curved wall made of metal chains threads its way around rotating handbag etageres and the Blister Wall emits short breath-like noises in order to hold the items of clothing on the acrylic sheets by means of a vacuum. But the fitting rooms are especially exciting: customers disappear behind rustling, light green fibre glass rods as if behind tall stalks of grass. This shop offers customers an opportunity for a voyage of discovery devoid of hurry or rush – a voyage through an entirely new product world and spatial universe.

1. Drehbare Treppe
2. Pinwand mit Metallstäben
3. Paletten-Tunnel
4. Inkubator
5. Gummibänder-Wand
6. Kleidercocon
7. Kassentheke
8. Anpass-Kabine
9. Vacuumwand
10. Epoxyschrank
11. Runde Tische
12. Metallene Vorhangwand
13. Socle
14. Fluo-Schränke
15. Spiegelboxen
16. Grasland – Umkleiden

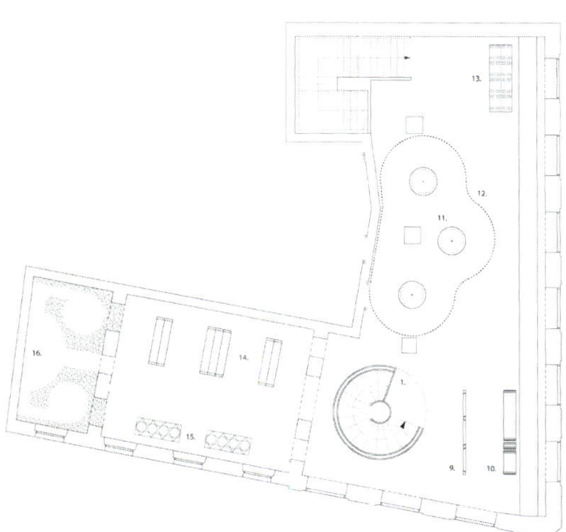

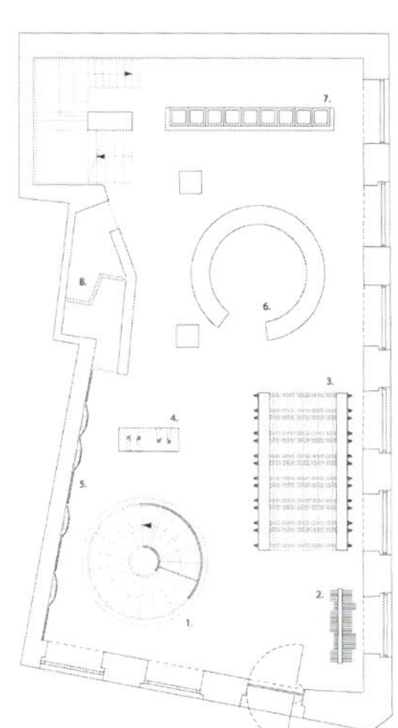

1. Revolving Stair
2. Pinwall
3. Pallet Tunnel
4. Incubator
5. Rubber Wall
6. Inverse Clothrack
7. Counter
8. Fitting Rooms
9. Vacuumwall
10. Epoxy-cupboard
11. Stacked round tables
12. Curtain Room
13. Socle
14. Fluo-cupboards
15. Mirrorboxes
16. Grassland

Project:
Mandarina Duck,
Paris/France

Design:
Droog Design
+ NL Architects,
Amsterdam/Nederlands

Area:
300 sqm, 2 floors

Photographer:
Mandarina Duck, Bologna

Missoni Shop System · New York

DESIGN
Matteo Thun
Mailand/Italien
Milan/Italy

Das traditionsreiche italienische Modeunternehmen *Missoni* steht für eine hochwertige, farbenprächtige Damen- und Herrenmode aus Maschenware, weltweit vermarktet und preisgekrönt. Matteo Thun entwickelte für und mit *Missoni* ein Shop Konzept, das in New York, Paris und Mailand umgesetzt wurde. Eine kreative Fröhlichkeit prägte nicht nur die Zusammenarbeit sondern auch die Designidee. Diese sieht für die hochwertigen farbigen Produkte eine neutrale Raumhülle vor, die durch geradlinige Wege und Lichtöffnungen in Wand und Decke betont wird. Die gewollte Heiterkeit des Raumes, die den Kunden willkommen heißen soll, wird durch Licht, Farbe und Materialien erreicht, die in ihrer Gesamtwirkung die Sensibilität der raffinierten Stoffe aufgreift. So stehen auf einem lackierten und polierten Betonboden verschieden hohe hinterleuchtete Kuben und erfüllen den Raum mit Leben. Fast wie Ikonen der Kollektion liegen nur wenige Produkte auf satiniertem Glas oder vor farbig hinterleuchteten Filmflächen. Diese Glasflächen, deren Farb- und Lichtqualität mit der Tageszeit und Modesaison wechseln, schaffen eine bauliche Entsprechung zu den raffinierten Farbeffekten der Ware. Daneben gibt es leicht gebogene Holztablare an der Wand, die durch ihren Lichtrahmen die Ware wie in einer Kunstgalerie präsentieren. Eine hinterleuchtete Säulenreihe zeigt die 40fache Vergrößerung der Maschenware. Der gesamte Raum atmet die Fröhlichkeit und Sensibilität der Ware und des Unternehmergeistes. Zugleich unterstützt er durch seine Materialien Idee und Qualität der Stoffe und verstärkt durch seine statische Anordnung den Galeriegedanken. Ein klares, heiteres Ladendesign für ein anspruchsvolles Publikum.

Missoni, an Italian fashion company which is rich in tradition, is a symbol of high quality and colourful women's and men's knit fashions – prize winning apparel that is marketed world wide. For and in co-operation with *Missoni*, Matteo Thun developed a shop concept that has been realised in New York, Paris and Milan. Creative cheerfulness not only characterised the co-operation effort, but has also permeated the design theme. This consists in a neutral interior space which highlights the colourful, high-quality products and which is reinforced by means of straight paths of movement and light openings in the walls and ceiling. The intended cheerfulness of the interior, which is meant to welcome customers, has been achieved by utilising light, colour and materials so that the overall impression reflects the sensitivity of the sophisticated fabrics. Back lit cubes of various heights have been arranged on the varnished and polished concrete floors so as to fill the interior with life. Almost like icons dedicated to the collection, a small number of products lie on satin finish glass or in front of transparent surfaces with colourful back lighting. The colour and type of light used for these glass surfaces vary according to the time of day and the fashion season, creating a structural effect that corresponds with the subtle and sophisticated colour effects of the merchandise. In addition, slightly curved wooden shelf elements affixed to the walls also display and highlight the merchandise by means of frame-like light halos – just like art in a gallery. A row of back lit pillars is sheathed in a replica of knit fabric magnified forty times its actual size. The entire interior exudes the cheerfulness and sensitivity of the merchandise and the entrepreneurial spirit behind it. At the same time, by means of the materials that have been utilised it underscores the idea and quality of the fabrics and intensifies the gallery theme by means of its static arrangement. This is a clear and cheerful shop design that is aimed at a sophisticated target group.

Schnitt und Grundriss des Eingangsbereichs

Section and Ground floor of the entrance area

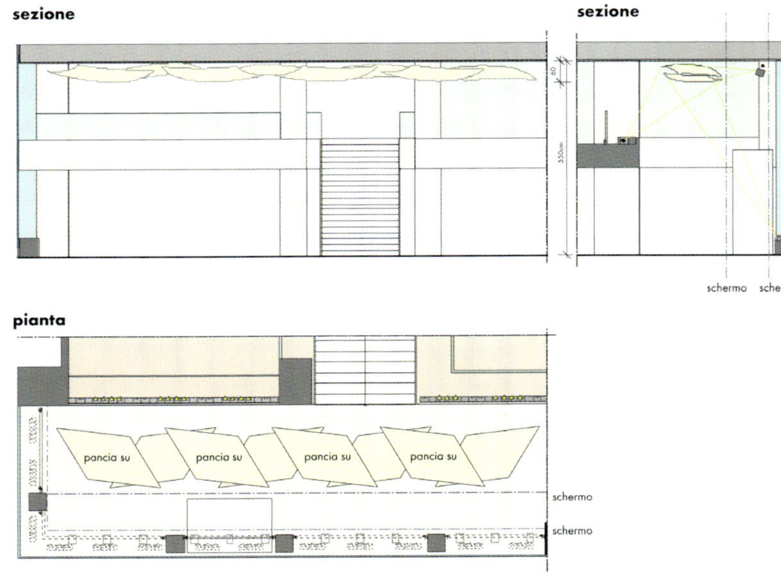

Hinterleuchtete Produktpräsentation wie in einer Galerie

Backlit product presentation like in a gallery

Erdgeschoss / Groundfloor

Obergeschoss / First floor

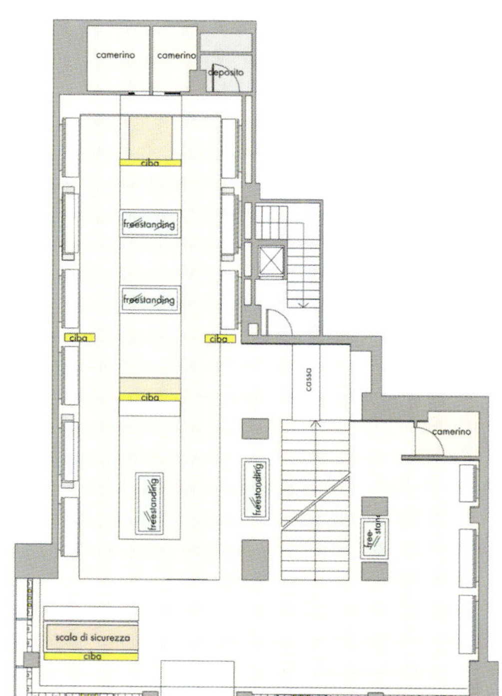

Project:
Missoni Shop System
New York/USA

Design:
Matteo Thun, Marco Rossi,
architects, Milan/Italy

Area:
400 sqm

Photographer:
Marc Craig, New York,
Gionata Xera, Milan,
(c) Missoni

Fila Sport.Life · Milano

DESIGN
Matteo Thun,
Marco Rossi,
Mailand

Fila steht für eine Welt des Sports, längst auch im Profilager. In Mailand hat das seit dreißig Jahren erfolgreiche Unternehmen nun seinen ersten Flagship-Store eröffnet, der allen Sportbegeisterten auf fünf Stockwerken eine neue ungewöhnliche Erlebniswelt eröffnet. Bereits an der Fassade machen in den oberen Fenstern Filme auf riesigen Bildschirmen Lust auf Freizeit und Sport. Und gleich hinter dem großen gläsernen Eingang tauchen die Besucher in einen unendlichen, immaterial wirkenden Raum ein ohne deutliche Dimensionen. Boden und Decke sind schwarz und verwischen die Raumgrenzen. Möbel und Wände scheinen zu glühen. Warenträger und Wandscheiben sind mobile Elemente, die beliebig nach Saison, Thema und Mode variiert werden können. Für die Möbel wurde ein semitransparenter Polycarbonat-Kunststoff hinterleuchtet und in Alurahmen eingespannt. Die Wandscheiben entpuppen sich als mobile hinterleuchtete PVC-Wandschirme, auf die Themenbilder, Farben und Special Effects projiziert werden. Themenbilder und Farben kennzeichnen die sieben Sportwelten *Filas* (Team, X-Training, Seasonal, Kids, Tennis, Running und Lifestyle) und führen den Besucher durch das ganze Haus, das alles rund um die Welt des Sports anbietet – von Sportartikeln, Reisen, Musik, Büchern und Filmen bis zu Speisen, ermöglicht durch Firmenpartner wie *Vitaminic, MV Agusta, Artemide,* Valtur und *Ferrero*. Bei *Fila Sport.Life* ist Sport ein Lebensstil, eine multisensoriale Erlebniswelt mit Licht, Ton, Bewegung und Düften, die ein Computerprogramm steuert und auch nach Ladenschluss noch weiterläuft. In einem Kiosk außerhalb des Hauses können 24 Stunden lang Bestellungen aus dem Katalog aufgegeben werden. Und im Internet geht das *Sport.Life* einfach weiter – mit neuen Dimensionen.

Fila represents the world of sports, even in the professional athletic sector. In Milan the company, which has been operating successfully for thirty years, has now opened its first flagship store. On five levels, a new and unusual realm of experience for all sports enthusiasts has been created. In the upper windows of the façade, enormous monitors show scenes that are intended to arouse people's appetite for leisure activities and sports. Directly behind the large glass entrance, visitors can submerge themselves in an endless, seemingly immaterial space without clearly delineated dimensions. Both floors and ceilings are black, thus blurring spatial boundaries. The furnishings and the walls appear to glow. The display fittings and wall panels are moveable elements that can be varied as desired according to the season, the theme or fashion. For the furnishings, a semi-transparent polycarbonate plastic was back lit and fastened into aluminium frames. The wall panels turn out to be moveable, backlit PVC wall screens on which thematic pictures, colours and special effects can be projected. Thematic pictures and colours signalise the seven *Fila* sports theme areas (Team, X Training, Seasonal, Kids, Tennis, Running and Lifestyle) and help visitors to navigate throughout the entire building. Any conceivable item associated with sports can be found, ranging from sporting goods and travel music, to books, films and food. All of this is made possible by corporate partners such as *Vitaminic, MV Agusta, Artemide, Valtur* and *Ferrero*. At *Fila Sport.Life*, sports essentially constitute a lifestyle. This is a multi-sensorial world of experience incorporating light, sound, movement and smell, which is controlled by a computer programme and continues on even after the store closes. At a booth outside the building, catalogue orders can be placed 24 hours a day.
Furthermore, *Sport.Life* has even expanded its existence to the internet – and thus opened up new dimensions.

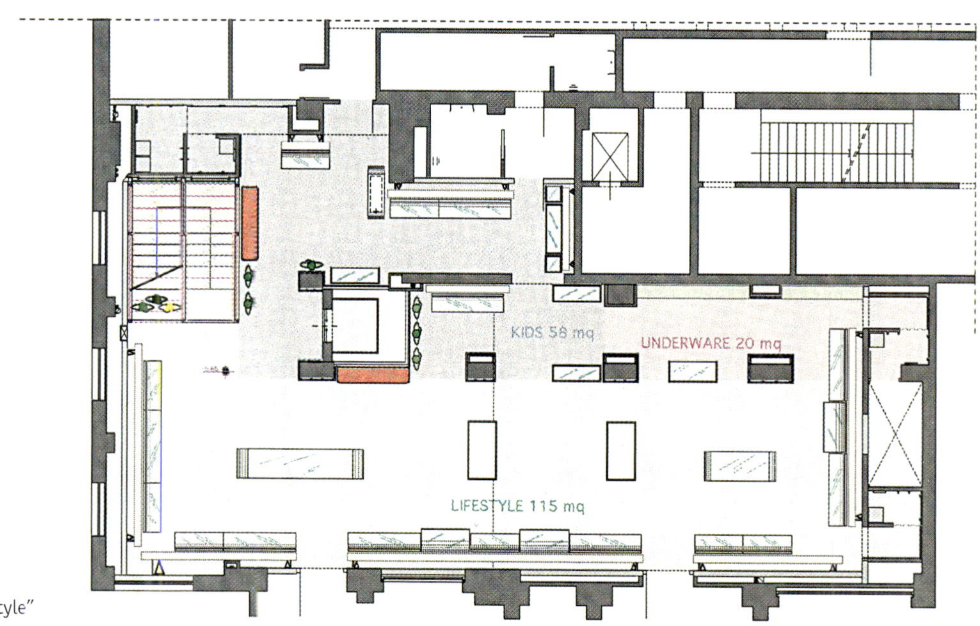

2. Untergeschoss / Second basement

Sportwelt / Sport theme world: "Lifestyle"

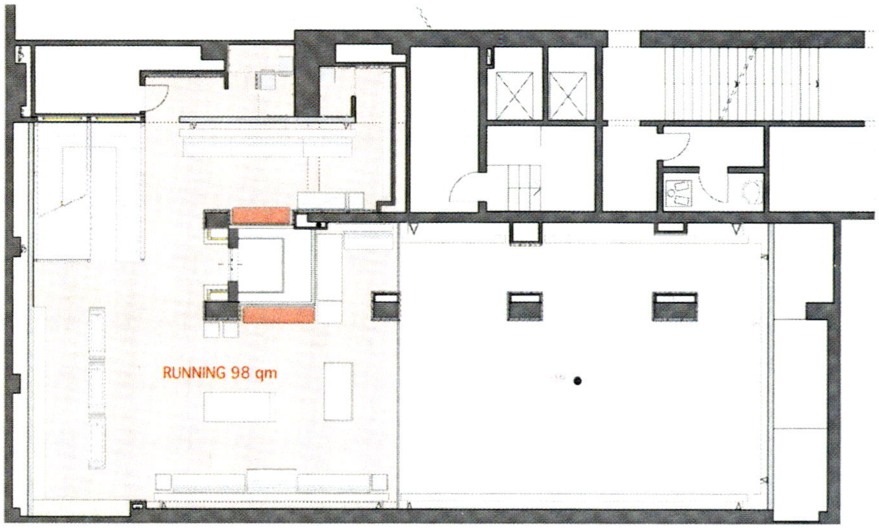

Untergeschoss / Basement: "Running"

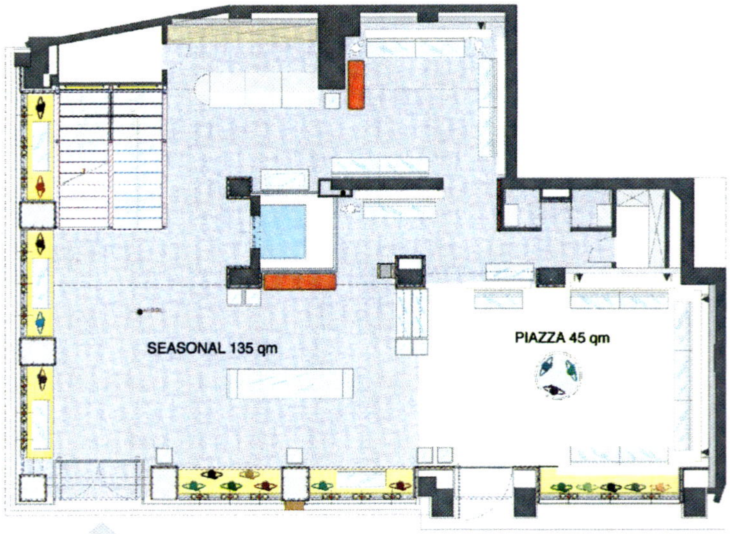

Eingangsgeschoss / Entrance floor: "Seasonal + Piazza"

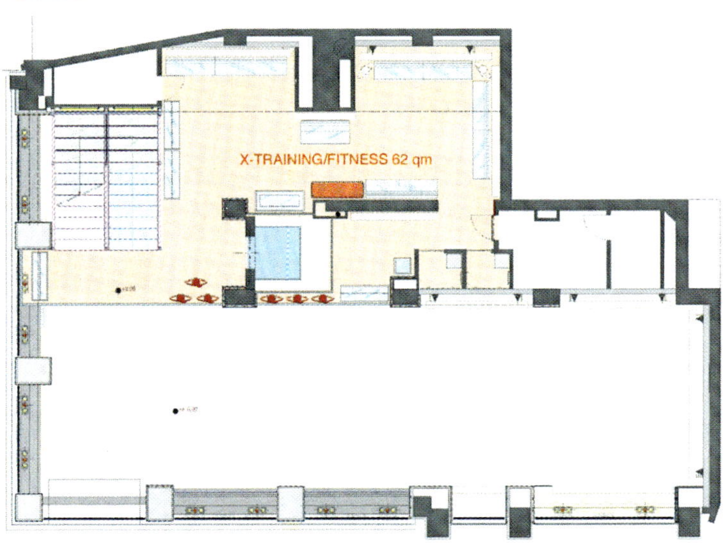

Oberes Zwischengeschoss / Upper Mezzanine: "X-Training / Fitness"

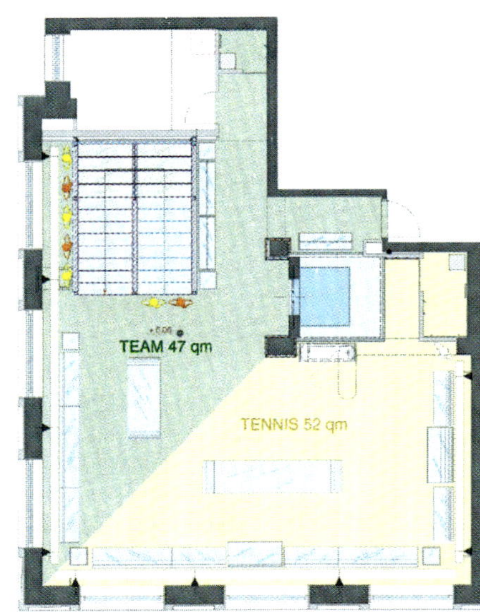

Obergeschoss / First floor: „Teamsport / Tennis"

Project:
Fila Sport.Life,
Milano/Italien

Design:
Matteo Thun, Marco Rossi,
architects, Milan

Area:
800 sqm

Photographer:
Fila, Biella/Italien

Sony Style Store · Berlin

DESIGN
Design Company, München

Mitten im Herzen von Berlin liegt das architektonisch reizvoll gestaltete *Sony Center* von Helmut Jahn mit Shopping, Unterhaltung und Gastronomie und dem neuen *Sony Style Store*, der neben New York, San Francisco und Sydney der erste Flagship Store in Europa ist. Auf vier transparenten Ebenen entfaltet sich hier eine Marken- und Lifestylewelt, in der für die Konsumenten die Produkte in Szene gesetzt werden. Mehr als in anderen *Sony*-Stores stehen hier neben dem Verkauf das Erleben, Ausprobieren und die Beratung im Vordergrund.
Bereits im Fensterbereich im Erdgeschoss werben Aktionen für die Unternehmen *Sony Deutschland, Sony Music, Sony Playstation* und *Columbia Tristar*. Schlichte hinterleuchtete Glas-Wände mit großen Bubbles aus Plexiglas-Halbkugeln und Kuben aus Mattglas bestimmten den Raum, präsentieren Produkte und Grafik im ganzen Haus. Farbige Gelkissen provozieren zum Anfassen. Cool, futuristisch und leicht geht es im 1. Obergeschoss weiter. Käferartige Lichtobjekte aus transluzentem Plexiglas und Aluminium zeigen Audio-Produkte, und Video-Kameras am Fenster erlauben einen Schwenk in den Raum. Klar, reduziert und elegant ist das Home-Entertainment im 2. Obergeschoss. Wohnliche Szenen mit bequemen Sesseln, Leuchten und Hifi-Anlagen und das High-End-Studio inszenieren das Heimkino. Playtime im obersten Stockwerk. Anders als in den meisten Spielen ist hier der Raum hell, futuristisch, abstrakt. Spielen und Anfassen der Playstations sind erwünscht und auch in relaxter Form möglich. Speziell entwickelte Titel-Präsenter an den Wänden zeigen aktuelle *Sony-Music*-Cover, die über Kopfhörer abgespielt oder als Video bzw. DVD in einem überkopf laufendem Monitor angesehen werden kann. Eine zentral gelegene runde Theke mit vier Metern Durchmesser ist Anlaufstelle für Informationen und bei Events als Bar der große Mittelpunkt.
Die Designfirma betreute den Store vom Rohbau bis zur grafischen Umsetzung der Shopping Bags und Preisschilder, wobei das grafische Konzept durch das ganze Haus führt, verbindet und den emotionalen Gegenpart zur puristischen Raumarchitektur darstellt.

Located right in the heart of Berlin – the architecturally fascinating *Sony Center* offers shopping, entertainment and gastronomic delights, as well as the new *Sony Style Store*, which is the first flagship store in Europe to be inaugurated after the ones in New York, San Francisco and Sydney. Four transparent levels open up a brand name and lifestyle oriented world, in which the products are dramatically presented for the consumers' benefit. More than in other *Sony* Stores, in Berlin the focus is on experiencing things, trying them out and consulting, in addition to sales. In the window area on the main floor special campaigns advertise *Sony Germany, Sony Music, Sony Playstation* and *Columbia Tristar*. Simple backlit glass walls with large bubbles fashioned out of Plexiglas spheres and cubes of frosted glass are the dominant element of the interior, serving to display the products and graphics throughout the premises. Colourful gel cushions just beg to be touched. On the first upper level the theme is cool, futuristic and light. Beetle-like illuminated objects made of translucent Plexiglas and aluminium are used to display the audio products. Video cameras at the window provide a panned view of the interior. The home entertainment area on the second upper level is clearly organised, pared down and elegant. Inviting, liveable arrangements with comfortable armchairs, lamps and hi-fi systems and a high-end studio incorporate the essence of a home movie theatre. "Playtime" is the motto of the uppermost level. In contrast with most of the games, the space is bright, futuristic and abstract. The relaxed atmosphere invites visitors to play and touch the Playstations. Specially designed title presenters on the walls show current *Sony music* that can be listened to on head phones or watched in the form of a video or a DVD on a monitor which is mounted above head height. A centrally located round counter that is four metres in diameter serves as an information centre and, during events, it constitutes a major focus when it is used as a bar. The design company was responsible for overseeing the entire store project – everything from the construction stage to the graphic realisation of the shopping bags and the price labels – whereby the graphic concept is continued throughout the building. It serves to connect the whole and create an emotional contrast to the puristic interior architecture.

KASSE
sony style
store

DURCHGEKNALLT

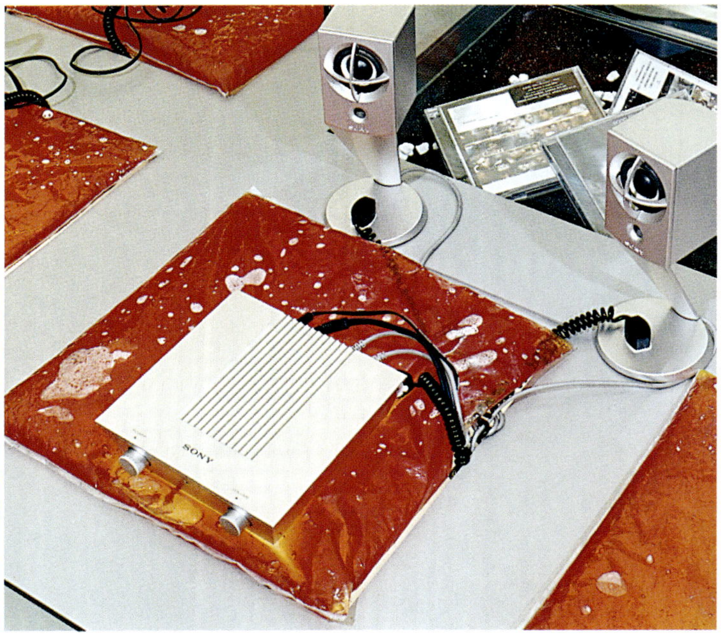
SONY

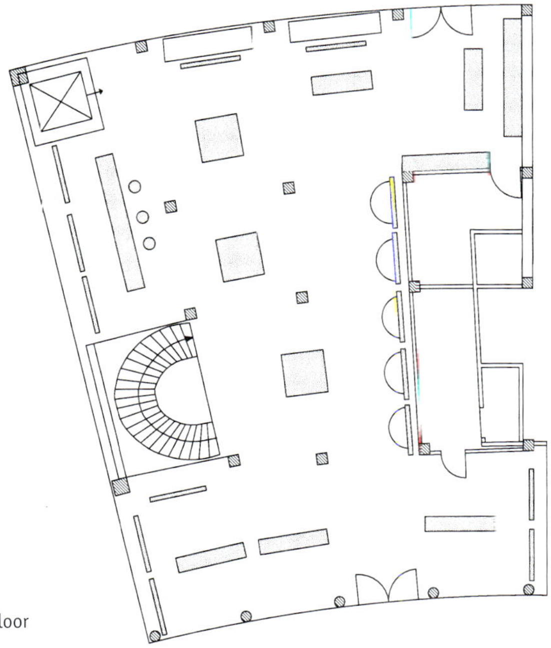

Erdgeschoss / Ground floor

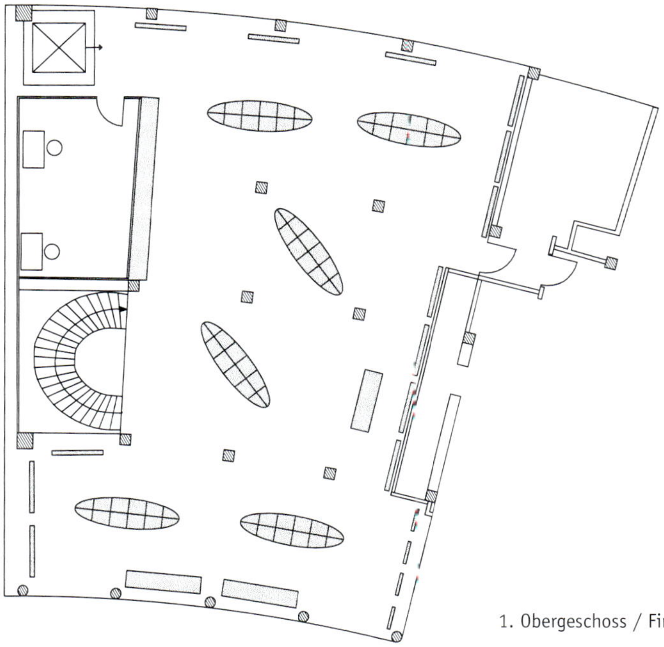

1. Obergeschoss / First floor

2. Obergeschoss / Second upper floor:
Home-entertainment + High-end studios

3. Obergeschoss / Third upper floor: Futuristische Playstations / Futuristic playstat ons

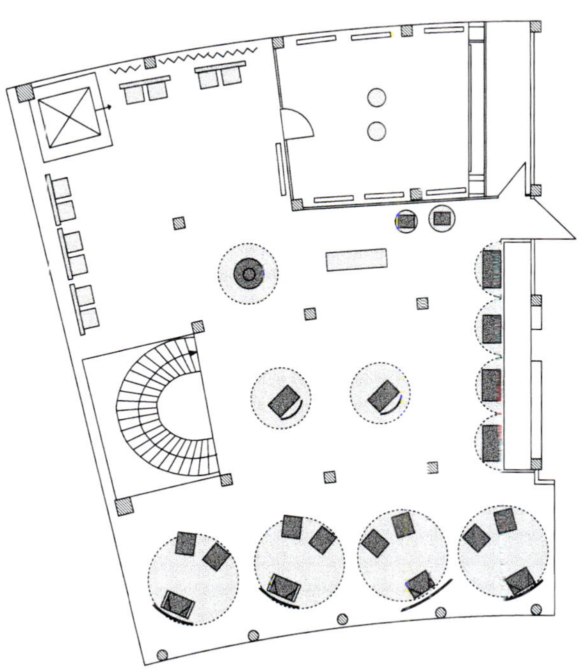

2. Obergeschoss / Second floor

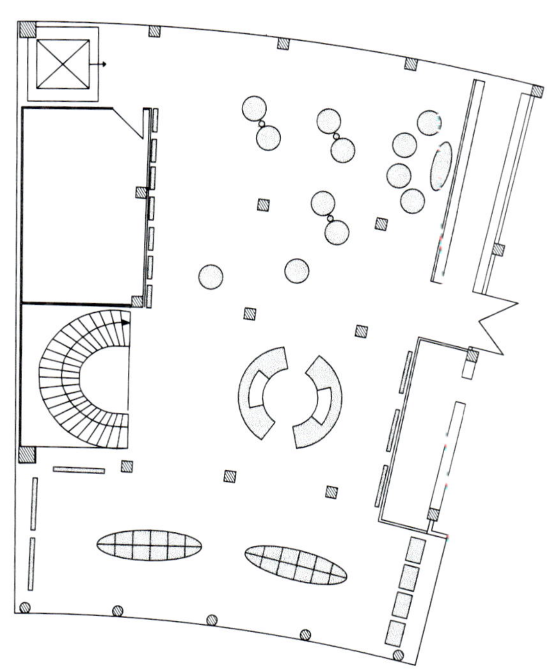

3. Obergeschoss / Third floor

Project:
Sony Style Store,
Berlin/Germany

Design:
Design Company, München

Area:
ca. 8100 sqm

Photographer:
Thomas Mira,
Stephan Rabold,
Alex Schelbert,
Wolfgang Schöbel,
München,
(c) Design Company

Läden wie Galerien und Showrooms

Es ist nicht die Enge und Dichtheit eines Marktes, die in diesen Läden gesucht wird, sondern der offene Raum für die Alleinstellung von Produkten, die verdeutlicht, dass diese Waren etwas Besonderes sind, ein Umfeld von Distanz und Weite brauchen, um ihre Eigenheiten herauszustellen. Mode, Schuhe und vor allem Schmuck im hochwertigen Bereich werden seit Jahren in dieser Form in Szene gesetzt, nicht zuletzt beeinflusst von der japanisch reduzierten Präsentationsform Produkte symbolhaft in den Mittelpunkt zu stellen.

Natürlich ist ein Laden wie *Bergman* ein Showroom. Hier schlendert man durch große weiße Räume ohne jedes Dekor. Die Atmosphäre ist ästhetisch, dezent, ruhig aber nicht elitär, eher unkompliziert. Wie selbstverständlich betrachtet man Möbel, Schuhe oder Accessoires, fühlt Materialien, sieht Details und hinterfragt Designer, Marken, Firmen-Geschichten, wird selbst ein Teil dieser Produktidentitäten. Es sind offene Räume, die Geschichten erzählen und allmählich eine eigene Geschichte erhalten. Auch *Zero-Lustrum-Pukeberg* ist eigentlich eine Galerie, in der eine lange interne Ladenstraße genutzt wurde, um den ungewöhnlichen Gläsern junger Designer durch die Präsentation einen besonderen Stellenwert zu geben. Und das geschieht hier vor allem durch reizvollen Materialwechsel und Lichteffekte in den Displays und Raumnischen. Die Galerie *Zebra* in Ljubljana ist nun tatsächlich eine Kunstgalerie mit Shop und Bar. Hier regten die kunstvollen Glasprodukte den Architekten dazu an, ganz sinnlich-ästhetische Raumerlebnisse zu schaffen, die die Besucher auf die Glasobjekte vorbereiten und sie in eine sensible Material- und Formenwelt einstimmen. Eine Perle in unserer Zeit. Dass durchaus auch ganz normale Kunden für eine Raumästhetik empfänglich sind, die so völlig anders ist als ihr privates Umfeld, beweist der Friseursalon *Aida* in New York mit seiner ungewöhnlich einfachen, gefalteten Raumarchitektur: weiß, sanft und einhüllend. Gerade in unseren dicht besiedelten Großstädten ist Platz zu haben ein Luxus, der nicht nur den Produkten sondern auch den Kunden „Raum gibt" für ein Lebensgefühl voller Großzügigkeit und dabei die Möglichkeit zum Schlendern, Verweilen, Anschauen, Anprobieren. Genau auf dieses Lebensgefühl spielt der Modeladen *More Majorum* in Sao Paulo mit seinen hellen sparsam möblierten Räumen an, die Eleganz und Komfort signalisieren. In dem kleinen Laden von *Tritec* in Basel hingegen werden die Kunden eher überrascht sein, einen Showroom für technische Solarprodukte anzutreffen – hier hilft die Architekur räumliche Weite zu erzeugen und zugleich eine neutrale Plattform für Fachgespräche anzubieten.

Beim Schuladen *Legrand* in Hamburg wird deutlich, dass es eben manchem Händler nicht reicht, nur einen schönen Laden zu haben. Legrand ist eine starke Persönlichkeit und selbst fast eine Marke und wollte für sich, seine exklusiven Schuhe und seine Kundinnen einen abgehobenen Raum im Raum – eine Bühne, eine Show. Und auch mit der *Fattoria Blu* in Zürich entstand nicht einfach ein Laden für Feinkostartikel – hier wurde die Idee des Modeagenten Cagol übersetzt, hochwertige Produkte in vernetzter Form zu präsentieren – in seinem Showroom für Mode, seinem Restaurant, seiner Firmencafeteria und dem Feinkostgeschäft. Und überall geht es um exklusive Inszenierungen – wie bei seiner Mode.

Shops like galleries or showrooms

In these shops, the focus is not on the compactness and density of a market sector, but rather on open space for highlighting products. This form of presentation makes it clear that this merchandise is something special, that it requires surroundings characterised by distance and spaciousness in order to effectively demonstrate its particular characteristics. For years, fashion, shoes and particularly jewellery in the high quality range have been displayed in this manner, not least because of the influence of the minimalist Japanese form of presentation which symbolically places products at centre stage.

Of course, a shop like *Bergman* is a showroom. Patrons stroll through large white rooms devoid of any decoration whatsoever. The atmosphere is aesthetic and discreet, tranquil but not elitist, with more of a tendency toward the uncomplicated. In a completely natural fashion, the customer views the furniture, shoes or accessories, feels the materials, examines details and wonders about designers, brand names, corporate histories – he himself becomes a part of these product identities. These are open interiors that convey stories and gradually develop their own story.
Zero-Lustrum-Pukeberg is also actually a gallery in which the long interior shopping aisle is exploited in order to – through the type of presentation – impart particular significance to the unusual glassware by young designers. In this shop, this is primarily achieved through the use of fascinating changes of materials and lighting effects in the displays and recessed alcoves. The *Zebra* gallery in Ljubljana is actually a genuine art gallery which includes a shop and a bar. The artistic glass products exhibited there inspired the architect to create quite sensually aesthetic spatial experiences, which prepare the visitors for the glass objects and put them in the mood for this sensitive world of materials and shapes. A modern day gem. The fact that entirely ordinary customers are definitely also receptive to particular spatial aesthetics that diverge completely from their own private environment is illustrated by the *Aida* hairdressing salon in New York with its unusually simple, folded interior architecture: white, soft and enveloping. Particularly in our densely populated metropolitan cities, having space is a luxury that not only gives products "space", but also affords customers space – space for a lifestyle feeling characterised by spaciousness, space to stroll and linger, to look and try things out. It is precisely this lifestyle feeling that is alluded to in the fashion shop *More Majorum* in Sao Paulo with its bright, sparsely furnished rooms that signalise elegance and comfort. By contrast, in the diminutive shop by *Tritec* in Basel customers are more likely to be surprised at discovering a showroom for solar technology products. There, the architecture contributes to creating a spatial feeling of largeness and at the same time provides a neutral platform for professional consulting discussions. The shoe shop *Legrand* in Hamburg clearly illustrates that some retailers are not satisfied with merely having a beautiful retail store. Legrand is a strong personality and almost a brand name in himself. For himself, his exclusive shoes and his customers he wanted an eccentric room in a room – a stage, a show. At *Fattoria Blu* in Zurich as well, what was created is not simply a delicatessen shop. Rather, the shop is an interpretation of the concept of Cagol, the fashion agent who envisaged presenting top quality products in an interlinked network context – in his fashion showroom, his restaurant, his company cafeteria and the delicatessen shop. Everywhere the theme is exclusive, theatre-like settings – just like his fashions.

Bergman · Frankfurt am Main

DESIGN
E15,
Florian Asche,
Philipp Mainzer,
Oberursel/Ts.

Mitten im Frankfurter Bankenviertel nahe des Opern- und Schauspielhauses eröffnete die deutsche Designergruppe *E15* ein ungewöhnliches und extravagantes Geschäft, um ihre eigenen sehr einfachen Massivholzmöbel in einem Umfeld zu präsentieren, das ihre Philosophie von Materialschönheit, handwerklichen Details und langer Lebensdauer durch andere Produkte unterstützt und verdeutlicht. *E15*, die heute mit ihren Produkten in großen Ausstellungen und Messen vertreten sind, gaben sich ihren Namen nach ihrer ursprünglich im Londoner Stadtteil Hackney angesiedelten Werkstatt.
Mit *Bergman* haben sich der Designer Florian Asche und der Architekt Philipp Mainzer eine Plattform geschaffen, auf der sie neben ihren eigenen Produkten hochwertige Markenprodukte aus den Bereichen Designermode, Streetwear, Möbel, Wohnobjekte und Accessoires einem Kundenkreis anbieten, der Spaß hat an Produkten, die über eine eigene Geschichte verfügen – qualitätvoll und mit schönen Details. Ganz dieser Idee verpflichtet ist auch der *Bergman Store* eine einfache weiße Hülle mit Betonboden und alter Holztreppe, die die drei Ebenen verbindet. Es ist eine ständig sich wandelnde Bühne, auf der die Modedesignerin und Creative Director Farah Abrahimi die Möbel und Produkte immer wieder neu arrangiert und in Szene setzt. Alles steht hier zum Verkauf an, selbst Regale, Tische, Hocker oder Bänke, auf denen andere Produkte präsentiert werden. Bereits in diesem Geschäft erfüllen die Massivholzmöbel von *E15* das, was sie auch sein sollen: Ruhender Pol in einem modernen, lebendigen Interieur, das licht und leicht ist, von leiser Musik durchströmt, ein wandelbarer Raum für Produkte und Ausstellungen und für viele kleine Geschichten von Menschen, Produkten und Unternehmen.

In the midst of Frankfurt's financial district and in close proximity to the city's theatre and opera houses, the German *E15* designer group opened an unusual and extravagant shop, in order to present its extremely simple solid wood furniture in a context that would support and illustrate its philosophy, which focuses on beautiful materials, finely executed details and long product life, supplemented by other products. *E15*, which exhibits its products at major exhibitions and trade fairs, named itself after its original workshop, which was located in London's Hackney district. At *Bergman*, the designer Florian Asche and the architect Philipp Mainzer have created for themselves a platform where, in addition to their own products, they can offer high quality brand name products from areas such as designer fashion, street wear, furniture, interior decorating objects and accessories to a clientele that enjoys products that tell their own story, by means of their high level of quality and exquisite detailing. A simple white shell with concrete floors and an old wooden staircase that connects the three levels, the *Bergman Store* subscribes to this idea completely. It is a continually changing stage setting in which the fashion designer and creative director, Farah Abrahimi, is constantly rearranging and effectively presenting furnishings and products. Everything in the store is for sale, even the shelves, tables, stools and benches on which other products are displayed. In this store, the solid wood furniture by *E15* achieves what it is intended to: it creates a stabilizing element in a modern, animated interior that is bright, ethereal and filled with gentle strains of music – an adaptable retail space geared to products and exhibitions, as well as the countless small stories behind people, products and companies.

Wandelbarer Raum für Produktgeschichten, schöne Materialien und handwerkliche Details

Changeable room for product stories, beautiful materials and skilled manual details

Der Galerieladen 1999 / The galleryshop in 1999

Project:
Bergman,
Frankfurt am Main,
Germany

Design:
E15,
Florian Asche,
Philipp Mainzer,
Oberursel/Ts.

Area:
400 sqm, 3 floors

Photographer:
Ingmar Kurth, E15,
Oberursel

Harriet Dorn · Santa Monica

DESIGN
Lorcan O'Herlihy Architects, Culver City

Im Edgemar Development von Frank Gehry aus dem Jahre 1988 in Santa Monica gibt es viele an den Süden erinnernde turmartige eckige Gebäude unterschiedlicher Nutzung, Läden und Cafés.
In einem der schmalen Türme hat sich der Modeladen *Harriet Dorn* angesiedelt. Kein leichtes Unterfangen bei einer Raumgröße von 19 Quadratmetern und 16 Metern Raumhöhe, die in einem filigranen Glaskubus endet und intensives Sonnenlicht einfängt.
Bei einer eleganten Mode für junge Damen zwischen 20 und 40 Jahren aber hat die Architektur Chancen für eine ungewöhnliche Präsentationsform. So wurde die Raumhöhe genutzt, um filigrane Metallgestänge vom Deckenkreuz der Lichtkuppel nach unten abzuhängen und als Aufhängemöglichkeit für die Kleidung zu nutzen. Birkenholztablare für Accessoires schweben wie ein Schaukelbrett zwischen den Stangen. Um die Großzügigkeit im Raum zu erhalten, wurde eine gefaltete Wand – auch aus Birkenholz – entwickelt, die Ausstellungsnischen, Lagerraum und die Umkleide aufnimmt. Sie wirkt im Raum wie eine sanfte Skulptur, vor der die dünnen schwarzen Metallstangen fast schwerelos wirken und alle Aufmerksamkeit der Besucher auf sich und die Produkte lenken. Um das starke Sonnenlicht zu filtern und die Raumhöhe zu reduzieren, wurde unter dem Glaskubus ein Fallschirm befestigt. Nimmt das Sonnenlicht ab, erzeugen darüber liegende Strahler diesen weichen Effekt. Der einfache polierte Betonboden setzt sich nach außen im Steinbelag fort. Ein wirkungsvolles und sehr preiswertes $ 8000 Projekt.

The Edgemar Development designed by Frank Gehry and built in the year 1988 in Santa Monica boasts of numerous square, tower-like buildings reminiscent of southern climes, which are used for various purposes, shops and cafés.
The *Harriet Dorn* fashion boutique is located in one of the narrow towers. This was not an easy task, in light of the 90 square metres of floor area and a 16 metre high ceiling that culminates in a filigree glass cube, which captures intensive sunlight. But the architecture of the premises, which are devoted to elegant fashions for young women from 20 to 40 years of age, opened up incredible potential for unusual forms of presentation. Thus, the height of the interior has been exploited to suspend filigree metal objects from the cross bracing of the translucent dome and to hang items of apparel. Birch shelves destined for accessories hover like swing seats between the rods. In order to preserve the spaciousness of the interior, a folding wall of birch plywood was designed to accommodate the exhibition areas, storage space and a changing room. Within the interior space, this wall creates a soft sculptural effect, making the thin black metal rods before it seem almost weightless and thus drawing the patrons' attention to itself and to the merchandise. In order to filter the strong sunlight and to reduce the height of the interior space, a parachute has been attached below the glass cube. When there is no sunlight, spotlights mounted above create the same soft effect. The simple polished concrete floor merges into stone underfoot outside. This is an effective and very budget priced $8,000 project.

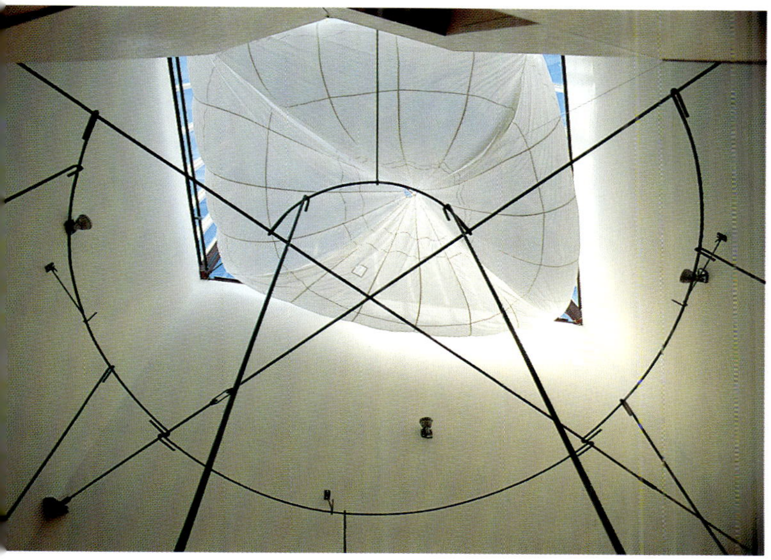

Faszinierender Blickfang: ein Fallschirm als Sonnenfilter

Fascinating eyecatcher: a parachute to filter the sunlight

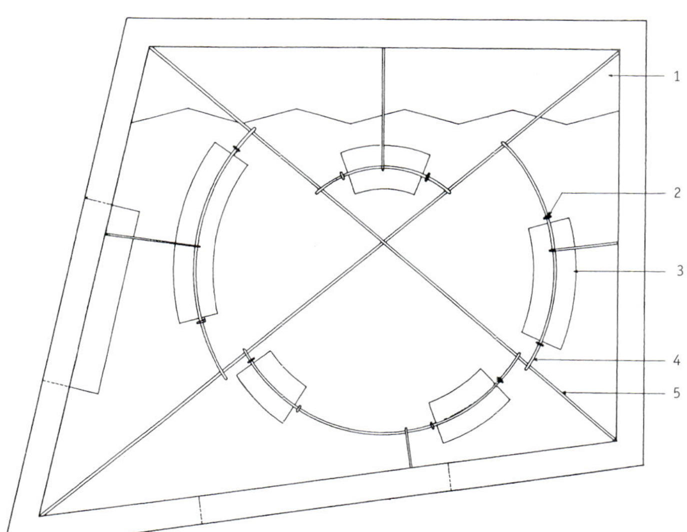

1 Top of Cabinet
2 Clothes Rack Suspension Point
3 Shelf Below
4 New Support Rod for Display
5 Existing Steel Rod

Project:
Harriet Dorn,
Santa Monica/USA

Design:
Lorcan O'Herlihy Architects,
Culver City

Area:
19 sqm

Photographer:
Grey Crawford, Los Angeles

Zero-Lustrum-Pukeberg · Stockholm

DESIGN
Rupert Gardner Design, Stockholm

In der Innenstadt Stockholms haben sich die drei Unternehmen *Zero*, *Lustrum* und *Pukeberg* zusammengetan, um mit ihren Leuchten, Glaswaren und Möbeln eine gemeinsame Kollektion anzubieten, die von einer kleinen Gruppe skandinavischer Designer entwickelt wird. Qualitätsvolle und preiswerte Produkte, die morgen Klassiker werden könnten. Ihr Domizil fanden die Unternehmen in einem 820 Quadratmeter großen Laden, der sich von der Straße aus 60 Meter nach innen ausdehnt und ausreichend Platz bietet, um neben dem Verkaufsgeschäft auch Showroom und Galerie zu sein und Veranstaltungen und Sonderpräsentationen zuzulassen. Um Abwechslung in die lange „Ladenstraße" zu bekommen, wurden die beiden Längsseiten völlig unterschiedlich gestaltet: Auf der linken Seite vom Eingang aus wurden beleuchtete Glasprodukte vor eine reliefartige Kiefernholzwand gestellt, kunstvoll von oben angestrahlt. Die andere Seite mutet eher industriell an und besteht aus hinterleuchteten Glasregalwänden mit silbergrauen Aluminiumborden. Eine spannungsvolle Präsentation für die Glasprodukte. Ein alle fünfzehn Minuten wechselndes farbiges Lichtspiel von rot zu gelb und blau verstärkt noch dieses Wanderlebnis. Um den Kunden den langen Weg zu verkürzen, haben sich die Architekten gestalterisch viel einfallen lassen: Kontrastierende Materialien wie Sandsteinplatten auf dem Boden, Mosaikfliesen an den Säulen, roher Beton und unbehandeltes Holz, glatte, raue oder gelochte Flächen sind zusammen mit der skulptural ausgebildeten Decke effektvolle Hintergründe für die Produkte. Der räumliche Wendepunkt wird durch das runde Büro eingeleitet, hinter dem sich der Raum weitet und allmählich in die L-förmige Galerie und den Showroom für Leuchten und Möbel führt. Hier erlauben Schiebewände und mobile Glasabtrennungen Vielfalt und Flexibilität für eine Kollektion, die sich ständig weiterentwickelt und verändert.

In Stockholm's city centre, three companies – *Zero*, *Lustrum* and *Pukeberg* – have collaborated in order to jointly present their collection of lamps, glassware and furniture. This collection was developed by a small group of Scandinavian designers and consists of high-quality and low cost products that may well become tomorrow's classics. The companies discovered a joint domicile in a 820 square metre store which extends 60 metres back from the street towards the interior and which, in addition to retail sales, provides sufficient space to function as a showroom and a gallery for events and special presentations. In order to ensure variety in this relatively long sales area, the two long sides were decorated in entirely different styles. On what is the left side when facing away from the entrance, illuminated glass products have been placed in front of a pine wall with a relief-like surface and artfully illuminated from above. The opposite side has more of an industrial flair and consists of back lit glass wall shelving elements with silver grey aluminium shelves on which the glass products are set off very effectively. A lighting system which changes colour from red through yellow to blue every fifteen minutes intensifies this wall experience even further. In order to make the relatively large longitudinal dimension appear shorter to the customers, the architects have exploited a large number of very inventive methods: contrasting materials such as sand stone slabs on the floor, mosaic tiles on the pillars, raw concrete and untreated wood. Smooth, rough or perforated surfaces combine forces with the sculpture like ceiling to provide an exciting background for the products.
The spatial turning point is signalised by the round office area, behind which the interior expands and gradually merges into an L-shaped gallery and showroom that is devoted to lamps and furniture. In this area, sliding partitions and portable glass dividers ensure variety and flexibility for a collection that itself is continually evolving and changing.

ASTO

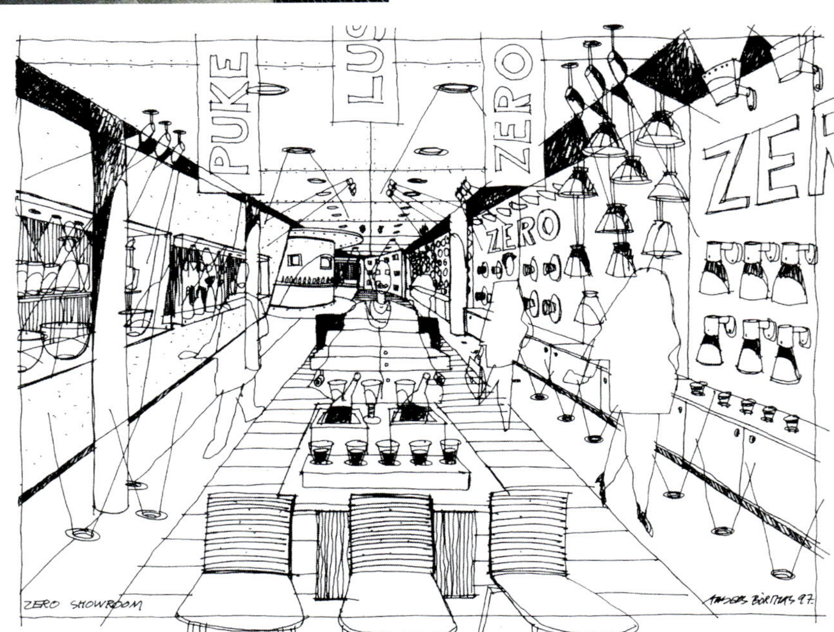
PUKE
LUS
ZERO
ZERO
ZER
ZERO SHOWROOM

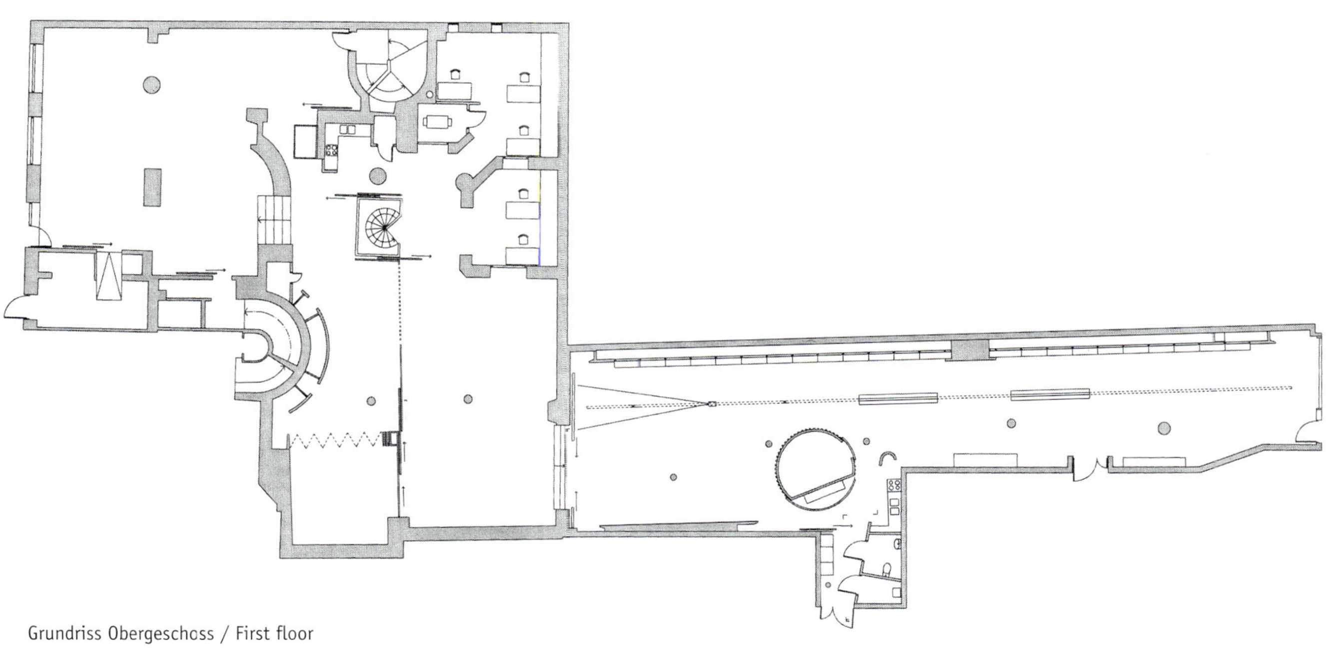

Grundriss Obergeschoss / First floor

Project:
Zero-Lustrum-Pukeberg,
Stockholm/Sweden

Design:
Rupert Gardner Design,
Stockholm

Area:
820 sqm

Photographer:
Ake E:son Lindman,
Stockholm

Zebra Galerie-Shop und Ze Bar · Ljubljana

DESIGN
**Nenad Fabijanic,
Zagreb, Kroatien**

Zwischen dem Uferdamm der Ljublanica und der Nationalgalerie (1936–40) liegen die wunderschönen Gebäude des kroatischen Architekten Joze Plecnik aus dem 19. Jahrhundert. In einem dieser Häuser befindet sich die Galerie *Zebra*, die Möbel und Glasobjekte des Künstlers Oskar Kogoj präsentiert. Neben dem Eingang im Erdgeschoss können in einem Shop seine Glasobjekte, Flaschen, Gläser und regionale Weine in Designflaschen erworben werden. Ein größeres Sortiment an Weinen und Spirituosen wird nebenan in der *Ze Bar* angeboten, ein Wortspiel von Zebra, ebenfalls vom Galerieinhaber betreut und krönender Abschluss so mancher Galerieevents. Im Innern des Hauses spürt man die mediterrane Idee der Gebäude-Architektur auf die neuen Raumideen und die kunstvoll sensiblen Räume übersetzt, die den Rahmen für die Objekt-Kunst bilden. Direkt am Eingang empfängt den Besucher ein rosafarbener Perlino Rosato Marmorboden, der sich in einer skulpturalen Wendeltreppe nach oben ausbreitet. Eine Wolke aus Eichenholz überrascht unter der Decke, schwebt, wirft Fragen auf. Oben in der **Galerie** ist alles hell und neutral für die vielfältige Kunst: der Boden aus Ahornholz. Wände und seidene Vorhänge im gleichen Farbton. Die Kargheit des Raumes wird nur unterbrochen durch Metaphern zum Thema Nature Design: Eine schmale Wandnische wird zur schrägen Ablage mit einem Onyxkubus ab Ende, gekrönt von einem Bonsaibäumchen; ein Schmetterling im Raum und ein Bündel Rohleder an der Studiodecke. Ein Treibholzbalken aus Ulme überdeckt hier die Tür.
Auch im **Galerieshop** im Erdgeschoss ist die Architektur kunstvoller Rahmen für die Produkte. Ein schwarzer glänzender Granit durchzieht den Raum, gleitet an den Wänden zum Fenster empor bis zu einer gebrochenen Steinkante, die die Schönheit der Steinstruktur offenbart. Es ist ein karger heller Raum mit dünnen weißen Metallborden für die kunstvollen Gläser. Wie eine Skulptur steht mitten im Raum ein Eichenholztisch für Verkauf und Präsentation.

The wondrously beautiful buildings that were built in the 19th century by the Croatian architect, Joze Plecnik, are situated between the bank of the Ljublanica and the National Gallery (1936–1940). One of these buildings is home to the *Zebra Gallery*, which exhibits furniture and glass objects by the artist Oskar Kogoj. On the ground floor next to the entrance is a shop where his glass objects, bottles, glasses and regional wines in designer bottles can be purchased. In the adjacent Ze Bar – a pun on *Zebra* – there is an even larger range of wines and liquor. The bar is also managed by the owner of the gallery and has often been often the setting for a splendid finale after quite a few gallery events. In the interior of the building, the Mediterranean theme of the building's architecture has been re-interpreted in the new concepts for the interior and the artistically sensitive rooms, which serve as the backdrop for the objects of art. Directly at the entrance, the visitor is welcomed by pink Perlino Rosato marble floor, which spreads upwards on a sculpturally shaped spiral staircase. A cloud of oak creates a surprising effect on the ceiling – floating and inspiring questions. Upstairs in the **gallery**, everything is bright and neutral so as to set off the varied objects of art. The flooring is maple and the walls and silk drapes pick up the same colour. The austerity of the interior is only interrupted by metaphors on the theme of "nature design". A narrow wall alcove becomes a tilted surface with a cube of onyx at its end, crowned by a bonsai tree. A butterfly hovers and a bundle of raw leather adorns the studio ceiling. A beam of driftwood from an elm tree arches over the door. In the **gallery shop** on the ground floor, the architecture also serves as an artful framework to set off the products. Gleaming black granite has been used throughout the room, climbing up the walls to the window and as far as a broken edge of stone which lays bare the beauty of the stone's inner structure. It is an austere white room with thin white metal shelving used to display the artistic glass objects. An oak table like a work of sculpture dominates the middle of the room and is utilised for sales and presentation.

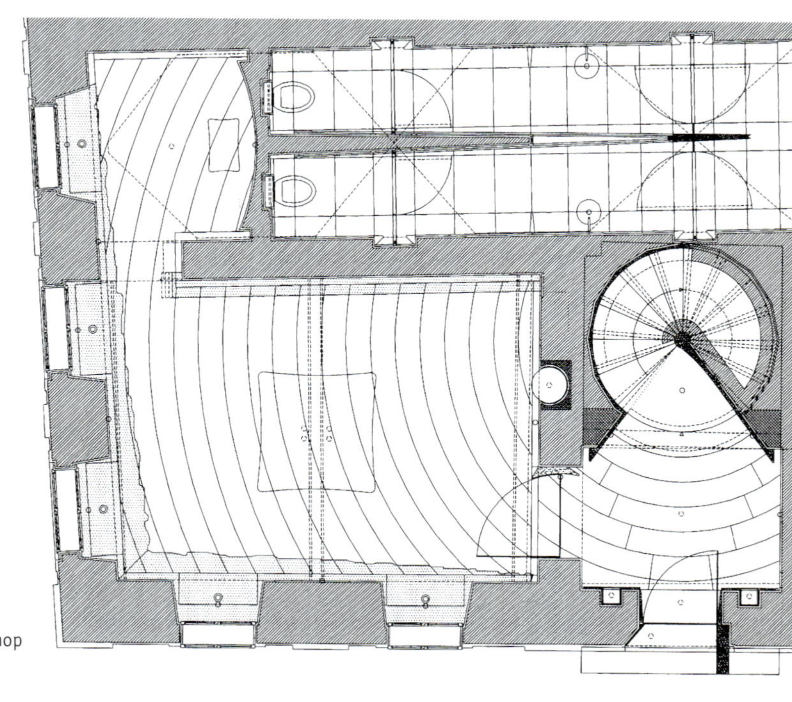

Galerieshop / Galleryshop

Schmale schräge Wandnische endet in einem Onyxkubus

Narrow wall alcove becomes a cube of onyx at its end

Lichtvolle Galerie im Obergeschoss mit hellen Wänden, Ahornboden, Seidenvorhängen und Glas

Bright gallery in the first floor with light walls, maple flooring, silkdrapes and glass exhibition cubes

Der „Rote Raum" mit alter Deckenmalerei, rotem Marmor, tropischem Holzboden und roten Brokatvorhängen – bühnenartiger Rahmen für Besprechungen

The "Red Room" with old ceiling paintings, red marmble, tropical wood floor and with red brocade drapes – theatrical stage for meetings

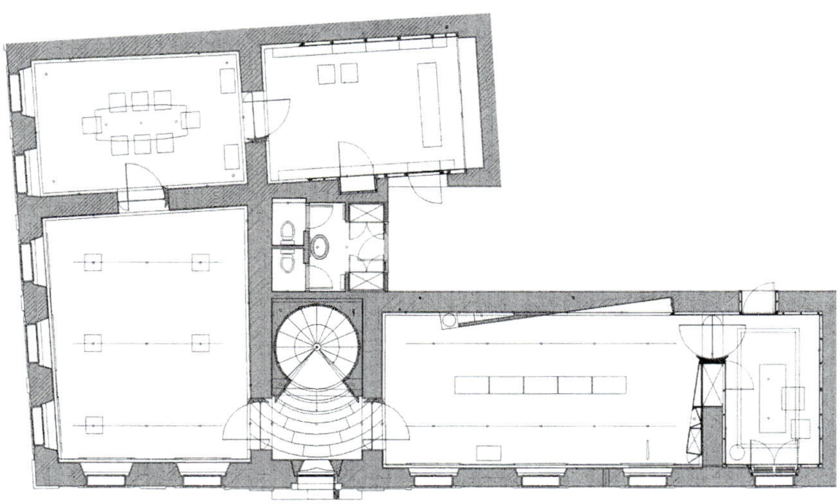

Im gleichen Gebäude einige Meter weiter betritt man vier Stufen unter Straßenniveau die **Ze Bar**. Schwarzer Marmor an Boden und Wand machen deutlich, dass die Bar der Nacht gehört. Kleine Lichter beleuchten Wandnischen und leiten den Gast über den tiefschwarzen Boden. Fast sakral ist der kleine Raum daneben mit schmalem elliptischem Mitteltisch und einer Wandlehne aus schwarzem Leder. Selbst die Toilettenanlagen erhalten liebevolle Details. *Zebra* und *Ze Bar* sind ein spannendes architektonisches Ensemble für die Präsentation und den Verkauf, für die Entspannung und Anregung der Sinne.

A few metres away in the same building, four steps lead the visitor below street level to the **Ze Bar**. Black marble on the floor and walls unmistakeably signalise the affinity of the bar with the night. Small lights illuminate wall alcoves and guide the guest across the deep black floor. The small adjacent room is almost sacral in character, with a narrow elliptical central table and black leather to lean on the wall. Even the restroom facilities are characterised by painstaking attention to detail. *Zebra* and *Ze Bar* form an exciting architectural ensemble geared to presentation and sales, as well as to relaxation and stimulation of the senses.

Project:
Zebra Galerie-Shop und Ze Bar, Ljubljana/Slovenien

Design:
Nenad Fabijanic + Sonja Tadej, Zagreb, Kroatien

Area:
total 195 sqm (Shop 24 sqm, Gallery 144 sqm, Bar 27 sqm)

Photographer:
Damir Fabijanic, Zagreb

Aida Hairsalon · New York

DESIGN
Archi-Tectonics, New York

In der enormen Dichte der Stadt New York spielen zunehmend die Innenräume eine Rolle. Mitten in Manhatten, umgeben von hohen Backsteinhäusern, hat die aus Skandinavien stammende Architektin einen Friseursalon wie eine moderne Raumskulptur geschaffen. Schon von weitem fällt die ungewöhnliche Fensterform auf, die ein amorphes Loch in die Fassade aus hellblauem New Yorker Stein schneidet. Links oben in der Ecke erinnert ein kleines hinterleuchtetes Fenster mit Logo an das traditionelle Barbier-Zeichen. In großen geätzten Lettern steht der Firmenname auf der Scheibe, wirkt elegant, modisch für ein recht bunt gewürfeltes Publikum. Der Raum dahinter ist ein kleiner Wartebereich mit Bank und Empfang, wird schmal und lang und endet in einem begrünten Hinterhof mit Schieferbelag und Sitzbänken zwischen alten Bäumen und wildem Wein. Ein angenehmer und kühler Warteplatz im Sommer. Im Rauminnern ist es vollkommen weiß, eine plastische gefaltete Hülle, die die Kunden sanft einzuwickeln scheint. Hinter der Verpackung aus Gipskartonwänden sind die gesamte Technik und Nebenräume verborgen. Gleichzeitig aber bietet die spannende Raumarchitektur den Kunden viel zum Schauen: Winkel, Ecken, Spiegelflächen, die den Raum spiegeln; der Friseursalon als „reality theater“.

In the midst of the incredible urban density of the city of New York, interior spaces are playing an increasingly important role. In the centre of Manhattan surrounded by tall brick buildings, the architect, who is originally from Scandinavia, has created a hair dressing salon that is like a modern work of spatial sculpture. From a distance even the unusual window shape attracts attention, slicing an amorphous gap in the façade which is sheathed in light coloured New York blue stone. At the upper left corner, a small backlit window displaying the logo fills in for the traditional barber shop sign. The name of the business establishment has been sandblasted on the glass pane in large characters – elegant and fashionable for a clientele that is nevertheless a quite heterogeneous mix. The space immediately behind the window consists of a small waiting area fitted with a bench and a reception desk. Beyond this the interior stretches into a long, narrow space that culminates in a garden courtyard: slate underfoot and bench seating arranged between mature trees and vines create a cool and pleasant waiting area in the summer. Within the interior everything is entirely restricted to white, forming a sculptural, folded wrapper that seems to gently envelope the customers. All of the technical facilities and the functional spaces have been concealed behind the enveloping surfaces constructed out of gypsum wallboard. At the same time, this stimulating interior architecture gives salon customers a great deal to look at: angles, corners and mirrored surfaces that reflect the room – a hairdressing salon in the guise of “reality theatre”.

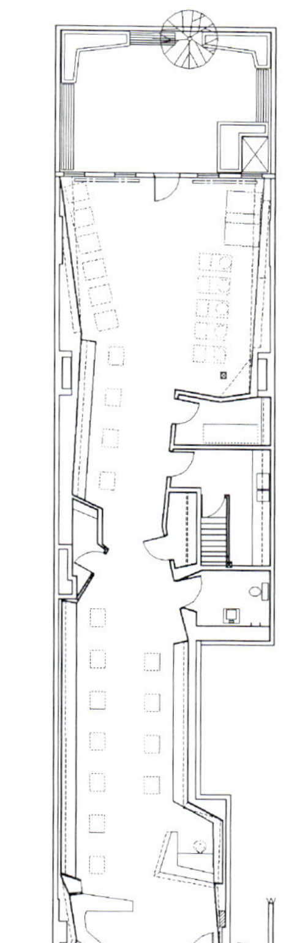

Project:
Aida Hairsalon, New York/USA

Design:
Archi-Tectonics, New York, Winka Dubbeldam

Area:
ca. 240 sqm

Photographer:
Paul Warchol, New York

Tritec · Basel

DESIGN
Pia Ziegler, Zürich

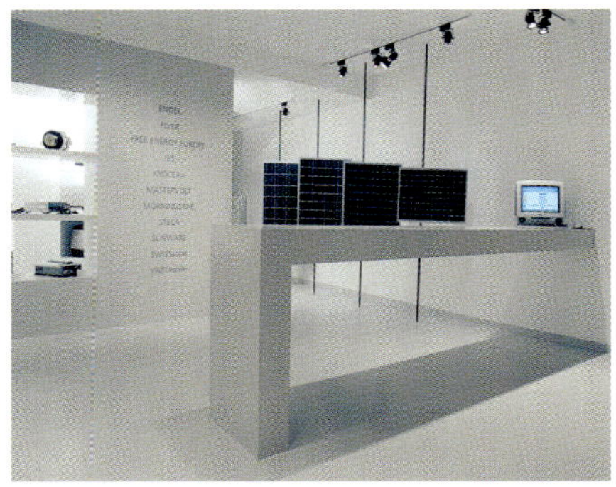

Tritec ist ein Unternehmen, das unabhängige Energiesysteme entwickelt, verkauft und montiert, von der Kühlbox für den Caravan und der Energiesparlampe für zuhause bis zum Solarmodul für das Boot oder Spezialteile für die Solaranlage. Der Umzug der Büros und der Werkstatt in ein gewachsenes Wohngebiet Basels mit nahe gelegenen Geschäften brachte neben Grosskunden nun auch private Laufkundschaft. Das führte zu der Idee einen Laden mit Showroomcharakter zu eröffnen, in dem eine intensive Beratung stattfinden konnte und all die Produkte vorgeführt werden, für die das Unternehmen die Generalvertretung innehat. Die verwinkelte Raumsituation mit kleinem Schaufenster war ideal, um Nischen, Ablagen und Raumteile zu schaffen, die allesamt für die Präsentation der Produkte genutzt werden können. Ein hellgrauer Kautschukboden korrespondiert mit der technischen Produktwelt und verstärkt die studioartige Atmosphäre des völlig weißen Raumes, in dem später auch Sonder-Präsentationen und kleine Veranstaltungen stattfinden sollen. Quer im Raum steht ein drei Meter langer schmaler Tisch für Beratung und Präsentation. Daneben gibt es Produktinformationen per Computer und Fachzeitschriften.
In den skulpturalen eingeschnittenen Regalnischen wird die Technik der kleinteiligen Produkte durch Licht besonders gut herausgestellt. Wie künstlerische Plastiken erscheinen die drei Solarzellen, die zwischen Decke und Boden verspannt sind. Selbst die unzähligen Zubehörteile verschwinden nicht in Kästen oder Firmenpräsentern sondern sind kunstvoll auf einer erweiterbaren Stahlwand im vorderen Raumteil angeordnet. Derzeitiger Blickfang ist das Elektrofahrrad Flyer im Schaufenster, das auf das ungewöhnliche Laden-Konzept des Unternehmens hinweist.

Tritec is a company that develops, sells and installs independent energy systems – everything from refrigerators for mobile homes and energy conservation lamps for the home to solar modules for boats or special parts for solar energy systems. Moving the office and workshop to an old established residential area in Basel close to a shopping district resulted in increased numbers of occasional private customers dropping by. That led to the idea of creating a shop with showroom character which is conducive to intensive consulting as well as to the display of all of the products for which the company acts as the general agent. The spatial situation with its many corners and a small display window has been effectively exploited to create alcoves, display surfaces and partitioned off areas which can all be utilised for the product presentation. Light grey rubber flooring is in tune with the technical range of products and underscores the studio-like atmosphere of the completely white interior, Plans foresee utilising the premises for special presentations and small events in the future. A three metre long narrow table placed crosswise in the room serves as a location for consulting and presentations, as well as for the display of professional journals. In the sculpture-like, carved out shelf recesses, the small technological components of products have been set off particularly effectively by means of the lighting. The three solar cells that are suspended between the ceiling and the floor resemble artistic sculptural objects. Even the innumerable replacement parts have not been concealed in boxes or company presentation elements, but are artfully arranged in an expandable steel wall in the front section of the interior. The current special focus is an electric bicycle in the display window, which signalises the unusual shop concept of the company.

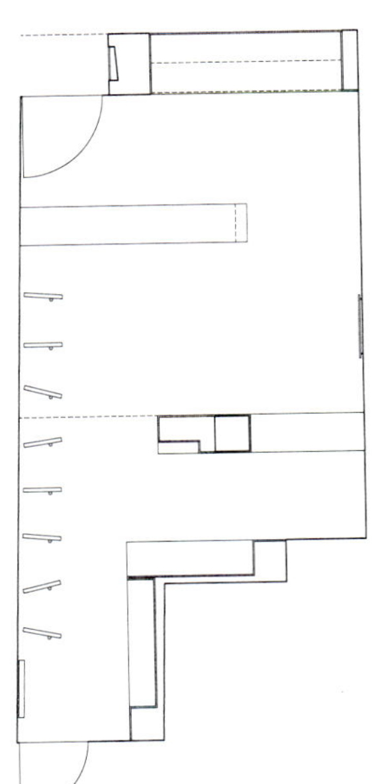

Project:
Tritec AG,
Basel/Switzerland

Design:
Pia Ziegler, Zürich

Area:
ca. 31 sqm

Photographer:
Delux, Zürich und Pia Ziegler, Zürich

More Majorum · Sao Paulo

DESIGN
Anastassiadis Arquitetos, Sao Paulo

In einer dicht besiedelten zehn Millionen-Stadt wie Sao Paulo sind Grünanlagen wahre Oasen zum Atmen und Entspannen. Brasiliens berühmter Gartenarchitekt Gilberto Elkis gab dem innerstädtisch gelegenen eleganten Modehaus *More Majorum* die Chance dazu und schuf ein reizvolles Entrée aus weißem Kies, Pflastersteinen und beleuchteten Buchsbaumhecken. Das Gebäude selbst ist lang und schmal, ein weißer Kubus mit schlanken Mauerscheiben und viel Glas, der die Idee der Mode transportiert: elegant, städtisch, modisch und leicht. Klassische Einstimmung bringt schon der helle Fassadenstein Pedra Mineira, eine Remineszenz an die 50er-Jahre Brasiliens. Im Innern überraschen hohe helle Räume mit vielen großen und kleinen beleuchteten Wandnischen für Mode und Accessoires. Manche sind gar von unten durch einen Glasboden beleuchtet, alle aber können ihr Licht je nach Jahreszeit verändern. Der Showroom löst ein, was die Mode verspricht: Eleganz mit Raffinesse. Ein weißer Terrazzoboden führt an den Guckkastenwänden vorbei, an der Tagesbekleidung und der Abendgarderobe bis hin zur Lounge mit Teppich und kleiner geschweifter Bartheke, wo den Kunden in bequemen Sesseln und Sofas Kaffee und Snacks offeriert werden. Komfort und Service werden hier großgeschrieben und alles erinnert eher an ein gepflegtes Hotel denn an ein Modegeschäft in einer stickigen City. Selbst die lange Empfangs- und Kassentheke, aus dem gleichen rötlichen Pau-Ferro-Holz wie die übrigen Möbel, ist einladend wie eine Hotelrezeption. Computer und Kassentechnik bleiben für die Kunden verborgen. Das Haus zeigt eine leichte Eleganz in Licht und Stein mit Komfort und Service.

In a densely populated city of ten million like Sao Paulo, park areas are truly awelcome oasis where people can breathe freely and relax. Brazil's most famous landscape architect, Gilberto Elkis, gave the elegant fashion shop *More Majorum*, which is situated in the inner city, this type of respite. He created an attractive entry area with white gravel, paving stones and illuminated box hedging. The building itself is long and narrow, essentially a white cube with slim wall slabs and a great deal of glass, which communicates the theme of the fashion style: elegant, urbane, fashionable and light. Pedra Mineira – the light stone of the façade – is reminiscent of Brazil in the fifties and engenders a classical mood. In the interior, bright rooms with high ceilings and numerous large and small illuminated wall niches for fashion and accessories create an element of surprise. Some are even illuminated from below through a sheet of glass, but in all of them the light can be varied according to the season. This showroom achieves what the fashion design promises: sophisticated, subtle elegance. A white terrazzo floor leads patrons along peephole walls, past daytime wear and evening dress, until they ultimately arrive in a carpeted lounge area with a small curved bar counter, comfortable armchairs and sofas, where coffee and snacks are served. Comfort and service are the watchwords here and everything is more evocative of a luxury hotel than a fashion shop in the stuffy city. Even the long reception and cash register counter, which is made of the same reddish Pau Ferro wood as the other furnishings, is just as inviting as a hotel reception desk. Computers and cash register technology are concealed from the customers' view. The building demonstrates an effortless elegance composed of light and stone and replete with comfort and service.

MORE
MAJORUM

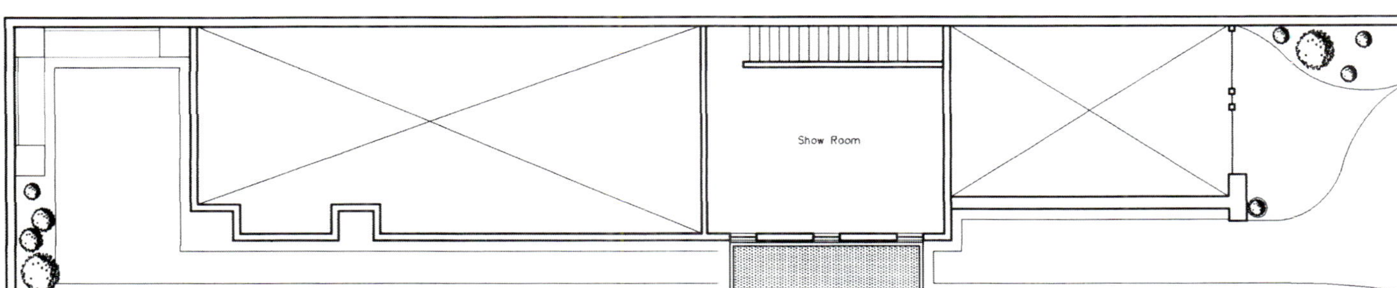

Obergeschoss / First floor

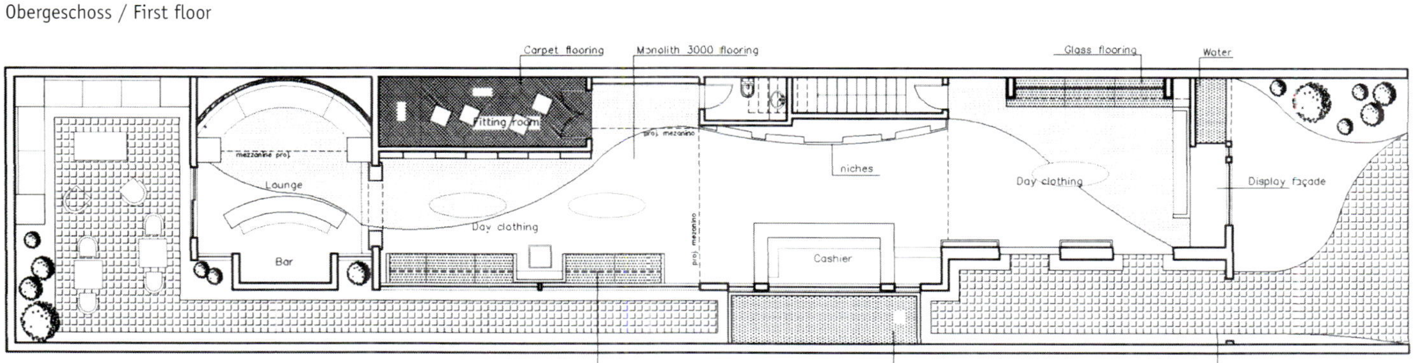

Erdgeschoss / Ground floor

Project:
More Majorum,
Sao Paulo/Brasil

Design:
Anastassiadis Arquitetos,
Sao Paulo

Area:
600 sqm

Photographer:
Ary Disendruck,
Sao Paulo

Legrand Shoes · Hamburg

DESIGN
Luxus,
Ulrich Vollborn,
Moritz Müller,
Hamburg

Hamburgs Edelmeile „Galleria", von den Schweizer Architekten Trix und Robert Haussmann gebaut, ist anspruchsvoll und hat genau das gewisse Etwas, das die avantgardistischen Schuhe von *Legrand Shoes* als Umfeld brauchen. Längst ist der Franzose Max Legrand über die Grenzen Hamburgs hinaus ein Begriff für Schuhmode, und sein großes Gespür für Trends beweist er auch in seinen Präsentationen im regionalen TV-Sender. Seine topmodischen Marken kommen aus Paris, New York und Mailand und ziehen TV-Prominenz, Schauspieler und Stylisten an, die sich nun den Weg nach Mailand oder Tokio sparen können. Etwas ganz Besonderes wie seine Schuhe sollte auch die Gestaltung des Ladens werden, etwas vom Baukörper abgehobenes, ein Raum in einem Raum, der nun von einer liegenden offenen Röhre gebildet wird. Die weichen Rundungen der Eichenschale wurden sowohl von den Produkten als auch vom weiblichen Klientel beeinflusst. Um die hölzernen Raumschale nun auch noch abzuheben und schwebend erscheinen zu lassen, wurde sie zur Decke hin mit Glasfaserlicht hinterleuchtet, das fließende Farbübergänge ermöglicht und Raumgrenzen verwischt. Der Raum ist nun offen und frei, fast meditativ. Die Schuhe werden auf schlichten Holzborden an den Längswänden präsentiert. Was diesen Laden prägt, sind nicht nur die ungewöhnliche Raumidee und die trendigen Schuhe sondern auch eine sehr persönliche und freundliche Bedienung, ein Konzept, das sich inzwischen bis zu den Pariser Einkäufern herumgesprochen hat.

Hamburg's elegant shopping arcade "Galleria", which was built by the Swiss architects Trix and Robert Haussmann, is sophisticated and has that special something that the avant-garde shoes of *Legrand Shoes* require as a backdrop. A Frenchman, Max Legrand has become a real name in shoe fashion well beyond Hamburg's city limits. He even demonstrates his incredible feeling for trends during his shows on regional television stations. The ultra fashionable brand names that he stocks come from Paris, New York and Milan and have been attracting TV celebrities, actors and stylists in droves. After all, now they no longer have to bother with a trip to Milan or Tokyo. Just like his shoes, the design of the store was supposed to be something special, something that clearly distinguishes itself from the rest of the building like a room within a room. This is precisely what has been created – by means of an open pipe like element lying on its side. The soft curves of the oak shell are meant to correspond with the products and the store's female clientele. In order to make the wooden room shell seem to float, the ceiling area has been backlit with fibre glass lighting fixtures. Among all of the myriad types of lighting, this is the only light that can also be utilised in problem areas and that makes seamless colour transitions possible. A perforated 500 by 500 millimetre grid accommodates merchandise display elements and the cash register and makes it possible to transform the wall utilisation arrangement very easily. This shop is not only especially unique because of its unusual spatial design and the trendy shoes, but also because of the extremely personal and friendly sales personnel, a concept that has even become the talk of Parisian purchasing circles.

GRAND
SHOES

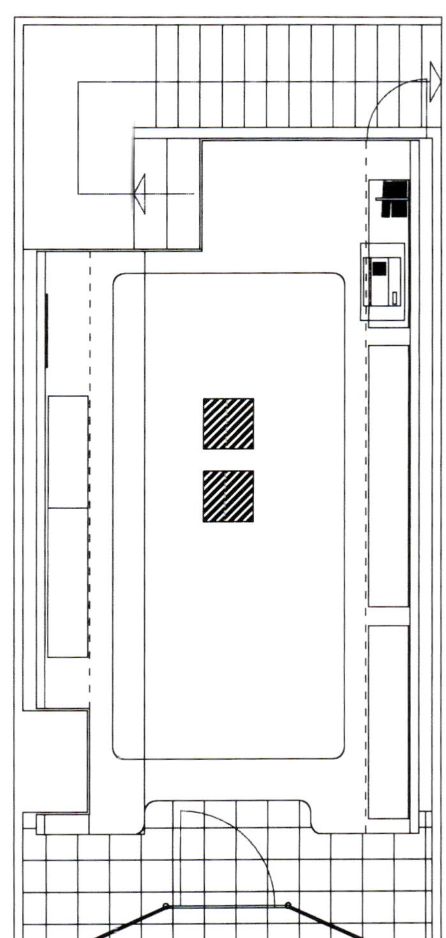

Project:
Legrand Shoes,
Hamburg/Germany
Design:
Luxus, Ulrich Vollborn
+ Moritz Müller, Hamburg
Area:
ca. 36 sqm
Photographer:
Philip Glaser, Hamburg

Fattoria Blu · Zürich

DESIGN

Angélil/Graham/ Pfenninger/Scholl, Zürich

fattoria ≈ blu

delikatessen caffè bar take away

Das Delikatessengeschäft *Fattoria Blu* ist Teil der umgebauten, ehemaligen Waschanstalt Zürich-Wollishofen, in der heute Wohnungen, Büros, Läden und ein Restaurant mit Bar ein städtisches Ensemble bilden. *Fattoria Blu* entstand als ergänzendes gastronomisches Element neben der angrenzenden Mitarbeiterkantine und dem Restaurant Blu, die allesamt zur Modeagentur Enzo Cagol gehören. Ungewöhnlich ist nicht nur die edle, wie eher in der Mode üblichen Präsentation der Lebensmittel-Produkte, sondern vor allem das gastronomische Konzept. Was im Laden als Gericht angeboten wird, kann in der Kantine gekocht werden oder die in der Kantine angebotenen Espressi kommen aus der Kaffeemaschine im Laden. Diese Synergieeffekte ermöglichen hohe Wertigkeit und Qualität bei optimaler Ausnutzung der Geräte. Auch zwischen dem Restaurant Blu und dem Laden gibt es Verbindungen: Was den Gast im Restaurant begeistert, kann er im Laden erwerben, in dem viele kleine Gerichte vor den Augen des Kunden zubereitet werden. Speisen und Getränke gibt es an Stehtischen direkt im Laden oder können im Take-Away mitgenommen werden. In der Gestaltung lehnt sich das Mode-Gastro-Ensemble an die bauliche Geschichte des Gebäudekomplexes an, lässt Betonstützen und polierten Betonboden bestehen und setzt dazu kontrastierend schwarze Holzregale für die farbigen Produkte und eine lange elegante Edelstahltheke für die Snacks.

The *Fattoria Blu* delicatessen is part of a remodelled former laundry in Zürich-Wollishofen, which now houses apartments, offices, shops and a restaurant with a bar, thus forming an urban focal point. *Fattoria Blu* came into being as a supplementary gastronomic catering element in addition to the adjacent employee cafeteria and the Restaurant Blu, which all belong to the Enzo Cagol fashion agency. What is unusual is not only the presentation of the food products in a sophisticated manner reminiscent of the fashion world but, particularly, the catering concept behind it. The dishes that are sold in the shop can also be prepared in the cafeteria, or alternatively, the espresso served in the cafeteria originates in the coffee machine in the shop. These synergy effects make it possible to offer high value and quality and ensure maximum capacity utilisation of the appliances. There are also links between the Restaurant Blu and the shop: in the shop where many tempting snacks are prepared right before the eyes of the customer, restaurant patrons can purchase the delectable food that they previously dined on in the restaurant. The food and beverages can either be enjoyed at a stand-up table directly in the shop or as take-away. The design of the fashion plus restaurant ensemble is attuned to the architectural history of the building complex itself. Concrete pillars and polished concrete floors are set off by contrasting black wooden shelving for the display of the colourful products and a long, elegant stainless steel counter for the snacks.

ANTIPASTI
VINI E BIRRA
APERITIVI
CAFÈ

Galerieartige Präsentation von Delikatessen

Delicatessen presented like in a fashion gallery

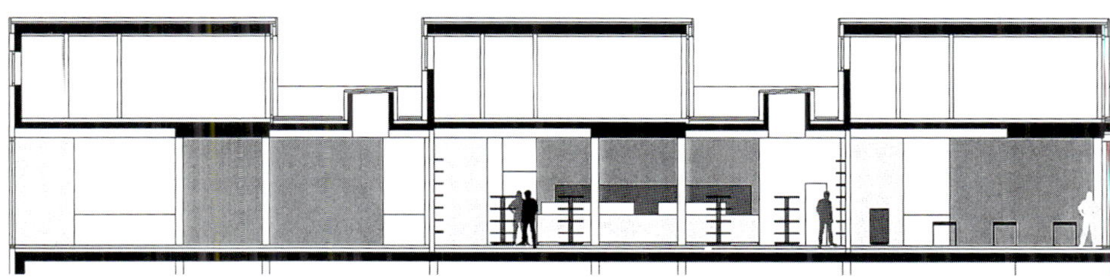

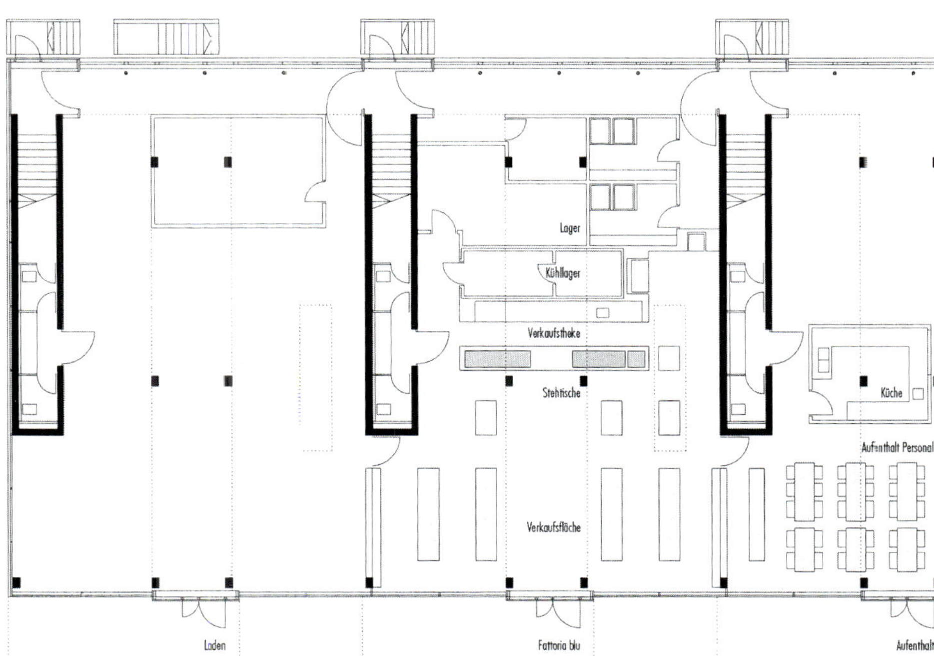

Project:
Fattoria Blu,
Zürich/Switzerland

Design:
Angélil/Graham/
Pfenninger/Scholl, Zürich

Gastronomyconcept:
Jürg Landert, Zürich

Area:ca. 145 sqm

Photographer:
Gaston Wicky, Zürich

Läden wie Verkaufsmaschinen

Natürlich geht es hier nicht um Verkaufsmaschinen oder gar um Automaten. Die Objekte, die ich hier vorstelle, sind meist kleine Läden, deren Gestaltung so optimiert wurde, dass Präsentation, Information und Beratung in dichter Form möglich sind.

25 Records in Hamburg ist wirklich ein winzig kleiner Shop, eher ein Kiosk, der auf nur fünf Quadratmetern Produktpräsentation, Beratung und Probehören anbietet. Es gibt hier ein kleines, speziell auf die Kunden zugeschnittenes CD-Sortiment mit einer fast privaten Betreuung. Das genau macht den Erfolg dieses kleinen Shops aus. Auch *The Klinik* ist ein recht kleiner Friseursalon in London. Fast klinisch nüchtern, technisch perfekt, ästhetisch, klar, mit einer Besonderheit: Der Kunde kann sich selbst beim Haareschneiden in einem Monitor von hinten sehen, ein Gag, der einen Bezug zum technischen Alltag bringt, über den man auch mit den Stylisten ins Gespräch kommt. Die gewünschte Kommunikation mit den Kunden wird auf der Website fortgesetzt: informativ und doch persönlich. Bei den *Lynx- Barbershops* hat man schon eher den Eindruck Verkaufsmaschinen vorzufinden, die für die jungen Männer ein ganzes Servicepaket parat haben, das aus einem großen Kasten, dem Pod, entnommen werden kann: Alles was zur Haarpflege gebraucht wird, verbirgt sich in diesen Kästen und dazu noch all das, was junge Kunden heute suchen: TV, Videospiele, Getränke. Bei anderen Friseursalons Londons kann man nebenbei noch telefonieren, übers Internet einkaufen, E-mails abrufen etc. Längst geht das Servicepaket weit über das eigentliche Anliegen hinaus. Die Wartezeit wird intensiv genutzt: sei es für Informationen, Einkauf und Business oder aber für ein Wellnessprogramm zur totalen Entspannung. Beide Konzepte scheinen erfolgreich zu sein. Das Uhrengeschäft *Watch2Watch* war von vornherein so konzipiert, modische Uhren an junge Leute zu verkaufen, zum An- und Ausprobieren bei einer Verlustrate von null. Der Anreiz dieses Geschäftes liegt in seiner Präsentationsidee, die originell und spielerisch ist, nicht nur junge Leute anspricht und zudem erfolgreich ist. So wie *Swatch* seit Jahren versucht seine Lifestyle-Idee in seinen Läden sichtbar zu machen, hat *Watch2Watch* mit seinen Läden einen ganz eigenen Stil entwickelt, der auf der Website in eine spannende Kommunikation mit den Kunden übergeht – auch nach Geschäftsschluss. Das *Microcenter* in Athen ist ein Laden für Computerzubehör und Spiele. Und wer diese Läden kennt weiß, dass es oft chaotische Läden sind, Läden zum Stöbern oder für Freaks. Hier ist sicher noch vieles möglich, um diese Ladentypen zu aktivieren. Die griechischen Architekten haben versucht einen Laden zu kreieren, der die Kunden durch architektonische und grafische Signale an die gewünschten Produktbereiche heranführt, wo sie von einer Beratung aufgefangen werden. Es ist in erster Linie ein Konzept, um sich im Laden orientieren zu können. Gerade Kunden dieser Läden kennen sich aber am Markt recht gut aus, suchen Vergleich, Information und Möglichkeiten die Geräte auszuprobieren. Es besteht allerdings großer Handlungsbedarf die Läden zu beleben und zudem über das Internet Verknüpfungen herzustellen.

Shops like vending machines

Naturally, this category does not actually include vending machines or automatic machinery. For the most part, the projects that I have selected are diminutive shops where the design has been optimised so that display, information and consulting are possible in concentrated form. *25 Records* in Hamburg is a really miniscule shop – more of a kiosk – which offers product presentation, consulting service and test listening in an area of only five square metres. The shop offers a small assortment of CD's, specially tailored to its customers, with almost private personalised service. That is exactly the reason for the success of this miniature shop. The *Klinik* hairdressing salon in London is also relatively small. It is almost clinically austere and technically perfect, aesthetic and clear – with a special added touch: while having his hair trimmed the customer can watch himself from behind thanks to a monitor. This gag serves as an allusion to the technical side of everyday life and also promotes conversation with the hair stylist. This welcome communication with customers is also promoted on the salon's web site, which is informative, but still personal. At the *Lynx Barber Shops* the impression created is really that of vending machines. The young male patrons are offered an entire service package that is contained in a large box-like element called a pod. Everything imaginable required for hair care is concealed in these pods, plus everything else that young customers of today appreciate: TV, video games, beverages. At other hairdressing salons in London, customers can also make telephone calls during their appointment, shop via the internet, access e-mails etc. The service package offered extends to much more than conventional hairdressing service. Waiting times can be intensively exploited: either for information, shopping or business, or even for a wellness programme aimed at total relaxation. Both concepts seem to be successful. Right from its inception, the *Watch2Watch* watch shop was aimed at selling fashionable watches to young people: it provides an opportunity to try everything on while ensuring a zero shop lifting rate. The attraction of this shop is its presentation idea, which is original and tongue-in-cheek. It not only appeals to young people – and it is successful as well. Just like Swatch, which has for years been aiming at making its lifestyle idea visible in its shops, *Watch2Watch* has developed a completely individual style, which merges into exciting communication with customers on the shop's web site – even after business hours are over. The *Microcenter* in Athens is a shop for computer accessories and games. Those who are familiar with this type of shop know that these are often chaotic stores, geared to rummaging or freaks. There is no doubt that there is a great deal of potential for activating this type of shop. The Greek architects have attempted to create a shop that directs the customer toward the desired product areas by means of architectural and graphic signals, where consulting service is then available. Mainly, this is a concept that promotes customer orientation within the store. However, particularly those customers that frequent these stores are relatively familiar with the market: they want comparisons, information and the opportunity to test use the hardware. In this area, there is still a great deal of scope for action, in order to infuse the shops with life as well create links via the internet.

25 Records, Hamburg

DESIGN
Luxus, Ulrich Vollborn +
Moritz Müller, Hamburg

In einer ehemaligen Sushi-Station in der exklusiven schwarz-weiß marmorierten Einkaufspassage an der Großen Bleichen in Hamburg liegt der wahrscheinlich kleinste Plattenladen der Welt. Für Innenstadt-Shopper mit Zeitnot und Unentschlossene hilft *25 Records* mit seinem knappen Angebot von 25 CDs durch den Angebotsdschungel. Von der musikbegeisterten Crew gemeinsam ausgesucht wird Musik quer durch die Bereiche Jazz, Elektro, Techno, House and Ambient angeboten. Die Crew sucht das Besondere für ihre Kunden, Musik, die sonst neben 10 000 Titeln unterginge: für Stimmungen, Situationen, zu speziellen Themen. Blickfang ist ein großes hinterleuchtetes Display an der Rückseite des Ladens mit den aktuellen Covers. Ansonsten ist der ganze Laden einfach weiß glänzend, abgerundete Kunststoffformen, in die alle Funktionselemente integriert sind. Platz zum Stöbern gibt es nicht. Auf rund fünf Quadratmetern Verkaufsfläche haben gerade ein Verkäufer, eine Theke mit Schubladen für die Warenlagerung und zwei Abhörstationen Platz. Die Kunden bleiben draußen vor dem Tresen stehen, können sich die Kopfhörer überstülpen und bequem an einen ausklappbaren Sitz lehnen. Mit einem Mini-Joystick können sie sich durch das Angebot klicken. Pro Tag werden ca. 30–40 Platten verkauft, meist an Stammkunden zwischen 25 und 55 Jahren. Die Idee wurde patentiert. Weitere Standorte für die Suchmaschine des guten Geschmacks sind schon in Planung.

A former sushi eatery in the exclusive black and white marble shopping passage on Hamburg's Große Bleiche thoroughfare is the location of the – in all probability – smallest record shop in the world. For downtown shoppers strapped for time and the chronically indecisive, *25 Records* makes sense of the prevalent jungle-like proliferation of music offers by restricting its selection to only 25 CDs. The musically enthusiastic crew handpicks the shop's selection, including jazz, electro, techno, house and ambient styles. The focus is on that something special for the shop's customers. This is music that would otherwise be overwhelmed if it were placed next to 10,000 other titles – special music attuned to a particular mood, situation or a special theme. The visual focus is a large backlit display on the back wall of the shop showing the current selection of covers. Otherwise, the entire shop is restricted to glossy white, rounded plastic shapes into which all of the functional elements have been integrated. There is no room for rummaging around or shuffling through merchandise. The roughly five square metres of retail area just barely accommodate one sales person, a counter with drawers for storing merchandise and two test listening units. Customers remain standing outside the shop in front of the counter, where they can don head phones and comfortably lean on a fold out seating element. A mini joystick allows them to click their way through the available selection. Per day, approx. 30–40 records are sold, for the most part to regular customers between the ages of 25 and 55. In the meantime, the idea has been patented and further locations for this "good taste" search engine are in the planning stage.

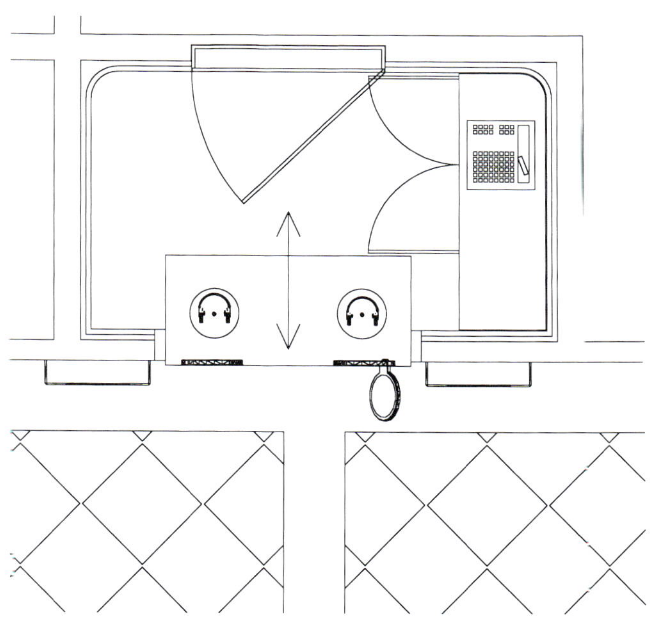

Project:
25 Records,
Hamburg/Germany

Design:
Luxus, Ulrich Vollborn
+ Moritz Müller, Hamburg

Area:
5 sqm

Photographer:
Klaus Frahm, Hamburg,
Philip Glaser, Hamburg

The Klinik, Hairsalon, London

DESIGN
Block Architecture,
Anna Forsling, London

Die schwedische Inhaberin Anna Forsling wollte mit Ihrem nur 36 Quadratmeter großen Friseursalon einen interessanten, unterhaltsamen Ort mit wirkungsvollem Service anbieten. Um die Raumgröße optimal zu nutzen, lehnte sie sich an die Funktionalität und medizinische Ästhetik einer Klinik an und übertrug diese Idee in enger Zusammenarbeit mit den Architekten auf die Atmosphäre und Grafik bis hin zum Firmenschriftzug. Überwiegend in Weiß gehalten erhielt der Raum klare grafische Linien durch schmale hohe Spiegel, lange Lichtbänder und karg verwendete Materialien. Die wenigen von den Architekten entworfenen Möbel lassen ihn größer erscheinen als er ist. Für die Stühle verwendeten sie Second-Hand-Rahmen und fügten weiße Lederpolster hinzu. Die weiße Ledercouch ist Sinnbild für Luxus und Funktionalität zugleich. Selbst die digitale Uhr erinnert noch an eine Klinik. Seine Theatralik aber erfährt der klinische Raum durch von der Decke herabhängende kleine CCTV-Kameras, die sich auf jeden Winkel einstellen lassen und dem Kunden die Möglichkeit geben, sich von allen Seiten zu sehen. Ein 9 Inch großer s/w-Monitor unterhalb des schmalen Spiegels gibt dem Kunden die Möglichkeit, ganz voyeuristisch dem Stylisten bei der Arbeit zuzuschauen und sich selbst zu beobachten. So klinisch der Salon erscheinen mag, ist er für die Kunden ein warmer willkommener Platz. Die Freitag-Abende werden oft zu Social Events komplett mit Wein und Unterhaltung, und die Bildschirme geben dann stimmungsvoll die clubbige Atmosphäre wieder. Ein kleiner, attraktiver Salon mit gutem Service.

Anna Forsling, the Swedish owner of this only 36 square metre large hair dressing salon, wanted to create an interesting, entertaining locale that offers effective service. In order to exploit the size of the interior to the optimum, she focused on the functionality and medicinal aesthetics of a clinic and, in close co-operation with the architects, she transferred this theme to the atmosphere and graphic design, including the company logo. The interior has been rendered in white, with clear graphic lines achieved by means of high, narrow mirrors, long bands of light and sparsely utilised materials. The few furnishings, which were also designed by the architects, make the interior seem larger than it really is. For the chairs they used second hand frames and added white leather upholstery. The white leather couch is simultaneously a symbol of luxury as well as functionality. Even the digital clock is reminiscent of a clinic. However, the room is given its theatrical atmosphere by means of small closed circuit TV cameras that are suspended from the ceiling and can be aimed at every imaginable angle, thus offering the customer the option of inspecting himself from all sides. A 9 inch black and white monitor below the narrow mirror makes it possible for the customer to observe his hair stylist at work and observe himself in pseudo voyeur-like manner. While the salon appears to be quite clinical, it is a warm and welcoming place for customers. Friday evenings often evolve into social events, complete with wine and entertainment, and the monitors reflect the mood of the club-like atmosphere. This is an attractive small salon with excellent service.

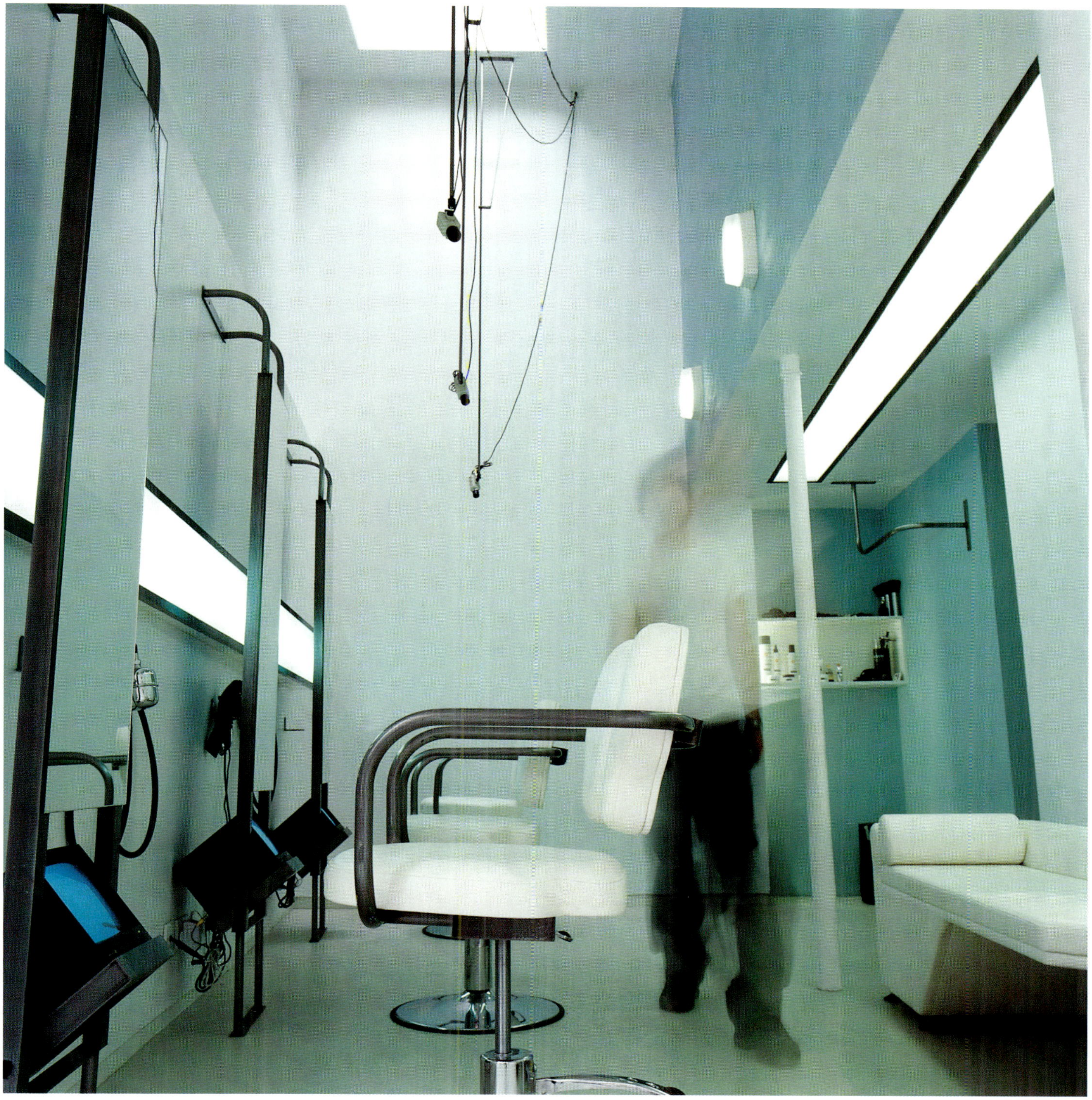

Voyeuristische Spielerei per Monitor: kleine hängende TV-Kameras geben dem Kunden die Möglichkeit, sich von allen Seiten zu betrachten

Voyeristic fooling via monitor: small hanging TV-cameras offer the customer the option of inspecting himself from all sides

Klinische Raumatmosphäre – selbst in der Zeit

A clinical atmosphere – even in the time

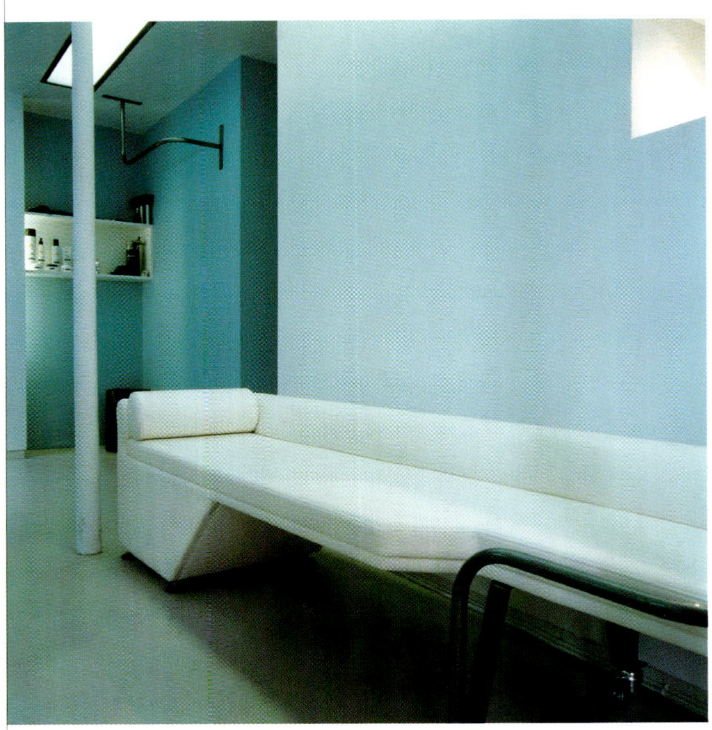

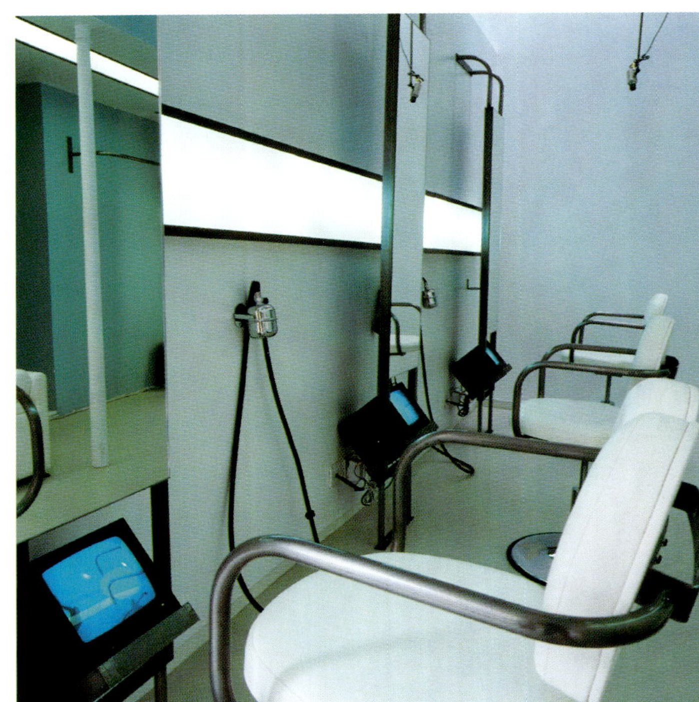

Für die Stühle wurden Secondhand-Rahmen verwendet und mit weißem Leder neu gepolstert

For the chairs second hand frames were used and added with white leather upholstery

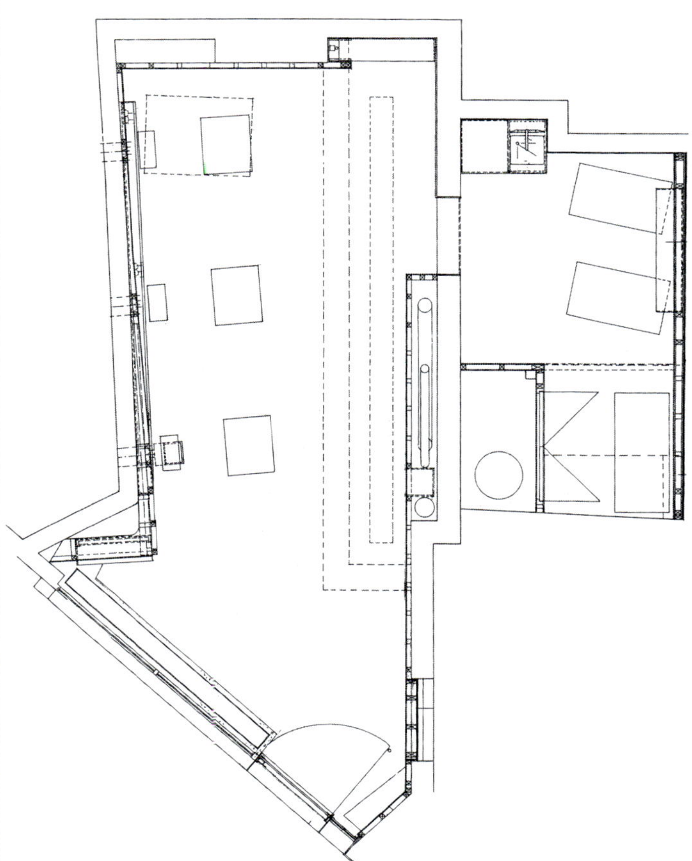

Project:
The Klinik, Hairsalon, London/UK

Design:
Block Architecture, Graeme Williamson, London + Anna Forsling, London

Area:
36 sqm

Photographer:
Leon Chew, London

Microcenter Koriasidis, Athen

DESIGN
Anamorphosis Architects, Athen

Koriasidis ist eines der größten griechischen Unternehmen, das sich auf Consumer-Elektronik spezialisiert hat. Sein Produktangebot umfasst seit 1999 Handys, Computer, Hightech-Artikel, Bürogeräte und Videospiele. Für seine zahlreichen Läden suchte das Unternehmen nach einem ganz neuen Designkonzept, das auch noch auf Shop-in-Shops übertragbar ist. Vor allem aber suchte es nach einem starken erkennbaren Erscheinungsbild, das besonders bei den 20–40-jährigen ankommt und den menschlichen Aspekt der Technologie und Firma heraushebt.
Für die Umsetzung bedienten sich die Architekten der Architekturelemente der Läden und der Firmenfarben Blau und Orange. So wurden bereits die Fassaden zum auffallenden Farbenspiel mit schrägen Flächen und balkenähnlichen Auslegern. Auf spezielle Schaufenster wurde verzichtet. Der ganze Laden sollte Schaufenster sein und die Kunden nach innen ziehen. Dafür wurden in den Steinboden Holzwege aus Eiche eingelassen, die direkt ins Ladenzentrum führen. Um die vier Produktkategorien sichtbar zu machen und schnell zu finden, wurden die Architekturelemente im Laden als Bedeutungsträger genutzt. Bestehende Stützen dienen als Service-Posten für Handys, durch eine blau-weiße Fotografik gekennzeichnet. Die Seitenwände im Raum nehmen die periphäre Ausstellung von Computern und Bürogeräten auf, in Szene gesetzt durch goldfarbene gewellte Stahlpaneele. Und die Glasfassade inspirierte zu den freistehenden hinterleuchteten Glaspaneelen für die Hightech-Gadgets. Selbst die Raumdecke regte dazu an, dem Kiosk, an dem Playstations und Videospiele verkauft werden, ein ganz markantes abgewinkeltes Dach in Orangerot aufzusetzen. Farbe und Architektur als Differenzierungsmerkmal für eine kleinteilige Produktwelt. Und nach Ladenschluss? Da setzt sich die Botschaft fort und an der Fassade werden Jalousien und Lichtspiele zum Firmenname in gerasterter Computerschrift.

Koriasidis is one of the largest Greek companies and specialises in consumer electronics. Since 1999, its range of products has included cell phones, computers, high-tech gadgets, office equipment and video games. The company was looking for an entirely new design concept for its numerous shops, a concept that could also be applied to a shop-in-shop retail set-up. In particular, the company wanted to find an easily recognisable corporate look, which would be well received especially among the twenty to forty year olds and which would highlight the human aspect of technology and of the company itself.
In order to realise this objective, the architects made use of the existing architectural elements of the shops and the company colours – blue and orange. The façades with diagonally delineated areas and beam like projections serve to call attention to the conspicuous use of colour. This concept dispenses with special display windows. The entire shop is intended to be a display window that entices customers inside. To this end wooden walkways in oak have been inlaid into the stone floor and lead directly into the centre of the shop. The architectural elements in the shop have been given a signal function in order to make the four product categories highly visible and easy to find. Existing pillars that serve as service posts for cell phones are highlighted by a special blue and white photographic design. The lateral walls of the interior are utilised for a peripheral display of computers and office equipment: they are effectively set off by gold coloured, corrugated steel panels. The glass façade was the inspiration for the free-standing backlit glass panels used for the high-tech gadgets. Even the existing ceiling prompted the creation of a kiosk with a striking angled roof in orange red,which is devoted to the sale of Playstations and video games. Colour and architecture have been used as differentiating characteristics for the myriad small product items. And after the store closes? The shop continues to broadcast its message: blinds and lighting effects highlight the company logo in grid based computer characters.

PlayStation
PlayStation
PlayStation
DURACELL

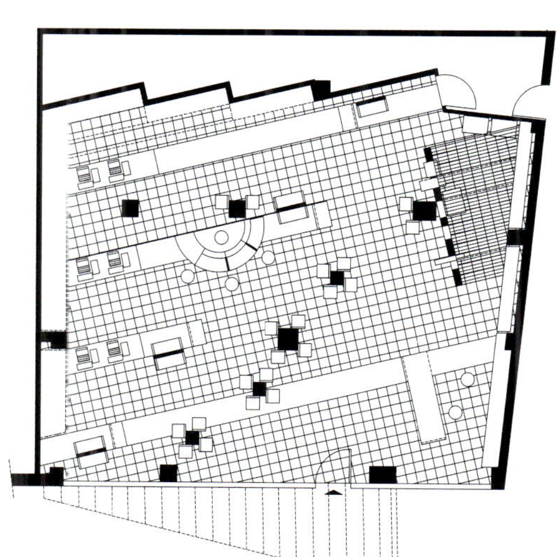

Project:
Microcenter Koriasidis, Athens/Greece

Design:
Anamorphosis Architects, Athens

Area:
200 sqm

Photographer:
Elias Nikolaidis, Athens

Watch2Watch, London

DESIGN
Cobalt Brand Development, London

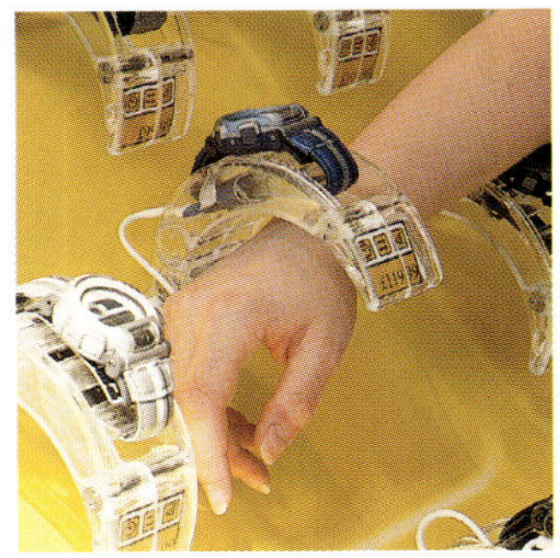

Ende der 90er-Jahre, als der Markt an jugendlichen Modeuhren explodierte, kam der Unternehmer Karl Oliver auf die Idee, Uhren völlig anders zu präsentieren als hinter Glasvitrinen. Nicht nur die Sperre zwischen Verkäufer und Kunde sollte verschwinden. Der Kunde sollte die Möglichkeit erhalten, anzuprobieren, was ihm gefällt. Eine intensive Marktrecherche in den USA und England untermauerte diese Idee: Uhr abnehmen, anprobieren – ohne zu stehlen. Die Agentur Cobalt, die an dem Unternehmen *Watch2Watch* beteiligt ist, entwickelte das Konzept dazu, das zur „Watch Banana" führte. Bei dieser Idee ist die Uhr auf einen bananenförmigen Plexiglashalter montiert und eng mit einem Sicherheitssystem verbunden. Der Kunde kann sein Handgelenk unter diesen Halter legen und eine Vorstellung von der späteren Wirkung bekommen. Geschwungen ist auch die gesamte Ladengestaltung. Sie nimmt die Formen und Materialien einer jungen Generation von Surfern und Skatern auf und übersetzt sie in konvexe Wandformen aus weißem Fiberglas mit ockerfarbenen Flächen als Untergrund für die Plexiglashalter. Das Licht hinter diesen schalenförmigen Wänden lässt den blaugrauen Boden und die Decke schwebend erscheinen und bringt Weltraumflair ins Geschäft. Surfbrettspitzen an den Regalwänden wurden zu Auslegern für die Markennamen. Inzwischen ist die Shop-Idee erfolgreich vervielfältigt worden und die anfänglich weißen Mitteltische mussten nun ockerfarbenen Torpedos weichen, die zwischen Decke und Boden verspannt sind. Das bedeutet noch mehr Freifläche zum Anschauen und Anprobieren. Verständlich und einfach wie die Form des Ladens wurden auch die Grafik und das Videoposter am Eingang, das dem Passanten digitale Markenbilder und Grafiken vermittelt. Mit dieser erfolgreichen Präsentationsidee hat Oliver die Chance seine Läden in A1-Lagen anzusiedeln und das breiteste Markenangebot an modischen Uhren zu führen.

In the late nineties, when the market for fashion watches for young people exploded, Karl Oliver had the idea of displaying watches in a completely different way than in glass cases. The intention was not only to eliminate the barrier between the salesperson and the customer, but also to give the latter the opportunity to try on whatever he likes. Intensive market research in the USA and England corroborated this idea: take off your watch, try another on – with no shoplifting. The Cobalt agency, which has a shareholding in the *Watch2Watch* company, developed the corresponding concept that resulted in "Watch Banana": the watch is mounted on a banana shaped Plexiglas holder and closely connected with a security system. The customer can place his wrist under the holder to get an impression of what the subsequent effect will be. The entire design of the shop utilises shapes and materials associated with the young generation of surfers and skaters and transfers them into convex wall shapes made of white fibre glass with ochre coloured areas as a back drop for the Plexiglas holders. Lighting behind these curved walls makes the blue grey floor and the ceiling seem to float and imparts an outer space flair to the shop. On the walls, the brand names jut out on the tips of surfboards. In the meantime, the shop concept has been successfully copied. The white central tables that were installed originally have now been replaced by ochre coloured torpedoes that are mounted between the ceiling and the floor, resulting in even more open space devoted to looking at the merchandise and trying it on. The simple and comprehensible shape of the shop has also been incorporated into the graphic design and the video poster at the entrance, which communicates digital brand name images and graphics to passers-by. This outstanding presentation idea has given Watch2Watch the opportunity of locating its shops in top locations and stocking the most extensive range of fashionable, brand name watches.

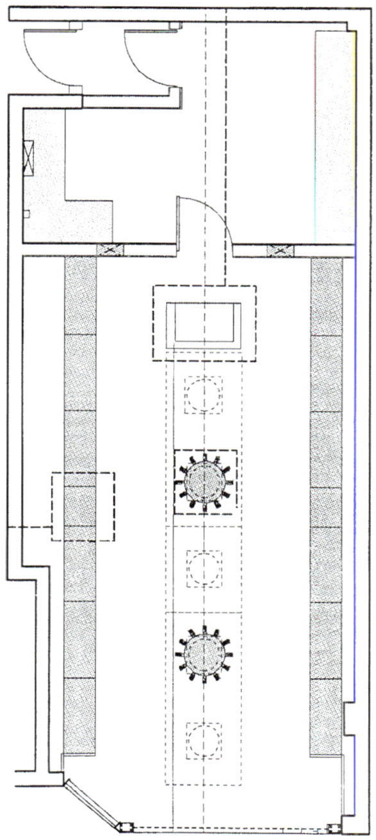

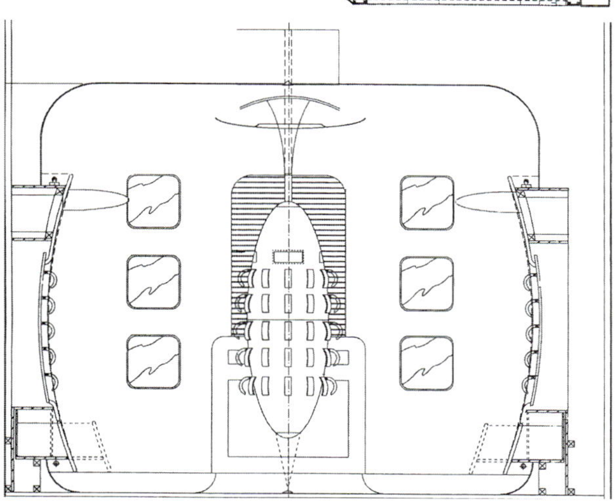

Watch Banana – der bananenförmige Plexiglashalter mit Sicherheitssystem

Watch Banana – the banana shaped Pexiglas holder with security system

Project:
Watch2Watch, London/UK

Design:
Cobalt Brand Development, London

Area:
ca. 30 sqm

Photographer:
Cobalt, London

LYNX Barbershop, Kingston und London

Für die Haarpflege und Pflegeprodukte junger Männer zwischen 18 und 25 Jahren entwickelten die Architekten im Auftrag von *Unilever* einen neuen spritzigen Haarsalontyp, der mit allen Konventionen bricht und eher an coole Bars und Clubs erinnern soll. Um den jungen selbstbewussten Herren die Peinlichkeit zu ersparen, mit nassen Haaren und Cape durch den Raum zum nächsten Platz zu wandern, wurde für sie eine Art kleine Weltraumstation entwickelt, ein *Pod*, von denen es mehrere im Raum gibt und diesen in intimere Bereiche einteilt. Die *Pods* sind große, schrankähnliche Magazine aus weißem Fiberglas, ähnlich wie riesige Armaturenbretter, in denen sich Waschbecken, Spiegel, Pflege- und Arbeitsprodukte und ein Hightech- Bildschirm befindet. Einmal am *Pod* kann der Kunde sitzen bleiben und während der Styling-Aktion Videos oder TV-Sendungen anschauen, an Playstations und Gameboys spielen und so für sich den Friseurbesuch zu einem vergnüglichen Erlebnis machen.

In **Kingston-upon-Thames** erinnert der Salon eher an den Showroom einer Werbeagentur mit runden Spiegeln an Decke und Wand – eine narzistische Männerwelt, in der Damen auf Großfotos für atmosphärische Stimmung sorgen.

In **London** stellt sich der Haarsalon über eine große Glasfassade zur Straße hin offen zur Schau. Eine raumhohe Barbier-Säule übersetzt das Traditionszeichen ganz neu. Besondere Attraktionen in diesem zweigeschossigen Salon sind hier farbige Wände, eine Wand mit runden Spiegeln, die den Raum kaleidoskopartig brechen und bequeme schwarze Ledersessel im Wartebereich – mit Flachbildschirm.

For hair care and personal care products aimed at young men between the ages of 18 and 25 and on behalf of their client *Unilever*, the architects have developed a fresh new type of hair salon that breaks with all convention and is intended to be somewhat reminiscent of cool bars and clubs. In order to spare the self-assured young men the embarrassment of walking around the room with wet hair and a protective cape to get to the next work area, a kind of miniature space station was developed: several of these *pods* have been installed throughout the interior, thus dividing the space into more intimate areas. The *pods* consist of large, wall unit-like elements made of white fibre glass, which resemble gigantic dashboards and accommodate sinks, mirrors, care products and working utensils, as well as a high-tech monitor. Once he is seated at a *pod*, the customer can remain in one place. During the styling process he has the option of watching videos or TV programmes, as well as diverting himself with a Playstation or Gameboy, thus making his visit to the barber an enjoyable experience.

The **Kingston-upon-Thames** salon, which sports round mirrors on the ceiling and walls,seems more reminiscent of an advertising agency showroom. This is a narcissistic male world, in which the females pictured on the photographic blow-ups serve as atmospheric mood makers.

The **London** hair salon has a large glass façade which is open to the street, providing a view of the interior. A ceiling high barber pole re-interprets the traditional symbol in an entirely new way. Special attractions in this two storey hair salon are the coloured walls, a wall with round mirrors that fractures the interior in a kaleidoscope-like manner and the comfortable black leather armchairs in the waiting area – all equipped with flat screens.

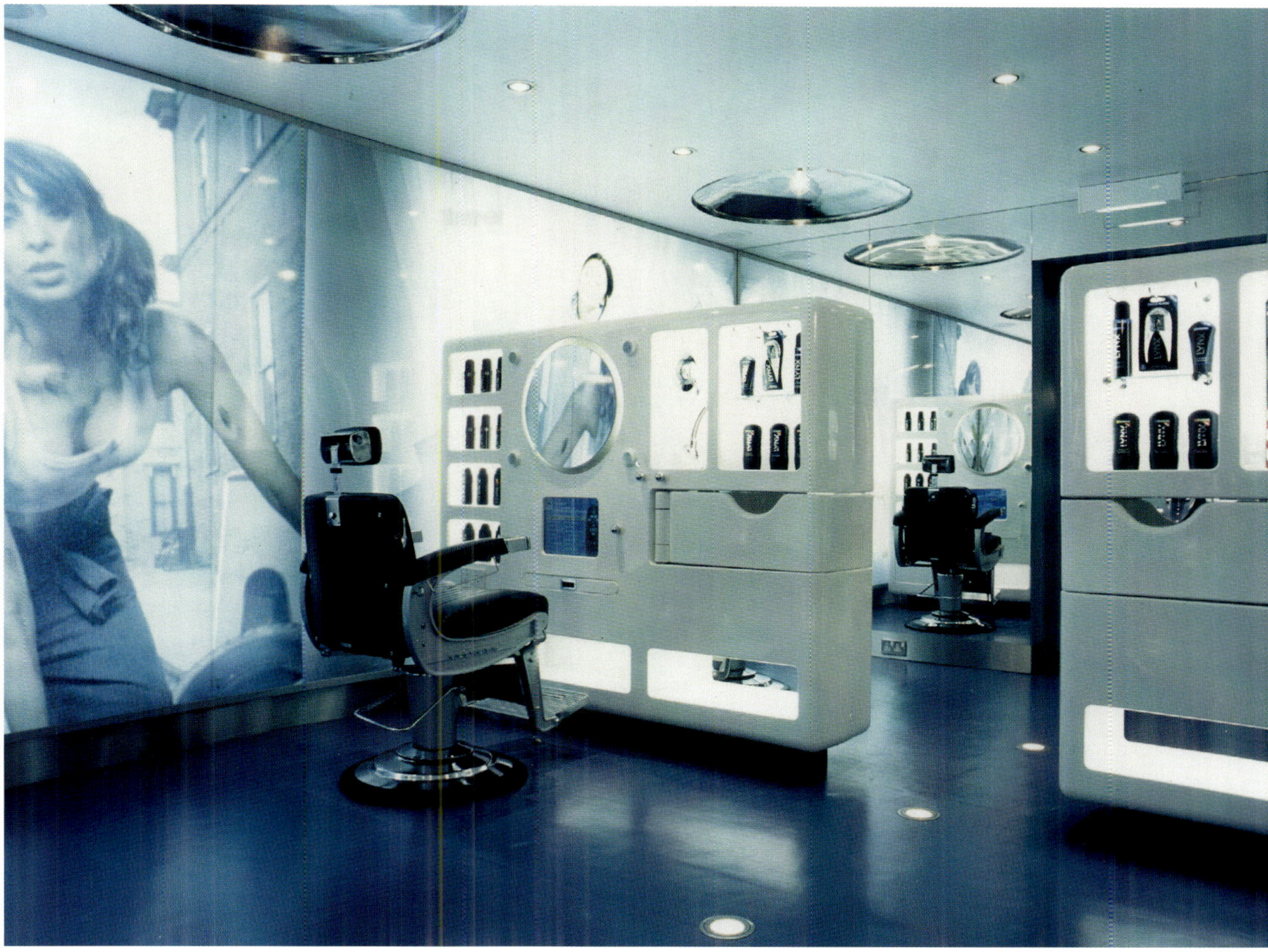

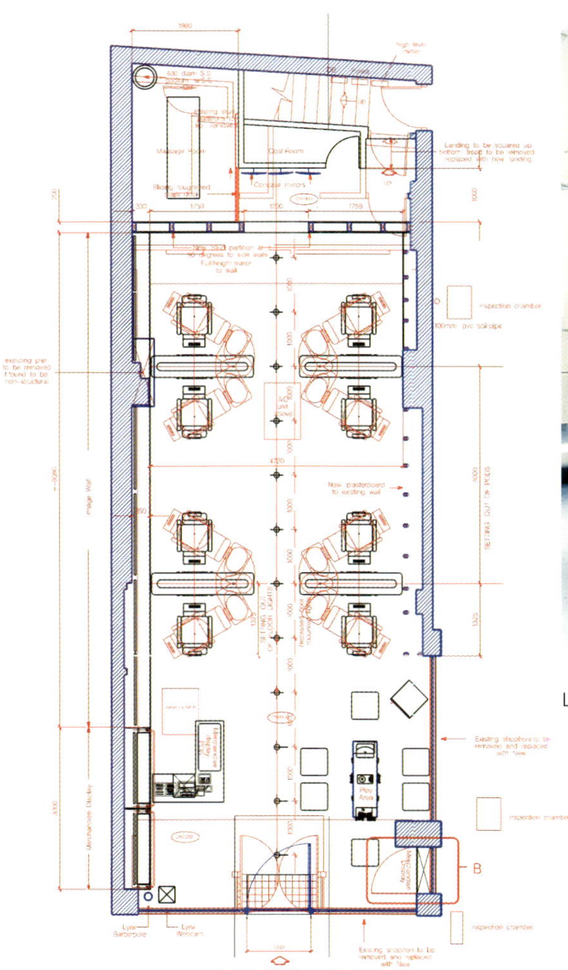

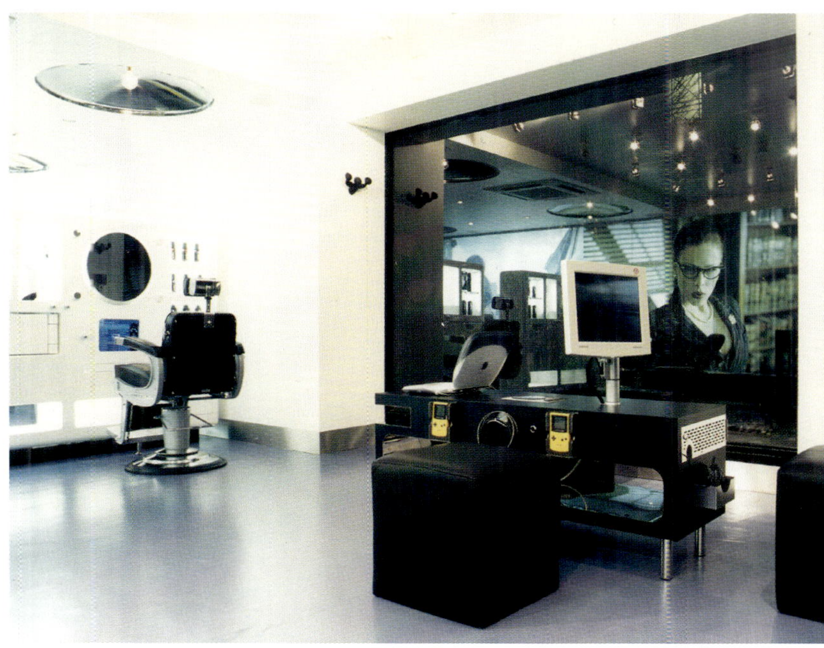

Lynx in Kingston-upon-Thames – wie in einer Werbeagentur / Like in an advertising agency

LYNX

THE MEGASTORE

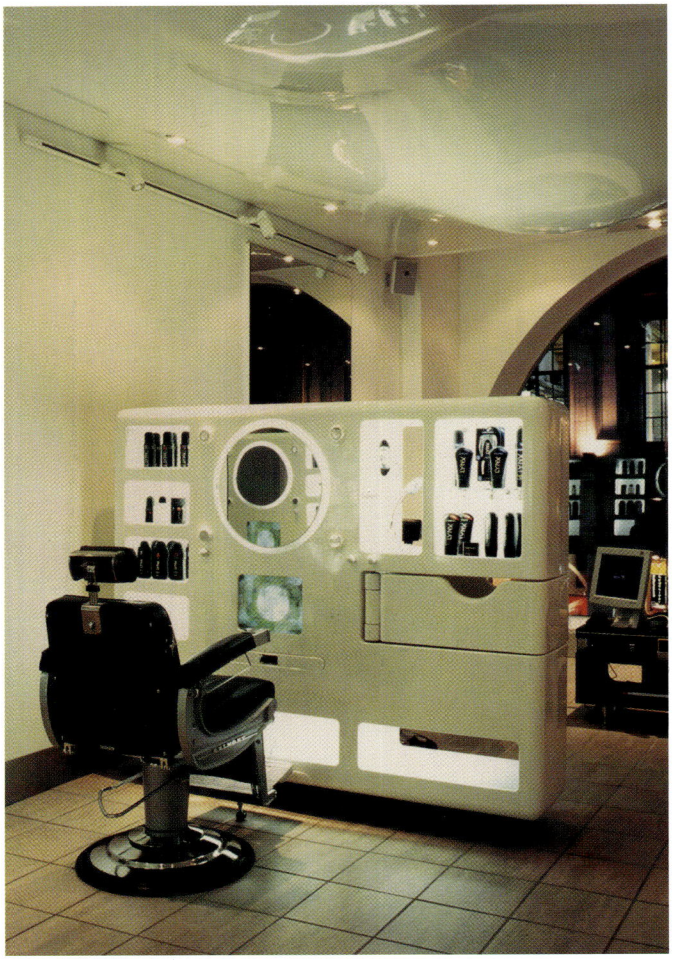

IE MEGASTORE

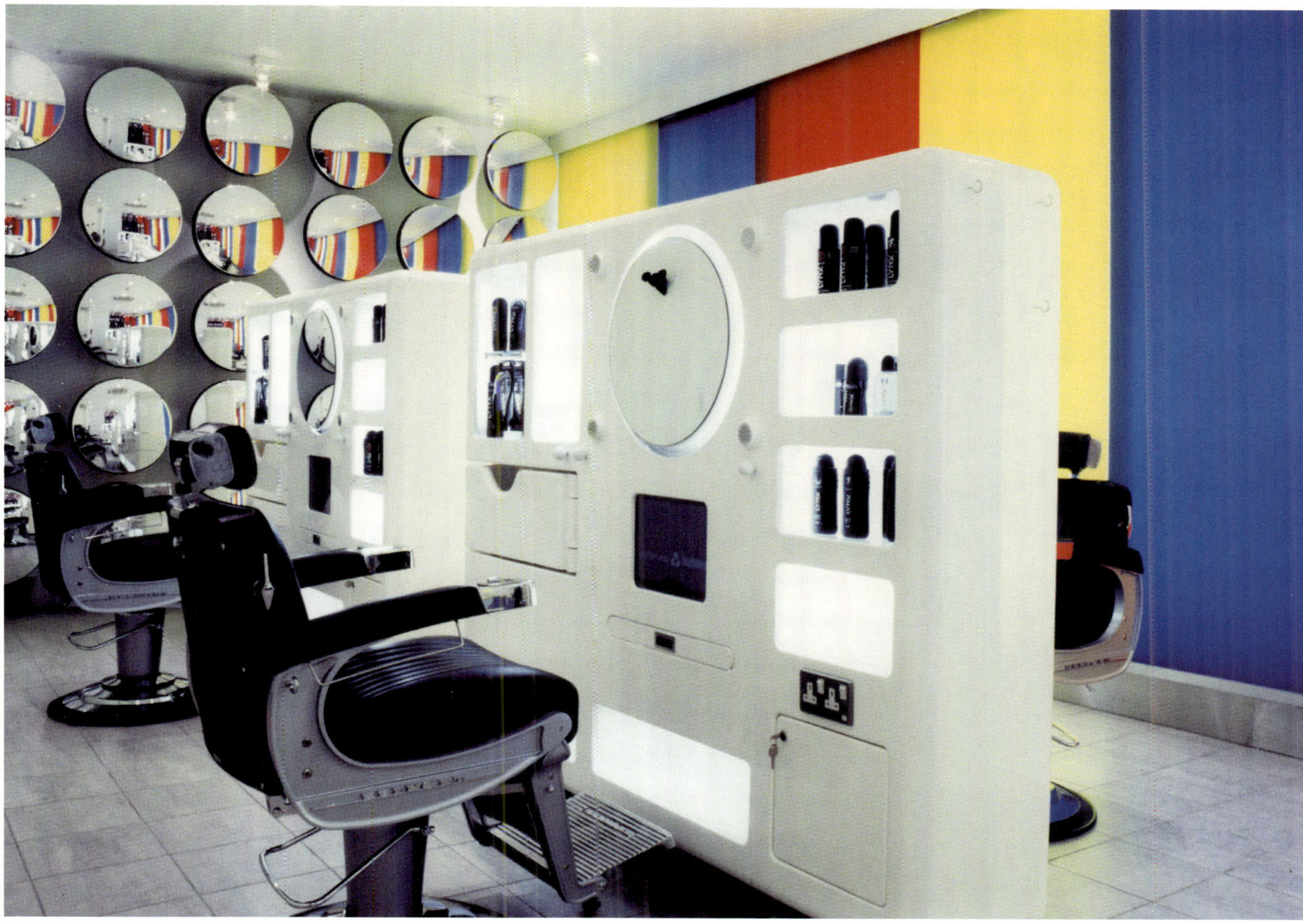

Lynx in London

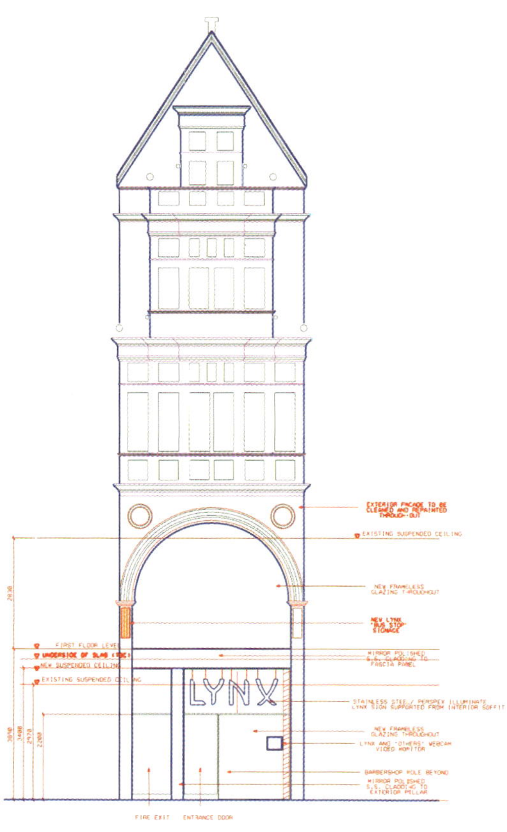

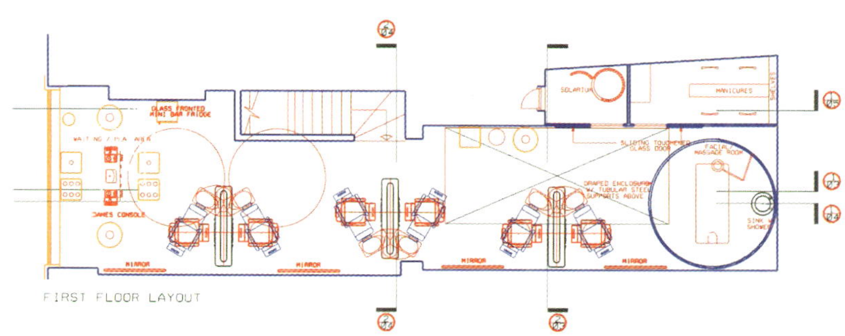

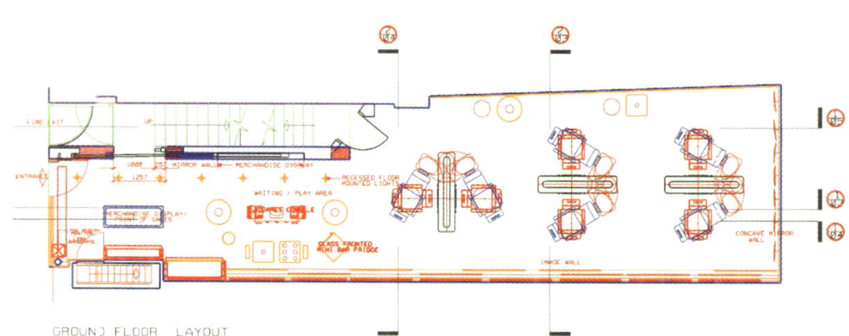

Project:
LYNX Barbershop, London und Kingston-upon-Thames, UK

Design:
Jump Studios, London

Area:
200 sqm in London,
80 sqm in Kingston

Photographer:
Mark York, London

Läden inspiriert durch Produkte

Sich im Handelskonzept auf das Produktangebot selbst zu beziehen, ist eigentlich das Naheliegendste, schafft Glaubwürdigkeit und Identität. Und hier gibt es viele Ansätze, Ideen für die Ladengestaltung und das Marketingkonzept zu entwickeln: Es können die Form sein, die Funktion, das Material, der Einsatzbereich oder auch die Inhalte und Ideologien, die mit einem Produkt verbunden sind. Bei dem brasilianischen *Banana Music Store* ist es bereits die Fassade, die an die Form einer Stereoanlage erinnert. Im Innern verweist der Store mit Materialien wie Glas, Metall und Terrazzoboden auf die Technik an sich und lehnt sich mit der Farbgebung des Raumes und der Lichtgestaltung an die den Kunden vertraute Discowelt an. Mit dem Modeladen *Mademoiselle* in Sorrent baute der Architekt eine Höhle aus gefaltetem grauen Samt, um den Kundinnen die Möglichkeit zu geben, sich ganz emotional und sensuell auf ein bevorstehendes Fest einzustimmen, das textile Material mit dem ganzen Körper zu spüren, bevor man sich für ein Stück entscheidet. Hier geht es nicht um Marken- oder Produktimage sondern um das eigene Empfinden, um die Fantasie, um ein sinnliches Erlebnis durch eine Raumgestaltung, die eine sehr spezielle Bindung zu einem Laden erzeugt. Dabei muss das Erlebnis sich nicht allein auf das ungewohnte Raumgefühl beschränken, sondern könnte durch Modepräsentationen, kleine Events live oder per Video angereichert werden. Für den Brillenladen *Basiliou* entwickelten die griechischen Architekten ein Ladenlayout, das das Material und die Form des Produktes Brille als Ausgangsbasis hat. Auch so ein Ansatz ist eigentlich recht neu. Meist werden in diesen Geschäften eher Präsentationsmöglichkeiten entwickelt, die es den Kunden erlauben, selbstständig auszusuchen, anzuprobieren und sich beraten zu lassen. Hier wurde versucht, ein Bezug zum Produkt Brille herzustellen, indem im Raum viel Glas verwendet wurde. Die elliptische Form der Linse wurde in Tischen, Regal- und Displayflächen übersetzt – alles ist leicht, durchscheinend und weit und symbolisiert damit die Funktion der Brille etwas sichtbar zu machen. Im Londoner *Breadshop* spielen Ladenidee und die Displayform der Backwaren auf den Herstellungsprozess und die Natürlichkeit der Produkte an. Ob bewusst oder unbewusst erinnert man sich bei den Plexiglaszylindern tatsächlich an große Getreidesilos, die für diese Form Pate standen, und Materialien im Raum wie Holz und Kalkstein verweisen auf die Natürlichkeit der Produkte. Es ist eine gelungene Präsentationsidee, die städtisch ist, über Zusammenhänge informiert und sich dabei nicht im ländlichen Holzlook verliert. Beim *Reactio Action Store* ist die Design-Strategie völlig anders. Hier ging es darum, die Produkte absolut in den Vordergrund zu stellen, sie durch nichts abzulenken. Die Architekten bauten daher eine ganz klare nüchterne Hülle aus Beton und Plexiglas, eher ein städtisches Element, das technische Details betont, um auf die Technik der Sportgeräte anzuspielen. Obgleich es sich hier um Lifestyle-Produkte handelt, ist das Umfeld völlig nüchtern – und funktioniert. Das gesamte Sortiment baut sich um das Thema Sport als Lifestyle auf und auch die Website trägt diesen Gedanken fort.

Shops inspired by products

A retailing concept that is directly based on the range of products itself is actually the most obvious way to proceed: it creates credibility and identity. This area offers abundant options for approaches, ideas for shop design and for developing marketing concepts: it can be the shape, the function, the material, the area of use as well as the content and ideologies that are associated with a product.

At the Brazilian Banana Music Store it is the façade that is reminiscent of the shape of a stereo. In the interior, the store creates allusions to technology per se through the use of materials such as glass, metal and terrazzo floors. It has borrowed the colour scheme for the rooms and the lighting effects from the disco world, which is familiar to its customers. In the fashion store, Mademoiselle in Sorrent, the architect constructed a cave using folded, grey velvet in order to give the female customers an opportunity to get into the mood – emotionally and sensually – for their upcoming festivity and to bodily experience the textile material before making a decision in favour of one particular piece of clothing. Here the focus is not on a brand name or a product image, but on the feelings of each individual, on fantasy, on a sensual experience created by means of the interior design, thus generating a very special bond with the shop. Furthermore, the experience is not necessarily restricted to the unusual spatial feeling; it could be supplemented by fashion presentations, small live events or videos. For the Basiliou optician's shop, the Greek architects designed a shop layout that took its inspiration from the material and shape of the product "eyeglasses" itself. This type of approach is actually quite new. Generally, for this type of shop, display options are developed in order to allow customers to independently pick what they like, try it on and then take advantage of consulting services. At Basiliou an attempt was made to create an allusion to the product "eyeglasses" through the utilisation of a great deal of glass. The elliptical shape of the lenses was translated into tables, shelving and display surfaces – everything is weightless, transparent and symbolic of the function of eyeglasses, which is essentially making something visible. At the Bread Shop in London, the shop idea and the form of display for the baked goods are an allusion to the production process and the natural quality of the products. Whether consciously or subconsciously, the Plexiglas cylinders actually do remind the viewer of large grain hoppers, which served as the inspiration for the shape, and the materials used for the interior, such as wood and limestone, create associations with the naturalness of the products. This is a successful presentation concept that is urban and informative, and does not fritter itself away in a woody, countrified look. At the Reactio Action Store the design strategy is entirely different. Here the emphasis is on highlighting the products to the utmost and ensuring that there are absolutely no distractions. For this reason the architects built an exceedingly clear, austere shell out of concrete and Plexiglas, a rather urban element that emphasises technical details in order to create an allusion to the technical aspect of the sports equipment. Although the focus is on lifestyle products, the setting is entirely austere – and it works. The entire range of merchandise revolves around the theme of sports as a lifestyle, and the web site takes this thought even further.

Banana Music Store, Sao Paulo

DESIGN
Anastassiadis Arquitetos, Sao Paulo

Wer in der Nobelgegend Sao Paulos, Jardins (die Gärten), an den eleganten Geschäften mit schönen Grünanlagen entlangschlendert, kann den *Banana Music Store* nicht übersehen. Bereits die Metall-Glas-Fassade erinnert in ihrer Form an eine Stereo-Anlage, die nicht nur auf die Technologie unserer Zeit sondern vor allem auf das Produktangebot im Innern verweist. Hier gibt es CDs und Zubehör und anders als in herkömmlichen Läden werden die jungen Leute immer mit ihrem Namen angesprochen. Die Basis für den unkomplizierten Kundenkontakt wird bereits durch die funktionelle Gestaltung des CD-Ladens und die visuelle Kommunikation durch Grafik gelegt. Sie ist Teil der Architektur, lässig, großzügig, informativ. Blau wie der Himmel und kühlend in der Hitze Sao Paulos ist der ganze Laden und lässt die farbigen Produkte besonders gut erkennen, aber er assoziiert auch Technik und Discowelt. Eher technisch und hart sind die Raummaterialien wie der gelbe und blaue Terrazzoboden, der rutschfeste Stahlboden im Zwischengeschoss, die aluminium- oder kunststoffbeschichteten Möbel und Glasabdeckungen auf der Theke. Sonnige Ausnahme zum coolen technischen Blau sind lediglich die gelben T-Shirts des Personals und natürlich das gelbe kreisrunde CD-Logo an der Glasfassade. Es ist wie eine Sonne, eine Mandela, die belebt, erfreut und gute Laune macht.

If you happen to stroll through the ritzy Jardins area of Sao Paulo (i.e. the gardens) past the elegant stores surrounded by beautifully landscaped greenery, there is no way you can overlook the *Banana Music Store*. Even the shape of themetal and glass façade is reminiscent of a stereo system, thus creating associations not only with the technology of our modern age, but also in particular with the products that are for sale inside. The shop sells CD's and accessories for young people who, in contrast with conventional retail stores, are always addressed by name. This promotes customer contacts, just as does the functional design of the CD shop and the visual communication which has been integrated into its interior architecture. The entirely blue shop not only sets off the colourful products particularly effectively, it also creates associations with technology and the world of disco. The materials selected for the interior, such as the yellow and blue terrazzo flooring, the non-slip steel floor of the mezzanine, the aluminium and plastic coated furniture and glass topped counter,evoke a technical, hard feeling. The only sunny exception amidst all of the technical blueis the yellow used for the T-shirts of the personnel and the circular yellow CD logo on the glass façade, which imparts a warm and exciting feeling to the interior.

Visuelle Kommunikation durch Graphikdesign

Visual communication by graphic design

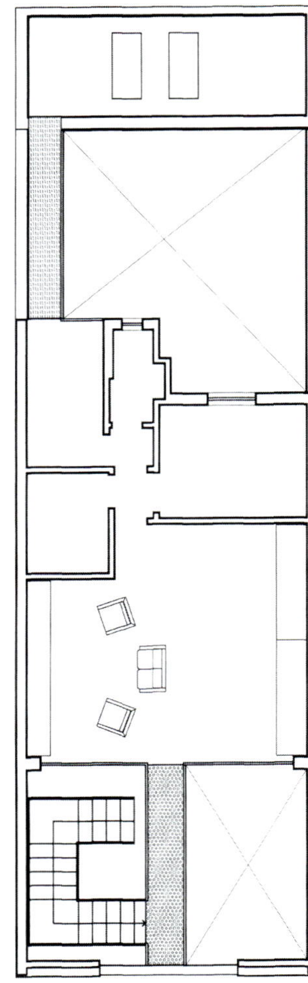

Obergeschoss / First floor

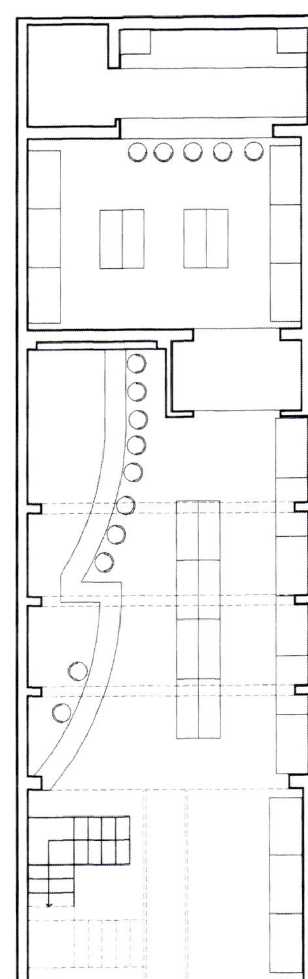

Erdgeschoss / Ground floor

Project:
Banana Music Store,
Sao Paulo/Brasil

Design:
Anastassiadis Arquitetos,
Sao Paulo

Area:
ca. 260 sqm

Photographer:
Sérgio Gikovate, Sao Paulo

Mademoiselle, Sorrento

DESIGN
Studio d'Architettura
Simone Micheli, Florenz

Meerluft, strahlende Sonne und ein blauer Himmel beleuchten den Hauptplatz von Sorrent, das auf einer Halbinsel direkt am Golf von Neapel liegt und zum bedrohlichen Vesuv emporschaut. Wer auf diesem Platz in den kleinen Modeladen *Mademoiselle* kommt, träumt nicht vom Meer oder den Gefahren des Vesuvs sondern von Hochzeit, von fröhlichen Festen und Feiern. Und ganz im Sinne einer Illusion wurde dieser Modeladen zu einem Traum aus Samt und Marmor. In allen fünf Räumen des Salons sind Wände und Decken nur mit grauem Samt eingehüllt. Während der Kunde über weißen arabeskischen Marmor wandelt, fühlt er in den Samthöhlen das weiche Material, das raffinierte Kleid, das bevorstehende Fest. Alles in diesen Räumen ist inszeniert. Die Modepuppen wurden mit Zeitungspapier umwickelt und auch einige Wände erhielten diesen ungewohnten Novitäten-Touch. Grau lackierte Deko-Podeste in Nierenform liegen wie schwimmende Inseln zu Füßen der Gewänder. Und aus der faltigen Samtdecke erscheinen die ovalen Keramikleuchten wie Tropfen an der Decke einer Tropfsteinhöhle. Doch jeder Kunde wird hier seine eigenen Träume und Gedanken haben. Es ist wie eine Reise ins Innere der Materialien und Objekte, die sich auf die festliche Bekleidung überträgt. Sie wechselt ihre Farben und Formen. Was bleibt, ist der Raumeindruck, das Erlebnis – die Einstimmung.

Sea air, sunshine and blue skies adorn the principal square in Sorrento, which is situated on a peninsula directly next to the Gulf of Naples with a clear line of sight to the threatening hulk of Vesuvius. Those who enter the small *Mademoiselle* fashion shop on the square are not dreaming of the sea or the dangers presented by Vesuvius, but of weddings, joyous festivities and celebrations. Entirely in the manner of an illusion, this fashion shop has been transformed into a dream concocted out of velvet and marble. In all five rooms of the salon, the walls and the ceilings are sheathed exclusively in grey velvet. While the customer strolls over the white, arabesque design of the marble floor and through the velvet "caves", she can feel the soft fabric and the sophisticated dress, as well as the excitement of the upcoming celebration. In these rooms everything is like a stage setting. The mannequins have been wrapped in newspaper and some of the walls have also been given this unaccustomed innovative touch. Decorative, kidney shaped slabs painted grey float like islands at the base of the garments. Suspended from the folds of the velvet ceiling, oval ceramic lamps resemble drops on the roof of a limestone cavern. But each customer can experience her own dreams and thoughts here. It is like a journey into the interior of materials and objects, which transfers itself to the festive apparel. The clothing itself may change colour and shape. What remains is the impression left by the interior, the memorable experience – and the mood that was conjured up.

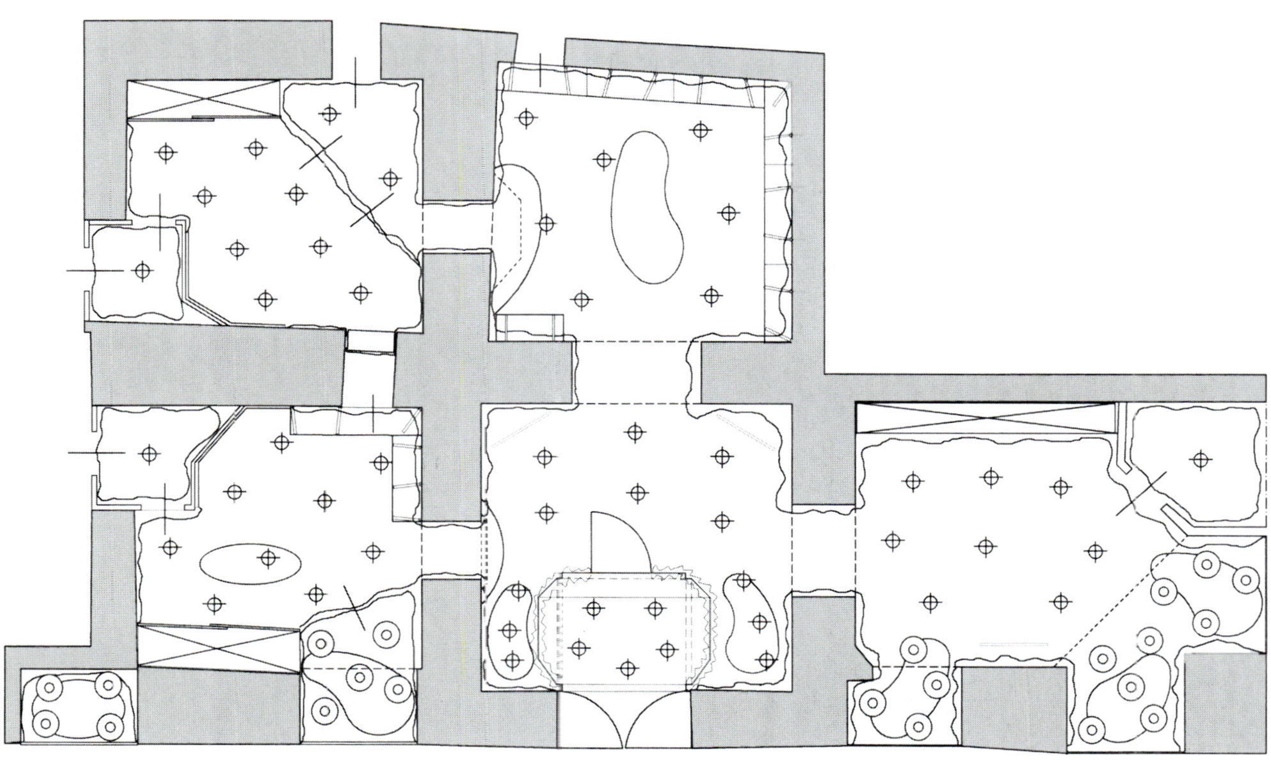

Project:
Mademoiselle,
Sorrento/Italy

Design:
Studio d'Architettura
Simone Micheli, Florence

Area:
ca. 90 sqm

Photographer:
Graziano Villa, Milan

Basiliou Optik, Athen

DESIGN
Anamorphosis Architects, Athen

Brillen dienen in zunehmendem Maße nicht nur der Seh-Korrektur sondern sollen auch modisch sein und die eigene Persönlichkeit unterstreichen – und das für die verschiedensten Anlässe. Wer eine Brille kauft, möchte erst einmal selbst ausprobieren und auswählen, um sich dann beraten zu lassen. Bei *Basiliou Optik* im Gebiet Maroussi in Athen wird genau diesem Wunsch Rechnung getragen, auszusuchen, anzufühlen und anzuprobieren. Das bedeutete, den verfügbaren Raum für die Produktpräsentation optimal auszunutzen, dennoch sollte alles leicht zugängig, sichtbar und großzügig sein. Einen solchen Anspruch in einer Stadt wie Athen umzusetzen hieß an Licht, Weite, Wärme, an das Meer zu denken, aber auch an Mythen und Metaphern. Die Brille selbst lieferte die Idee für das Konzept: die charakteristische Form und das Material der Linse war morphologische Inspiration für das Design: transparent, lichtdurchlässig, reflektierend. Ein hochglänzender Steinboden spiegelt Tageslicht und Raumlichter und geäzte Glaspaneele in versetzter Form sind Warenträger und Raumtrenner zugleich. Alles im Raum dreht sich um das Thema Glas und Durchsichtigkeit, selbst bei den Glas-Displays im Schaufenster, die in ihrer Form auf ein Brillenmodell des französischen Herstellers Briot zurückgehen, eine zweifach elliptische Fläche als Tableau. Die elliptische Linsenform stand Pate nicht nur für Displays sondern für Beratungstische, Spiegel und Spiegelträger, Griffe und Minidisplays. Basiliou verkauft Brillen, Beratung und handwerkliches Know How aber auch Licht und Tansparenz, Glanz und Weite für das Sehen.

Increasingly, eyeglasses not only serve to correct vision deficiencies, but also are a fashion statement, purchased for the most various of occasions. People purchasing eyeglasses prefer to try them on first and pick out what appeals to them before they take advantage of consulting services. At the *Basilou optician's* shop in the Maroussi district of Athens, every aspect of this wish is fulfilled: you can pick glasses out, feel them and try them on. This entailed utilising the available space to the optimum, while keeping everything easily accessible, visible and spacious. Realising this objective in a city like Athens meant incorporating light, space, warmth and the sea, as well myths and metaphors. Eyeglasses themselves provided the inspiration for the concept: the characteristic shape and material of lenses was the morphological model for the design, which is transparent, translucent and reflective. High gloss stone flooring reflects daylight and the artificial light of the interior fixtures. Etched glass panels in a staggered arrangement have been used as display elements as well as room partitions. Every element in the interior incorporates the theme of glass and transparency, even the glass display units in the front window: the shape of these was derived from a style of eyeglasses by the French manufacturer Briot – a double curved elliptical surface. The elliptical lens shape was not only the inspiration for the display units, but also for the consulting tables, mirrors and mirror brackets as well as the handles and mini-displays. Basilou offers eyeglasses, consulting service and professional know-how, as well as light and transparency, radiance and unimpeded vistas of vision.

Βασιλείου
οπτικα - φακοι επαφης

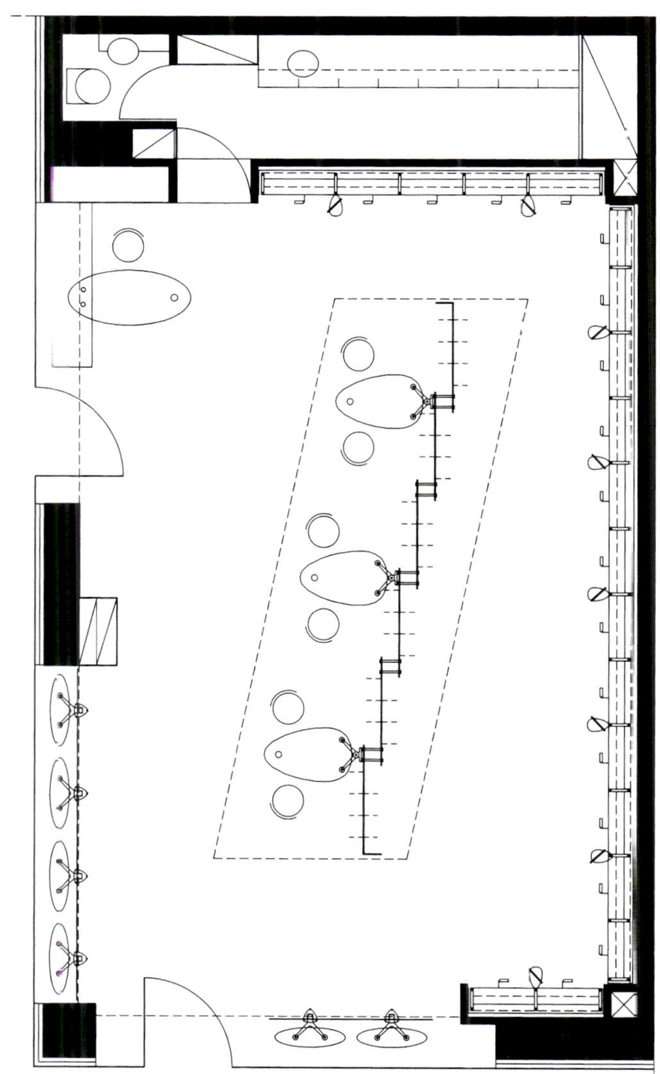

Porject:
Basiliou Optik,
Athens/Greece

Design:
Anamorphosis Architects,
Athens

Area:
81 sqm

Photographer:
Dimitra Georgantopoulou/
Phellipe Tsolakian, Athens

Bread Shop, London

DESIGN
The Formation Creative Consultants, London

Mitten im Herzen Notting Hills, dem Londoner Stadtteil, der durch den gleichnamigen Film berühmt und beliebt wurde, liegt der kleine Brotladen des in Israel geborenen Jonathan Cohan. Seine Erfahrung mit europäischen Backwaren brachte ihn auf die Idee einen Breadshop aufzumachen, in dem täglich über 30 verschiedene Sorten Brot und Backwaren angeboten werden, vom Siebenkörnerbrot bis zum Kartoffelbrot, vom italienischen Ciabatta bis zu den französischen Croissants, von deutschen Brezeln bis zu dänischen Puddingstückchen.
Die Gestaltung des Ladens greift natürliche und mechanische Elemente des Mehlmalens und Brotbackens auf. So erinnern Plexiglaszylinder hinter dem Eingang an Getreide-Einfülltrichter, unter denen die Backwaren auf zwei Etagen zwischen Lochblechen präsentiert werden. Ähnlich wie auf einem Marktstand entnimmt der Kunde mit speziell entwickelten Papieren und Tüten die Ware, legt sie in einen handgeflochtenen Spankorb und bezahlt im hinteren Teil des Ladens, wo das „Schauspiel des Backens" im großen Backofen erlebt werden kann. Auf den weiß verputzten Wänden erzählen reliefartige Schriften Philosophien vom Brot und Brotbacken. Bezug zur Natur haben auch die Materialien im Raum: Kalksteinfliesen für den Laufweg, dunkles Holzparkett und warme Holztöne des Walnussbaumes, der Kirsche und Eiche für die Möbel. Weiches indirektes Licht unterstreicht das einladende Flair, das schon die Fassade signalisiert: Das Logo lehnt sich an alte europäische Holzschnitt-Buchstaben an und auf die Glasfassade sind zahlreiche Backarten geätzt. Die Londoner sind begeistert und weitere Breadshops bereits in Planung.

Right in the heart of the London district of Notting Hill, which has become so famous and popular in the aftermath of the film Notting Hill, is the location of the small Bread Shop that belongs to Jonathan Cohan, who was born in Israel. His experience with European baked goods inspired him to open up a Bread Shop in which over 30 different types of bread and baked goods are offered on a daily basis – from seven grain bread to potato bread, from Italian ciabatta to French croissants, from German pretzels to Danish pudding pastries. The design of the shop incorporates references to the natural and mechanical elements of flour milling and bread baking. The Plexiglas cylinders just beyond the entry area are reminiscent of grain hoppers: below them the baked goods are displayed on two levels of shelving, separated by perforated metal dividers. Similarly to market stall shopping, the customer selects what he wants using the specially designed wrapping paper and bags, places the baked goods in a hand woven basket and pays for his purchase at the rear of the shop, where a large exposed bake allows him to experience the "drama" of baking. The white plastered walls serve as a canvas for the presentation of philosophical quotes involving bread and bread baking in relief characters. Natural materials such as limestone for the walkway, dark wooden parquet flooring, warm wood tones for the furnishings and soft indirect lighting underscore the inviting flair which is already signalised in the façade. The logo evokes the style of old fashioned European wood cut letters and the names of the numerous types of baked goods are etched into the glass façade. Londoners are raving about the shop and additional Bread Shops are already in the planning stage.

Bread Shop Roll
45p
Bavarian Loaf
Genetztes
A moist centre and well baked crust. Made from Rye-wheat corns ground together and sourdough.
SOME OF OUR PRODUCTS CONTAIN NUTS. PLEASE ASK.
1·80

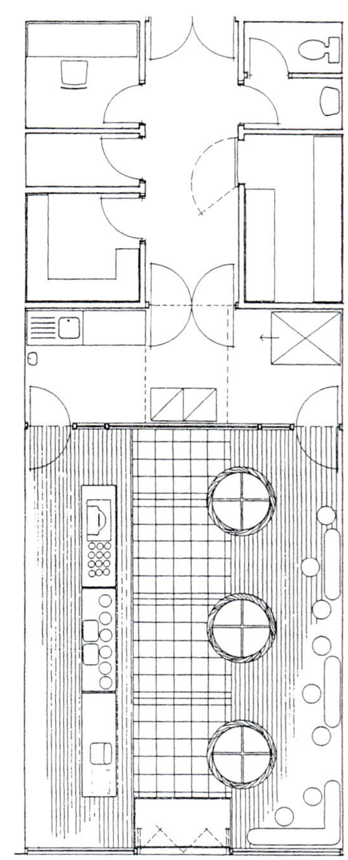

Project:
Bread Shop, London/UK

Design:
The Formation Creative Consultants, London

Area:
ca. 40 sqm

Photographer:
The Formation Creative Consultants Ltd., London

React Action Store, Stockholm

DESIGN
Sandell Sandberg AB, Stockholm

Für Sportbegeisterte und all jene, für die Sport zum Lebensstil gehört, bietet *React* Sportbekleidung und Sportschuhe, Skateboards und Snowboards, Fahrräder, Sonnenbrillen und sogar MP3-Player. Dieser Laden in der Innenstadt Stockholms ist das dritte Geschäft des jungen Unternehmens. Fünf weitere sollen demnächst dazukommen. Das Design für das erfolgreiche Handelskonzept stammt von den Designern und Architekten Sandell Sandberg, die das Thema Sport ganz funktionell, klar und produktbetont auffassen. Sie haben dafür ein dreigeschossiges Gebäude entwickeltet, in dem geneigte Ebenen die Stockwerke miteinander verbinden, als seien es Einschnitte in den Betondecken. Schmale farbige Rinnen trennen und betonen die Bauteile. Wände und Decken sind weiß und neutraler Untergrund für die farbigen Produkte. Das ganze Gebäude ist durchsichtig und sofort überschaubar, optisch eher kühl und im Hinblick auf die Sportgeräte technisch betont mit raffinierten Details. Um die Transparenz im Gebäude zu erhalten, sind die Möbel mobil, aus mattem Chromstahl oder klarem Acrylglas. Sportgeräte werden kaum sichtbar durch Magneten gehalten. Selbst Farbe wird nur sparsam verwendet: in Rinnen, hinter Paneelwänden und in Schaukästen. Sie kennzeichnet zugleich Warengruppen für Jungen, Mädchen und Teens. Neonleuchten und einzelne Strahler betonen das sachliche Flair, das bei den Stockholmern sehr gut ankommt. Wie gut diese „Close-to-the-Consumer-Philosophie" funktioniert, wird auf der Website www.react.se mit online-shop deutlich: Produktangebote sind in Lifestyle-Aktivitäten eingebettet, Infos berichten über Stars und Sportveranstaltungen sowie Gewinnspiele und das alles comicartig und unterhaltsam aufgemacht.

For sports enthusiasts and people for whom sports constitute an important lifestyle element, *React* offers sportswear and sports shoes, skateboards, snowboards and sunglasses, bicycles and even MP3 players. This shop located in downtown Stockholm is the third retail store of the young company. In the near future, five additional stores are supposed to be opened up. The design for the successful retail concept was developed by the Sandell-Sandberg designer and architect firm. The sports theme has been interpreted in an entirely functional, clear manner with a focus on the products. To this end, they designed a three storey building with inclined ramps which connect the various levels and resemble incisions made in the concrete slab ceilings. Narrow channels separate and emphasise the structural elements. The walls and ceilings are all in white, serving as a neutral background which highlights the coloured products. The entire building is transparent and can be viewed in its entirety at a glance. The result is a rather cool visual effect that creates a technical atmosphere which is attuned to the sports apparatus and underscored by sophisticated details. In order to preserve the transparency of the building, the furnishings are moveable and made of matt chromed steel or clear acrylic glass. Sports equipment is gripped by magnet fastenings that are barely visible. Even colour is only used sparingly – in the channels, behind the wall panelling and in the display cases. It also serves to indicate the merchandise departments aimed respectively at boys, girls and teenagers. Neon lighting fixtures and individual spotlights emphasise the austere flair that has been well received by Stockholm's inhabitants. This "close to the consumer" philosophy works very well, as is obvious on the website which includes an online shop. Product offers are embedded in life style activities and information is provided on stars, sporting events and contests – all presented in an entertaining comic-like style.

LIMITE

Transparenz durch Produkthalter und Möbel aus Acrylglas

Transparency by product displays and furniture made of acrylic glass

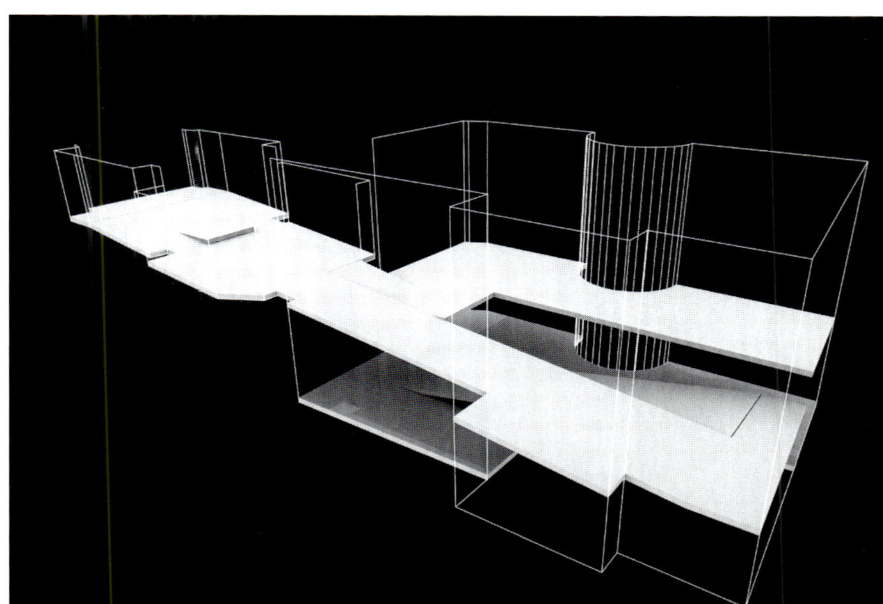

Geneigte Ebenen verbinden die drei Geschosse miteinander als seien es Einschnitte in den Betondecken

Inclined ramps connect the three levels and resemble incisions made in the concrete slab ceilings

Project:
React Action Store, Stockholm, Sweden

Design:
sandellsandberg AB, Thomas Sandell, Stockholm

Area:
350 sqm

Photographer:
Ake E:son Lindman, Stockholm

Themenläden

In der Gastronomie sind Themen eine bewährte Marketingidee aus der Anonymität herauszutreten und einem Lokal ein Profil zu geben, mit dem sich der Gast identifizieren kann. Läden ein Thema oder eine Story zugrunde zu legen, ist hierzulande selten. Dabei hat auch ein Showroom oder selbst ein Supermarkt eine Art Story, in die man als Kunde eintaucht, um für die Zeit des Einkaufs diese Welt zu erleben. Bei Themenläden sind die Geschichten bewusst inszeniert und ablesbar.

Z. B. im Gitarrenladen *guitar gallery* in Florida. Nun sind Läden für Musikinstrumente meist recht nüchterne Verkaufsstätten, die eigentlich in keiner Weise die Welt der Konzerte widerspiegeln. In diesem Shop werden nicht klassische Instrumente sondern Show-Gitarren verkauft und somit ist die Show das Thema in der Ladengestaltung, der Materialien. Und selbst die Art der Gitarren-Präsentation ist Show bis hin zu der Möglichkeit Videoclips zu sehen, selbst Musik zu machen oder gar auf einer kleinen Bühne Promis zu treffen. Hier zu kaufen gibt das Gefühl, ein Stück vom Showbusiness mitzubekommen. Beim *Cirque de Soleil Shop* ist das Thema der Zirkus, das man versteht, wenn man dort im Hotel oder im Casino ist und gleich nebenan den Zirkus auf dem Wasser erlebt. Der Laden ist nicht einfach irgendein Hotelshop, sondern nimmt Bezug zur Nachbarschaft auf, baut mit seinen Displays, den Raummaterialien und Farben eine Analogie zu den Artisten und der Zirkuswelt auf. Es ist eine ganz spezielle Welt, die den Kunden und Gästen in Erinnerung bleibt, Spaß macht, sie vielleicht wieder zum Zirkus zurückbringt und damit ein Gewinn bringendes Wechselspiel erzeugt. Beim Schuhhaus *Deerberg* versuchte ein Schuh-Versender eine Plattform für seine Kunden zu schaffen, die er sonst nie sieht. Er verkauft nicht nur Produkte für die ganze Familie sondern wollte mit seinem Laden auch seine persönliche Auffassung von Kundenbetreuung und Gastfreundschaft dokumentieren, indem er sich einen familiären, wohnlichen Rahmen bauen ließ – zum Wohlfühlen, Anprobieren, Informieren, Spielen, Träumen, zum Kaffeetrinken in einer unbeschwerten Atmosphäre. Mehrere Angebote von Ladenbauunternehmen scheiterten. Erst die Bilder des schwedischen Malers Carl Larsson überzeugten und lieferten wohnliche Raumideen, die überaus erfolgreich sind. Auch die Bäckerei *Backoase* hat sich das Thema aus einem anderen Land geholt: Bilder einer Oase zum Ausruhen, Verweilen, Entspannen. Das Ambiente mag theatralisch sein, gibt aber dem Laden dennoch ein unverwechselbares Gesicht, das Bäcker und Kunden brauchen, um sich damit identifizieren zu können. Dies ist besonders wichtig angesichts zahlreicher Bäckereiketten, die kaum zu unterscheiden sind. Im Weingeschäft *Im Fürstenhof* ging es darum, eine Verbindung zwischen dem umliegenden Stadtteil mit Rotlichtmilieu und dem angrenzenden Bankergebiet zu schaffen, um beide Kundenbereiche anzusprechen. Die Elemente des Rotlichtmilieus werden sehr dezent und gekonnt in das Weingeschäft integriert, illustrieren, erzählen, machen neugierig und sind zugleich lebendiger Hintergrund mit Lokalcolorit.

Theme Shops

In the restaurant sector, using a specific theme is a well-tried marketing idea that serves to liberate an eatery from its anonymity and give it a profile with which patrons can identify. In Germany basing a shop on a theme or a story is relatively uncommon, whereby even a showroom or a supermarket has a story to tell, a story in which the customer immerses himself so as to experience a specific shopping world during the time he is there. In theme shops, the story settings are purposefully created and easily interpreted.

One example is the *Guitar Shop* in Florida. Generally, stores for musical instruments are quite austere sales locations, which do not reflect the world of concerts in any way whatsoever. Instead of classical guitars, this guitar shop sells show guitars and so the theme of the retail design and the materials is "show". Even the manner in which the guitars are displayed is essentially show, including the possibility of watching video clips, playing music or even meeting celebrities on the small stage. Purchasing something here conveys a feeling of taking part in a piece of show business. At the *Cirque de Soleil* shop the theme is the circus, which is quite understandable for the hotel guests and casino visitors, who can experience a real circus in a water setting immediately adjacent. The shop is not merely an ordinary hotel shop: it is full of references to the immediate vicinity, creating an analogy with the artists and circus world with its displays as well as the materials and colours used for the interior. This is a quite special world which customers and guests are not likely to forget: it is fun and may well lure them back to the circus, thus generating profitable interaction synergy benefits. At the *Deerberg* shoe company, the mail order shoe retailer wanted to created a platform for the customers that he normally never sees. He not only sells products for the entire family; in his shop his intention was to document his personal attitudes with regard to customer service and hospitality, by commissioning the construction of a family oriented, cosily liveable setting – where customers can feel comfortable, free to try things on or get information, to play or daydream, or simply enjoy a cup of coffee in a casual atmosphere. Several proposals tendered by retail construction companies failed. Finally, convincing inspiration was found in the pictures of the Swedish painter Carl Larsson, which were the source of liveable room design ideas that are extremely successful. The *Backoase* bakery also found its theme in another country – pictures of an oasis that entice patrons to rest, relax and linger. Admittedly, this ambiance is theatrical. However, it gives the bakery shop an unmistakeable appearance that the baker and his customers need to identify with, something which is particularly important in light of the innumerable bakery chains that are barely distinguishable. At the wine shop *Im Fürstenhof*, the objective was to create a connection between the surrounding city area with its red light district and the nearby banking district so as to appeal to both customer groups. The red light milieu elements have been integrated into the wine shop in a very discreet and skilful manner: they illustrate, narrate, arouse curiosity and at the same time they provide an animated background of local colour.

Ace Architects, The Leviathan, Oakland

Guitar Gallery, Lake Buena Vista

Für die *Walt Disney World* in Florida eine Gitarren-Gallerie zu entwickeln, heißt sich vollkommen auf das Showbusiness einzulassen – auf die Show von Musikern und Marken. Der Gitarrenspieler über dem Eingang in Neonlinien hat seine Dauer-Performance, während auf der anderen Seite der Fassade die sechs größten Gitarrenmarken als leuchtende Gitarrenhälse in Intervallen blinken. In diesem Shop werden akustische und elektrische, alte und neue Gitarren verkauft, für alle denkbaren Ereignisse. Jede der sechs Marken erhielt eine eigene Wand zur großflächigen Präsentation der verschiedenen Gitarren, die auf raumhohen stilisierten Gitarrenrücken in Holz oder glänzendem Fiberglas präsentiert werden. Vor jeder Markenwand stehen zylindrische Verkaufsboxen mit einer Ausstellungsgitarre. Die Preziosen hängen an der Wand hinter der gitarrenförmig geschwungenen Info- und Verkaufstheke: Sammlergitarren auf dem riesigen Rücken einer Gitarre in dunkelrotem Samt. Gegenüber auf der großen Mittelbühne sprüht die Jukebox, flankiert von großen Lautsprechern, die auf den großen Auftritt warten: Signierstunden von Musikern, kleine Konzerte und Performances der Kunden. Wie bei Life-Konzerten sind am Rande der Bühne unter Leuchtenrags sechs Videomonitore angebracht – eine nachgestellte Bühnensituation für kleine Auftritte und große Marken, deren Storys hier als Videoclips ablaufen. Auch die verwendeten Materialien im Raum sind bühnenreif: eine Gitterkonstruktion aus Edelstahl für die Deckenstrahler, hochglänzende Lacke, silbergrüne Metalleffekte als Hintergrund für die Markenpräsentationen und zwischen dem grauen Fliesenboden betont ein schwarzer Stein mit Tausenden von sprühenden Perlmuttsternchen den Laufsteg der Gitarrengalerie. It's showtime in the summertime, wenn 4000 Leute am Tag hier hindurchpendeln.

Designing a guitar gallery for *Disney World* in Florida meant complete immersion into the world of show business – the show put on by musicians and by brand names. Over the entrance, neon notes hover over the guitar player that performs on a permanent basis, while on the other side of the façade the six major guitar brand names flash at intervals in the form of illuminated guitar headstocks. This shop sells acoustic and electric guitars – old and new instruments – for all conceivable purposes. An entire wall has been devoted to each of the six brand names: the large scale display areas exhibit the instruments on ceiling high stylised guitar backs made of wood or fibre glass. Cylindrical sales cases exhibiting guitars are positioned in front of each brand name wall. Special treasures hang on the wall behind the curved, guitar shaped information and sales counter: vintage collectors' guitars are displayed on a 75 foot high guitar shaped panel sheathed in dark red velvet. On the large central stage on the opposite side a jukebox glows and plays exuberantly, flanked on each side by enormous loudspeakers awaiting their big moment: autograph sessions with musicians, small concerts and performances by customers. Just like at live concerts, below the spotlight trusses beside the stage six video monitors have been mounted facing in all directions – creating a pseudo stage situation for small performances and big brands with perpetual non-stop video clips. The materials utilised for the interior are also stage-like in character: high gloss paint surfaces; a grid construction made of stainless steel used for the ceiling spot lights; silver green metallic effects used as a background for the brand name displays; and the grey tile floor is enlivened with black stone inlaid with thousands of glittering mother of pearl stars which underscores the main aisle of the guitar gallery. It's show time – when 4,000 people stream through here on a daily basis in the summertime.

Guitar
GALLERY

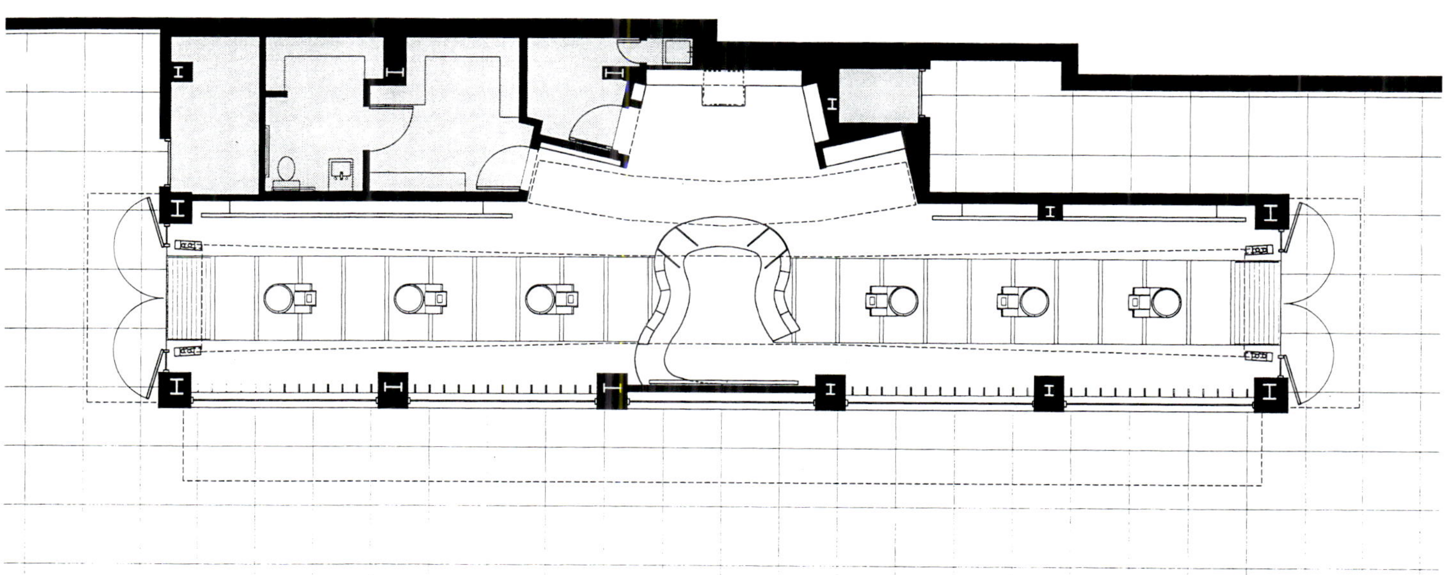

Martin & Co.
EST. 1833

Showbusiness für Musiker und Gitarrenmarken in Materialien und der Produktpräsentation. Selbst die Verkaufstheke ist eine gitarrenförmig geschwungene Plastik

Show business for musicians and guitar brands visualised by materials and the way of product presentation. Even the sales counter is a guitar shaped sculpture

Project:
Guitar Gallery,
Lake Buena Vista,
Florida/USA

Design:
Ace Architects,
The Leviathan, Oakland

Area:
ca. 160 sqm

Photographer:
Alan Weintraub,
San Francisco

Cirque de Soleil, Las Vegas

DESIGN
Jordan Mozer + Ass., Chicago

Jordan Mozer ist für seine ungewöhnlichen und vermenschlichten Interieurs bekannt: eine Welt voller Farben, Spaß, Comic und Metaphern. Für einen der großen Unternehmer und Visionäre in Las Vegas, Steve Wynn, hat er einen Hotelshop in eine Zirkuswelt verwandelt. Der Laden befindet sich am Nordende des Bellagio Hotels, von dem Wynn sagte, er wolle mitten in der Wüste das luxuriöseste und romantischste Hotel-Casino der Welt haben. Zu einer Zeit, als Las Vegas zum billigen Mafia-Platz verkommen war, investierte er in kühne Hotelideen mit viel Stil und Niveau. Als Attraktion und Anziehungspunkt für sein Casino holte er sich den kanadischen Zirkus *Cirque de Soleil*, der ohne Tiere arbeitet und alles selbst entwickelt, und baute für ihn ein eigenes Theater auf dem Wasser. Als Mozer für das Hotel einige Einrichtungen plante, schaute er den Zirkusleuten zu und beschloss, im Laden eine Analogie der Zirkus-Figuren zu bauen. Der Raum selbst ist elliptisch wie die ovalen Pools des Wasser-Theaters was ihn auch für den Teppich inspirierte. Unter der Decke leuchten dreidimensionale Sonnen, eine Interpretation der Sonne im Zirkus-Logo. Und selbst balancierende Artisten beleben als Warenträger den gesamten Raum. Alte Grammophone und TVs erhalten Arme und Beine und scheinen zu tanzen. Sie kennzeichnen zugleich, wo es CDs oder Videos zu kaufen gibt. Kunden die hierher kommen, sind gerade Gäste im Bellagio Hotel oder Casino, kommen vom Zirkus oder aber sind Touristen in Las Vegas.
Der Umsetzung der komplizierten Figuren gingen viele Aquarellskizzen und Computermodelle voraus. Als Materiallien wurden Aluguss, Stahl, Kevlar und Ahornholz verwendet.

Jordan Mozer is famous for his unusual, strikingly humanized interiors, which create a world of colour, fun, comics and metaphors. He has transformed a hotel shop into a circus world for Steve Wynn, one of the major entrepreneurs and visionaries of Las Vegas. The shop is situated at the north end of the Bellagio Hotel, which Wynn planned to make into the most luxurious and romantic hotel casino in the world, right in the middle of the desert. At a time when Las Vegas had degenerated into a cheap and tacky Mafia locale, he invested in daring hotel ideas characterised by style and sophistication in abundance. As an attraction and focus of attention for his casino, he commissioned *Cirque de Soleil*, the Canadian circus troupe that works without animals and develops all of its show numbers itself. Wynn built a special theatre on the water for the circus performers. When Mozer was planning some of the facilities for the hotel, he watched the circus troupe and decided to base the design of the shop on the circus artist analogy. The room itself has an elliptical shape that echoes the oval shape of the pool which the water theatre floats on, which also served as the inspiration for the carpet. Below the ceiling hang three dimensional illuminating stars, in interpretation of the sun in the circus logo. Balancing acrobats have also been used as merchandise display fixtures throughout the interior. Arms and legs have been grafted onto old gramophones and TV sets, so that they seem to be dancing and prancing while simultaneously announcing where the CDs or the videos available for sale are located. The customers that frequent the shop are either guests of the Bellagio Hotel or casino, circus spectators or tourists visiting Las Vegas. Preliminary water colour sketches and computer models were done in preparation for the realisation of the complicated figures. The materials used include cast aluminium, steel, Kevlar and maple wood.

Warenträger als Analogie zu den Zirkusfiguren des *Cirque de Soleil* in der Nachbarschaft

Merchandise elements analogous to circus artists of the neighbouring *Cirque de Soleil*

Zirkus, Tanz, Balance, Wasser und Spiel

Circus, dance, balance, water and play

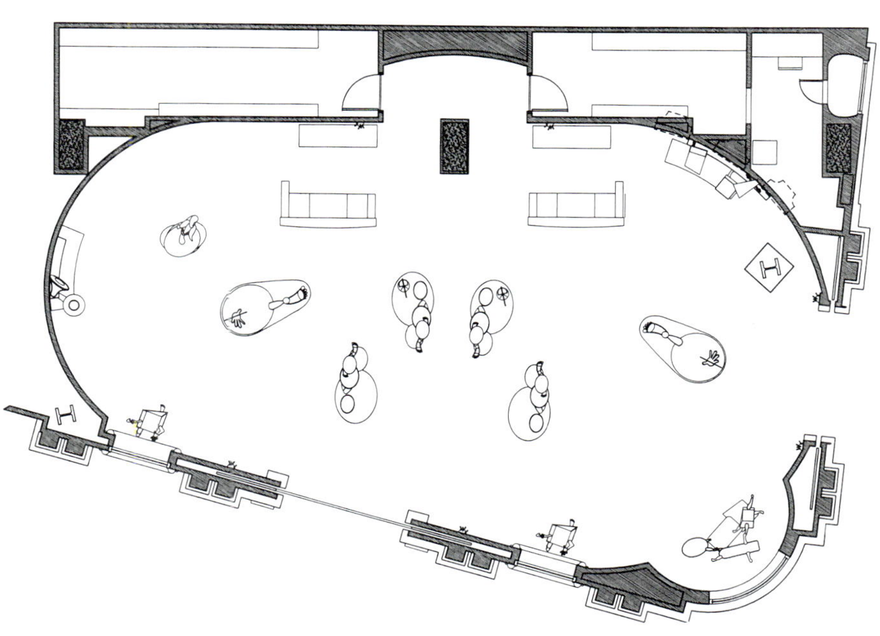

Project:
Cirque de Soleil,
Las Vegas/USA

Design:
Jordan Mozer + Ass.,
Chicago

Area:
ca. 280 sqm

Photographer:
Doug Snower, Chicago

Deerberg-Schuhversand, Hanstedt

DESIGN
Tromberend und Bathen, Lüneburg

Farbenfroh, hochwertig und bequem sind die Öko-Schuhe und die Bekleidung aus Naturfasern, die Deerberg per Versand deutschlandweit vertreibt. Ein Ladengeschäft an seinem Standort in der Nähe von Lüneburg sollte die Möglichkeit geben, alle Produkte vor Ort kennen zu lernen, auszuprobieren und die Philosophie des Unternehmens zu erleben: Familienfreundlich und bequem, dabei hochwertig mit modischer Eleganz. Diese Wertigkeiten auf einen Laden zu übertragen führte zu einer ungewöhnlichen Lösung, die die Architekten und die Inhaber in den wohnlichen Bildern des schwedischen Malers Carl Larsson fanden. Entstanden ist ein helles Haus mit gelber Holzfassade im Schwedenstil und einem farbenfrohen Innenleben aus sichtbarem Fachwerk, mit hölzerner Innentreppe, Kinderhaus und vielen Produktnischen mit bequemen Sitzbänken und Sofas zum Verweilen, Ausprobieren, Schauen und Träumen. Regale, Präsentationstische und Kleinmöbel in Buche und weiß lasierter Kiefer werden mit vielen Pflanzen, Dekoration und einem stimmungsvollen Licht in eine legere Wohnwelt verwandelt. Bei Bedarf gibt es Wasser und Säfte, Kaffee und Kuchen vom Bäcker aus der Nachbarschaft. Diese Annehmlichkeiten und die unkomplizierte Einrichtung lassen selbst Kinder und Großeltern stundenlang verharren, sodass manche Kunden 200–300 km auf sich nehmen, um den Großeinkauf für die ganze Familie zu tätigen. Öko heißt hier familienfreundlich, natürlich und zeitgemäß. Daher gibt es viele auch durch Computer unterstützte Produktinformationen, persönliche Beratung und ergänzende Produkte durch Bekleidung und saisonal bedingte Accessoires von Kerzen bis zum Biowein, vom Gartengerät bis zur Wanderflasche. Ein Laden, der die Schönheit und Qualität der Produkte und Landschaft nutzt, um eine Unternehmensidee zu transportieren und dabei Kunden Freude zu bereiten.

The ecological shoes and apparel made of natural fibres that Deerberg distributes throughout Germany by mail order are colourful, high-quality and comfortable. A retail store located not far from Lüneburg was created to provide an opportunity for customers to see and try out all of the products live and to experience the company's philosophy first-hand: family oriented and comfortable, as well as high-quality and fashionable elegance. The objective of applying these values to a retail store resulted in an unusual solution, for which the architects and Deerbergs discovered their inspiration in the eminently liveable pictures of interiors by the Swedish painter, Carl Larsson. The result is a bright house with a yellow wood façade in the Swedish style and a colourful interior with visible structural timbers, an interior wooden staircase, a children's playhouse and countless product alcoves with all manner of benches and sofas that literally seem to invite customers to stop and try things out, to linger and look, or just to dream. Shelves, display tables and small furnishings in beech wood and white stained pine have been combined with large numbers of plants, decorative elements and mood lighting to create an informal interior. If they wish, customers are served water and juice, or coffee and cake from the neighbourhood baker. These amenities and the uncomplicated furnishings are such that even children and grandparents are willing to stay for hours. Some customers even drive 200 to 300 km for a shopping trip to deck out the entire family. Ecological in this context means family oriented, natural and in tune with the times. So naturally, there is a wealth of computer supported product information, personal consulting and supplementary products ranging from clothing and seasonally oriented accessories to candles and biologically produced wine, as well as gardening tools and hiking flasks. This is a family oriented store that exploits the beauty and quality of its products and the countryside in order to convey its corporate idea and to offer its customers an enjoyable outing.

Familienfreundlich und bequem, hochwertig und modisch – ökologische Produkte in schwedischem Flair

Family-oriented and comfortable, high-quality and fashionable – ecological shoes in Swedish atmosphere

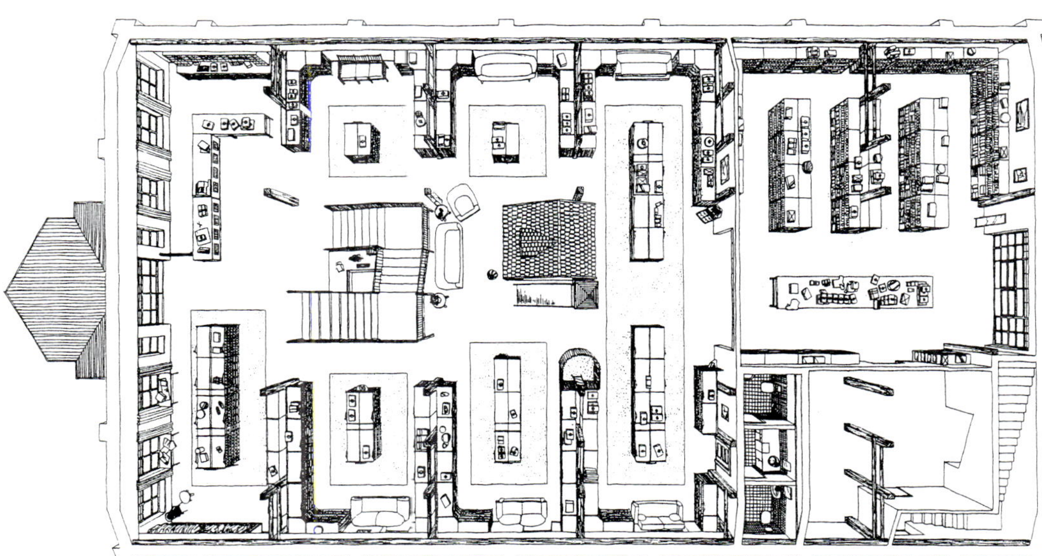

Project:
Deerberg-Shoes,
Hanstedt/Germany

Design:
Tromberend und Bathen,
Lüneburg

Area:
ca. 300 sqm

Photographer:
Antina Wolff,
Pen Werbeagentur,
Velgen/Hanstedt

Backoase, Arnsberg

DESIGN
E.T. Equipment Team, Leopoldshöhe

Hochwertige Backwaren in einem herkömmlichen Bäckerladen anzubieten, war den Inhabern nicht genug. Sie suchten nach einem Konzept, in dem die Produkte, der Kauf selbst und das Ausprobieren zu einem ungewöhnlichen Erlebnis werden und dem Unternehmen selbst ein einprägsames Firmen-Image verleihen. Unter dem Thema *Backoase* – Genuss für die Sinne, wurde von den Gestaltern und Ladenbauern eine Backstube mit Café geschaffen, die den Eindruck erweckt, inmitten einer Oase zu sitzen, umgeben von Schatten spendenden Palmen mit Blick auf eine ägyptische Landschaft mit Wüste, Tempeln, Pyramiden und dem Nil. Theatermaler setzten diese Idee in Acryltechnik auf Wänden, Decke und Teilen der Möbel um und übertrugen sie sogar auf die Verkaufsbereiche wie Theke, Preisauszeichnung und Regale für die Produktpräsentation. Sandfarbener Fliesenboden und geölte Massivholzmöbel lassen an Sitzplätze im Süden denken, an Produkte der Natur, wenngleich diese hier bildhaft hereingeholt wurde. Selbst das Licht unterstützt mit seinen starken Licht- und Schatteneffekten diesen Eindruck im Freien zu sitzen. Das für Deutschland eher ungewöhnliche Erlebniskonzept führte nicht nur zu einer starken Kundenbindung sondern verhalf diesem Bäckereiladen auch zu ungewöhnlichem Erfolg.

For the owners, merely offering high quality baked goods in a conventional bakery shop was not enough. Their aim was to develop a concept which would transform the products, the purchase transaction itself and taste testing the wares into an unusual experience, while at the same time ensuring an unmistakeable corporate image for the business itself. By embracing a theme – *Bake Oasis* – a pleasure for the senses – the designers and shop construction professionals have created a bakery plus café which conjures up the impression of sitting in the midst of an oasis – surrounded by shady palm trees and a view of an Egyptian landscape replete with desert, temples, pyramids and the Nile. Using acrylic painting techniques, theatrical stage prop painters have realised this idea on the walls, the ceiling and parts of the furnishings. It has even been transferred to sales areas, such as the counter, the price labelling and the product display shelving. Sand coloured tile floors and solid wood, oil finished furniture evoke visions of southern patios and associations with products derived from Nature, although in this case they have been achieved up by pictorial means. Even the lighting, with its pronounced light and shade effects, underscores the illusion of sitting outdoors. This successful concept, which is relatively unusual for Germany, has not only resulted in increased customer loyalty, but has also led to extraordinary business success for the bakery shop.

Muzen
+
Muzenmandeln
OasenBrot
500g 3,75
750g 5,25
Coca-Cola

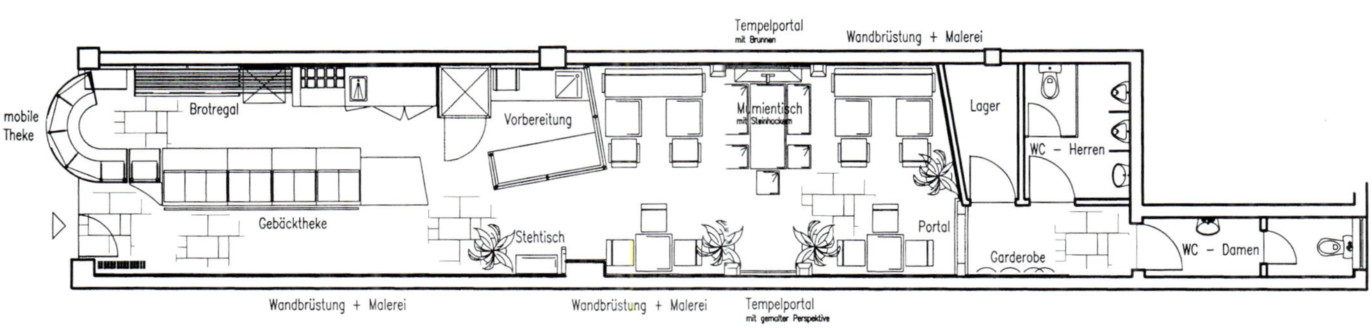

Wüstenoase als Erlebniskonzept für ganz normale Backwaren

Desert oasis as theme concept for quite normal bakery goods

Project:
Backoase, Arnsberg, Germany

Design:
E.T. Equipment Team, Leopoldshöhe

Realisation:
Aichinger MP, Einrichtungsbau, Wendelstein

Area:
ca. 86 sqm

Photographer:
ET-Equipment Team GmbH, Leopoldshöhe

Im Fürstenhof, Frankfurt am Main

DESIGN
Volker Bender, Kaiserslautern

Seit 25 Jahren war diese Weinhandlung mit Gross- und Einzelhandel in Frankfurt gegenüber dem Hauptbahnhof ansässig. Eine Umstrukturierung des Sortiments in hochwertigere Produkte und eine Erweiterung des Feinkostbereiches erforderten einen neuen repräsentativen Standort. Dieser wurde in den Räumen des ehemaligen Fürstenhofes im gleichen Stadtteil gefunden – in einem Milieu, das neben Geschäftsbauten vor allem von Sexshops und Bars geprägt ist. Eine neue Ladengestaltung und ein neues Erscheinungsbild sollten die gewachsenen Geschäftsbeziehungen erhalten und zugleich die Kunden des nahe gelegenen Bankenviertels erreichen. Herzstück des Ladens wurde eine große Weinprobiertonne, die von dem Künstler Wolfgang Carra mit einem rundumlaufenden Wandbild von der Milieuszene bemalt wurde. Während die runde rote Lederbank im Innern der Rotunde ganz milieugemäß ist, ironisieren die geflügelten Deckenleuchter Bird-Bird-Bird von Ingo Maurer die Szene. Raumprägend aber ist ein 7,50 mal 4,20 Meter großes Weinregal aus einem diagonalen Stahlgitter für 1425 Weinflaschen. Weine, vor allem kostbare, haben unterschiedliche Lagerformen und so stehen z.B. Weißweine auf Regaltischen aus Schiffsmahagoniholz, der Champagner ruht in Ledergurten. Rote Wände und ein dicker roter Teppich führen die Kunden ins Obergeschoss in ein Separé mit einer lippenförmigen Besprechungskoje aus schwarzem Leder und einer ausfahrbaren Minibar. Das Büro daneben ist eher eine Überwachungsstation in Glas mit hellen Ahornholzmöbeln, um Kunden und Laden im Auge zu behalten.

For over 25 years this Frankfurt retail and wholesale wine store was located opposite the main train station. The re-organisation of the range of products to include higher quality products and the expansion of the delicatessen area necessitated a new and more impressive location. The right venue was found on the premises of the former Fürstenhof, which is situated in the same part of the city – a district that is characterised by commercial buildings and in particular by sex shops and bars. The new shop design and new appearance was aimed at conserving the store's existing business relationships and at the same time targeting potential customers from the nearby financial district. The heart of the store is a large wine tasting barrel which the artist Wolfgang Carra adorned all the way around with a mural depicting scenes from the local red light milieu. This milieu theme is also underscored by the round red leather bench in the interior of the rotunda, as well as by two 'Bird-Bird-Bird' chandeliers designed by Ingo Maurer, which consist of wire arms and winged light bulbs. However, the interior is dominated by a huge 7.5 by 4.2 metre wine shelf consisting of a diagonal steel grid which can accommodate 1,425 bottles of wine. Wines, especially valuable wines, have varying optimum storage conditions. For this reason, white wines, for example, are displayed on shelving tables made of marine mahogany wood and champagne bottles are suspended in leather straps. Red walls and thick red carpeting entice customers upwards to the upper floor where a séparée boasts of a lip shaped private discussion cabinet and a retractable mini- bar. Appointed in glass and light maple furniture, the adjacent office exhibits a certain resemblance to a surveillance station, seeing as it does actually facilitate an overview of the customers and shop itself.

MASI
NOVAL

Weinverkauf mit erotischem Flair

Wine selling with erotic atmosphere

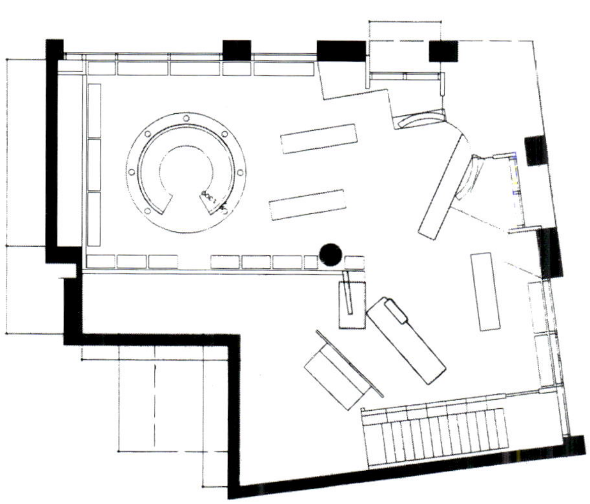

Erdgeschoss / Ground floor

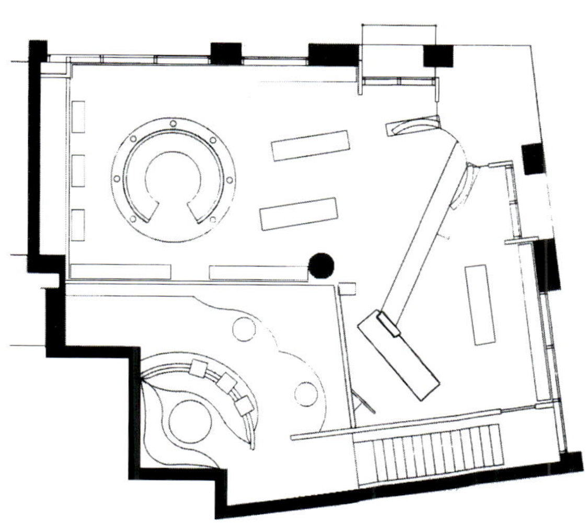

Obergeschoss / First floor

Project:
Im Fürstenhof,
Frankfurt am Main/Germany

Design:
Volker Bender,
Kaiserslautern

Area:
130 sqm, Empore 40 sqm

Photographer:
Jens Willebrand,
Köln/Cologne

Läden mit Service und Wellness

Freundlichkeit ist hierzulande nicht unbedingt oberste Devise im Verkaufsgeschehen, ganz anders als in den USA und in Japan, im Land der aufgehenden Sonne. Hier ist Freundlichkeit ein bewährtes kulturelles Konzept, Kunden zu gewinnen und zu halten. Auch für den Optiker *Niwaka* in Kyoto ist dies Unternehmensstrategie – Einfachheit im Ladendesign mit sensibel wirkenden Materialien und einem raffinierten Licht, das diesem Konzept entspricht. Freundlichkeit ist einfach, zeigt sie doch den Kunden, dass sie gern gesehen sind, sich wohl fühlen sollen und damit Anerkennung erhalten – emotionale Werte, für die Kunden in unserer hektischen Zeit besonders empfänglich sind. Service und die Bemühung um den Kunden haben im Handel Tradition, wenngleich dies durch Massenproduktion und anonyme Ketten in Vergessenheit geraten ist. Kenntnis der Kunden bringt auch Kundentreue. Das haben wohl am ehesten die handwerklich orientierten Serviceunternehmen begriffen wie Kosmetikgeschäfte und Frisörsalons.

Im Kosmetikgeschäft *Studio W* in Sao Paulo wird bereits mit der Raumgestaltung versucht, den Kunden etwas Gutes zu tun, sie mit Farben, gedämpftem Licht und großen weichen Sofas zu verwöhnen, ihnen eine Atmosphäre zu bieten, die den Alltag vergessen lässt. Auch die Läden des englischen Kosmetikherstellers *Space NK Apothecary* spiegeln diese Strategie wieder, durch sanfte, helle Räume auf das Thema der Haut- und Körperpflege vorzubereiten. Die fast weiße ruhige Raumgestaltung hebt die Produkte gut hervor, regt zum Herumschlendern und Ausprobieren an. Und wem es nicht genügt die Produkte nur zu kaufen, sondern ihre Wirkung am ganzen Körper spüren möchte, der kann in den dahinter liegenden Spa-Räumen auch dieses erfahren. Der Erfolg dieser Spa-Läden, die eine Erholung für Stunden oder einen ganzen Tag anbieten zeigt, wie groß der Bedarf ist, in unserer komplexen hektischen Zeit einen Ausgleich für Körper und Seele zu erhalten. Die Beliebtheit von Wellness- und Relaxprogrammen in Beautycentern und Hotels dokumentieren das Bedürfnis danach.

Auch der amerikanische Salon *Ajune daySpa* entspricht dem Konzept, kurzfristig dem Alltagsstress entfliehen zu können. Hier sind die gestalterischen Mittel etwas anders gelagert: Die Farben beziehen sich mehr aus der Natur und erzeugen zusammen mit weichfallenden Vorhängen und Kerzenlicht eine Atmosphäre der Entspannung, die fast an mythische Räume erinnert. Der Erfolg aber besteht im Zusammengehen medizinischer Hautbehandlung, Schönheitspflege und einem Entspannungsprogramm.

Das ein Kosmetikgeschäft Wohlbehagen und Wellness anbietet, erscheint angesichts ihres Produktangebots sinnvoll und selbstverständlich. Inzwischen haben aber auch manche Frisöre diese Möglichkeit entdeckt, ihr Servicepaket der Haarpflege mit Körper- und Schönheitspflege und Wellness anzureichern. Der junge Friseursalon *BrockmannundKnödler* in Chemnitz machte diesen Versuch auf eigene Weise. Nicht weich und hell sind hier die Räume, sondern eher in einer gedämpften warmen Atmosphäre aus dunklem Eichenholz, dunklen Rottönen und Weiß mit hotelartigem Flair. Ihre Konzeptbausteine sind Freundlichkeit, fachliche Kompetenz, Beratung, Wohlfühlen und Verwöhnen durch sanfte Düfte und Musik, natürliche Farben, kleine Getränke und Snacks und Öffnungszeiten mit open end. Ein Verwöhnprogramm, das Kunden von weit her anzieht.

Shops with Service and wellness

In Germany, cordial courtesy is not necessarily the top priority in sales transactions, in contrast with the USA and the land of the rising sun – Japan – where cordial courtesy is a tried and true cultural concept that is useful in to gaining and retaining customers. For the optician *Niwaka* in Kyoto this is the corporate strategy: the shop design is characterised by simplicity, sensitively selected materials and sophisticated lighting, and it corresponds to the concept. Courtesy is simple: it demonstrates to customers that they are welcome and respected, and are meant to feel at ease. Thus, it conveys emotional values that customers in our hectic day and age are particularly susceptible to.

Service and special efforts aimed at customers have a tradition in the retail sector, although this aspect has fallen into oblivion as a result of mass production and the proliferation of anonymous retail chains. Knowing the customers leads to customer loyalty. In particular, this fact has been recognised by service companies with a skilled trade background, such as cosmetics shops and hairdressing salons.

At the cosmetics shop, *Studio W* in Sao Paulo, the interior design itself is an attempt to promote customer well-being, to pamper them with colours, soft lighting and large soft sofas, to offer them an atmosphere which allows them to forget their daily cares. The shops of the English cosmetics manufacturer, *Space NK Apothecary*, also reflect this strategy, with tranquil, bright rooms initiating the theme of skin and body care. The almost exclusively white, peaceful interior decor effectively focuses attention on the products and invites the patrons to stroll and try things out. For those who not only wish to make a purchase, but would also like to feel the effect of the products in the form of a total body experience, there are spa facilities located behind the retail area. The success of these spa shops, which offer respite and relaxation for a few hours or a whole day, demonstrates how great the need is for compensating balance for the body and soul in our complex and hectic age. The popularity of wellness and relaxation programmes in beauty centres and hotels is ample evidence that this need does exist.

The concept of the American *Ajune mediSpa* salon is also geared to escaping day-to-day stress for a short time. In this case the design elements employed are somewhat different. The colours are derived more from nature and, together with soft draperies and candlelight, they create an atmosphere of relaxation that is almost reminiscent of mystical rooms. However, the salon's success is rooted in the combination of medical skin treatment, beauty care and a relaxation programme.

In light of the range of products offered, it seems quite sensible and natural for a cosmetics shop to focus on well-being and wellness. However, in the meantime some hairdressers have also discovered this potential for supplementing their hair care service package with body and beauty care, as well as wellness. The newly established hairdressing salon *BrockmannundKnödler* in Chemnitz attempts to do this in a very individual way. The interior is not softly tranquil and bright: on the contrary, it exudes a warm, subdued atmosphere concocted of dark oak, dark red hues combined white and a hotel-like flair. The elements of their concept are courtesy, professional competence, consulting service, a feeling of well-being and pampering achieved with soothing fragrances and music, natural colours, light beverages and snacks, and open end business hours. This is a pampering programme that attracts customers from near and far.

Studio W, Sao Paulo

DESIGN
Anastassiadis Arquitetos, Sao Paulo

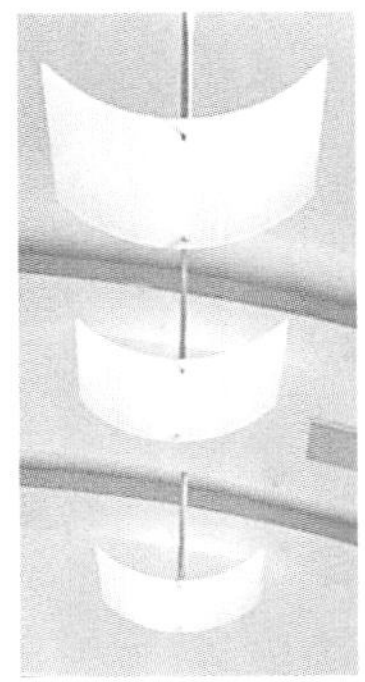

Das nach dem Vornamen des Inhabers benannte Haar- und Kosmetikstudio liegt in Higienopolis, einem hochwertigen Shoppingcenter Sao Paulos, das sich durch viel Grün, schöne Läden und gute Restaurants auszeichnet. Eine großzügige Treppenanlage bringt die reichen und oftmals berühmten Kunden in das großzügige weiße Studio, dessen Glasfassade einen totalen Einblick in das Innere des Geschehens erlaubt. Hier bekommen die Kunden nicht nur perfektes Haarstyling, sondern auch Hand- und Fußpflege, dekorative und heilende Kosmetik wie Lasertherapie. Die Produkte hierfür werden in offenen hellen Holzregalen wie in einer Galerie oder in hinterleuchteten Wandnischen mit Glasborden präsentiert. Alles im Studio ist großzügig, elegant und weiß: die Wände, der Marmorboden und die Möbel. Violegardinen vor den riesigen Glasfenstern filtern das Tageslicht und selbst das Licht an den Arbeitsplätzen schmeichelt der Haut. Gegenüber der Rezeption hängen Fotos berühmter Kunden, durch Spiegel und Produktnischen ergänzt und belebt. Am Empfang vorbei durchschreitet der Kunde oder die Kundin einen langen Gang, dessen Wände für Produktpräsentationen und kleine Beratungsplätze genutzt werden. Eine gebogene Deckenbeleuchtung gibt dem Raum von oben her einen tunnelartigen Schutz. Besonderer Blickfang und ruhender Pol im Salon ist das große weiße Ledersofa im Wartebereich, von dem aus man das ganze Treiben beobachten kann. Hier und auch an den Arbeitsplätzen werden kleine Getränke und Snacks gereicht, um den Aufenthalt so entspannend wie möglich zu gestalten.

This hair dressing and cosmetics studio, which was called after the first name of the owner, is situated in Higienopolis – a high-quality shopping centre in Sao Paulo, which is characterised by abundant greenery, beautiful shops and good restaurants. A generously dimensioned staircase structure leads the wealthy and frequently famous customers into the spacious white studio, where a glass façade provides an unimpeded view of what is happening within the interior. Studio customers are not only provided with perfect hair styling, but are also pampered with manicure and pedicure treatments. The products used are displayed on light coloured, open wooden shelving similar to those in a gallery or in back lit wall niches fitted with glass shelves. The spaciousness and elegance of the interior rooms has been achieved through the use of white for the walls, marble for the floor and white furniture, reinforced by soft indirect lighting for the work areas and by sheer curtains in front of the windows, which serve to gently filter the remorselessly harsh daylight. Opposite the reception area, a display with photographs of famous customers is supplemented and enlivened by mirrors and products arranged in recesses. Immediately behind the reception area, the customer proceeds through a long passageway where the arched ceiling lighting makes the space seem like a tunnel. The lengthwise walls are utilised for product presentation and consultation areas. The large white leather couch in the waiting area, from where you can observe all of the surrounding activity, is one of the particularly eye catching features in the salon. In order to ensure that the customers' stay is as relaxing as possible, beverages and light snacks are served in the waiting area as well as the work areas.

In Marmor gefasste Durchgänge sind Tor zu Schönheit, Entspannung, und Wellness

Marble framed passages are gates to beauty, relaxation and wellness

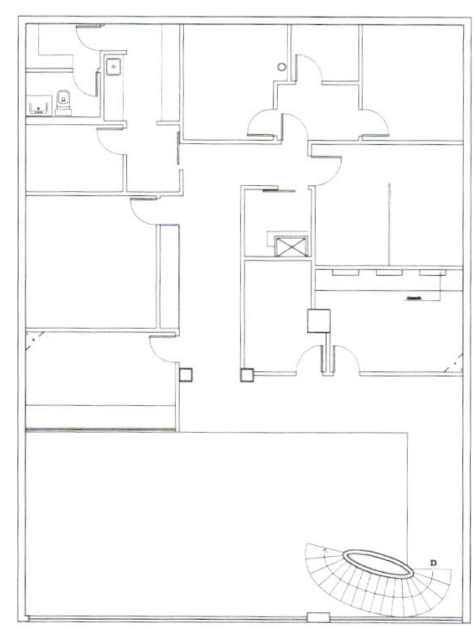

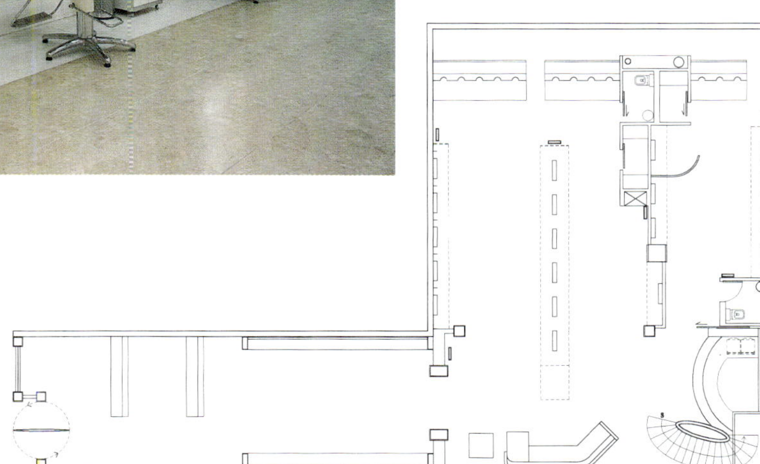

Obergeschoss / First floor

Erdgeschoss / Ground floor

Project:
Studio W, Sao Paulo, Brasil

Design:
Anastassiadis Arquitetos,
Sao Paulo, Brasil

Area:
ca. 220 sqm
plus 150 sqm Behandlungs-
räume/treatment rooms

Photographer:
Ary Disendruck, Sao Paulo

Optique Niwaka, Kyoto

DESIGN
Tsujimura Hisanobu Design Office

Mitten in Kyoto an einer der großen Hauptstraßen liegt das Optik-Geschäft *Niwaka*. Runde Fenster in der Fassade sind Sinnbild für den Blick durch die Brille, die hier die Sicht in den Innenraum ermöglichen. Und somit hat die ganze Fassade Zeichencharakter. Der Innenraum ist schlicht und prägnant und besteht genau genommen nur aus der langen Theke mit einer 30 cm dicken massiven Ahornplatte und der Brillenwand gegenüber, die aus geflochtenem Bambusmaterial besteht und daher ein besonders reizvoller Untergrund für die modischen Brillengestelle darstellt. Dies umso mehr, als die Bambuswand Ajiro hinterleuchtet ist und abends die Lichtfarbe wechselt. Was hier so einfach aussieht, ist Konzept: Simplicity and Politeness entspricht der Firmenstrategie *Niwakas*, der als Juwelier begann und nun drei Läden in Japan und New York besitzt. Er gehört zu denjenigen japanischen Händlern, die in den frühen 90ern eine Alternative zu den weit verbreiteten Franchise-Läden suchten und den Concept-Store-Typ entwickelten: individuelle hochwertige Läden, in denen nur wenige Marken angeboten werden wie Alan Mikli oder 9999 und in denen den Kunden besonders viel Aufmerksamkeit geschenkt wird. Auch hier in Kyoto führt *Niwaka* populäre junge Markenmodelle in Kunststoff und Metall und bietet natürlich Fullservice an von Augentests bis zum optischen Labor und einer persönlichen Beratung inklusive.

The *Niwaka* optician's shop is located right in the middle of Kyoto on one of the principal thoroughfares. Round window openings in the façade provide of view of the interior and symbolically duplicate the act of peering through eyeglasses. Thus, the entire façade is imbued with a symbolic character. The interior is simple and clearly defined: strictly speaking, it consists solely of a long counter with a 30 cm thick, solid wood maple slab and on the opposite side a display wall for eyeglasses made of woven bamboo material, which is a particularly attractive background for the fashionable eyeglass frames. The effect of the Ajiro bamboo wall is reinforced by backlighting and the colour of the light changes in the evenings. Everything looks so utterly simple, but it is based on a design concept: "Simplicity and Politeness" is the corporate strategy of *Niwaka*, who started out as a jeweller and now owns three shops in Japan and New York. He is one of the Japanese retailers who started looking for an alternative to the wide spread franchise shops in the early nineties and developed the concept store type: individual, high quality shops where the selection includes only a few brand names such as Alan Mikli or 9999, in which a great deal of attention is devoted to the customers. In Kyoto, *Niwaka* also offers popular, young fashion styles made of plastic and metal. Quite naturally, he also provides the full range of services – including vision tests, optical laboratory services and personal consulting service.

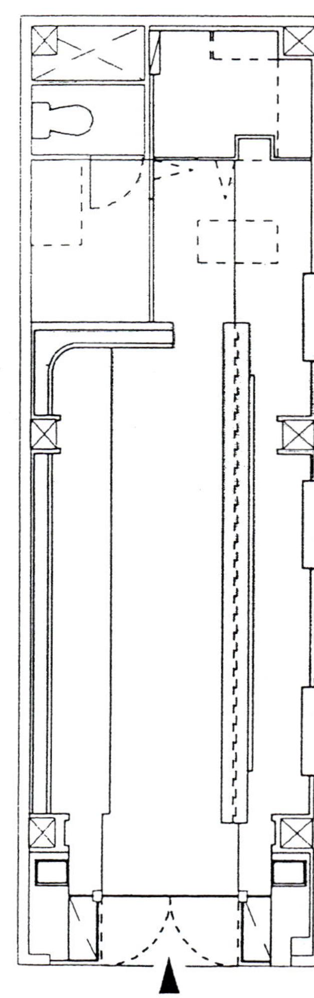

Project:
Optique Niwaka,
Kyoto/Japan

Design:
Tsujimura Hisanobu
Design Office
+ moon balance,
Kyoto

Area:
ca. 55 sqm

Photographer:
Kozo Takayama, Tokyo

SPAce.NK, London

DESIGN
Virgile and Stone Asssociates Ltd., London

Der englische Kosmetikhersteller *SPAce.NK Apothecary* besaß bereits einige Filialen in London, als das Designunternehmen *Virgile and Stone* beauftragt wurde, ein neues gemeinsames Erscheinungsbild der Läden zu erarbeiten. In West London entstand nun der neueste Flagship Store, der neben dem Einzelhandelsgeschäft auch über einen großen Spa-Bereich mit Behandlungs- und Entspannungsräumen verfügt. Hinter der völlig verglasten Fassade sprechen der weite offene Laden und die Produkte für sich. Eine helles einladendes Ambiente spiegelt Schlichtheit und Wohlbehagen wider, Qualitäten, für die die Produkte bekannt sind. Im Laden kann sich der Kunde völlig frei bewegen, sich umsehen und ausprobieren. Die Produktbereiche sind leicht zu erkennen: Regale mit quadratischem Raster enthalten Hautpflege und Herrenkosmetik, farbige Regale stehen für Make-up-Produkte, Bad- und Körperpflege findet man in einem gläsernen Umfeld. Trotz dieser Unterschiede ist der gesamte Raumeindruck cremig zart und hell. Der 530 Quadratmeter große Spa-Bereich ist über den Laden oder einen gesonderten Eingang zu erreichen. Auch hier soll die Atmosphäre einladen, Ruhe und Entspannung bringen. Über einen hellen Eichenboden gleiten die Kunden durch sensibel gestaltete, schlichte Räume. Sanftes Licht, Lichtnischen und dezente Dekoration sollen helfen das innere Gleichgewicht wiederzufinden, um Körper- und Schönheitspflege für einen Tag des Wohlbehagens zu bekommen.

The English cosmetics manufacturer, *SPAce.NK Apothecary*, already owned several branch outlets in London when the *Vigile and Stone* design firm was commissioned to design a new unified look for the stores. The newest flagship store has now been completed in West London. In addition to the retail store it also includes an extensive spa area with treatment and relaxation rooms. The spacious, open concept store behind the entirely glassed in façade and the products speak for themselves. A bright and inviting ambiance reflects the simplicity and feeling of well-being that the products are famous for. The customer can walk around the store freely – browsing and sampling everything. The product areas are easy to distinguish: shelves with a square grid contain skin care products and men's cosmetics and coloured shelving signalises make-up products, while bath and body care products are displayed in glass surroundings. All of the room elements have been rendered in pale colours, creamy white and pleasant. The 530 square metre spa area can be reached through the store or via a separate entrance. The atmosphere there is also intended to be welcoming and to radiate an aura of calm and relaxation. With light coloured oak flooring underfoot, patrons pass through the sensitively appointed, quiet rooms. Soft lighting, recessed light niches and unobtrusive decorating effects are aimed at helping customers retrieve their inner balance, in order to thoroughly enjoy body and beauty care for a day of well-being.

fresh
diptyque
JAS MIN

Erdgeschoss / Ground floor

Obergeschoss / First floor

Project:
SPAce.NK, London/UK

Design:
Virgile and Stone
Asssociates Ltd., London

Area:
ca. 800 sqm

Photographer:
Chris Gascogne, London

Ajune Day-Spa, New York

DESIGN
Robert D. Henry,
New York,

Ajune ist einer der vielen Day Spas in den USA, in denen Patienten einen Tag für Schönheit und Wohlbefinden opfern, um dem Alltagsstress zu entfliehen. Und doch ist *Ajune* weitaus mehr: Hier haben sich der Schönheitschirurg Mauro Romita und der befreundete Dermatologe Michael Albom zusammengetan, um einen Wellness-Platz zu schaffen, der ideale Bedingungen für eine gezielte Nachbehandlung ermöglicht und neben Schönheitspflege auch eine medizinische Behandlung anbietet. Das von einer Krankenschwester betreute Programm reicht von Hautanalysen bis zu Laser- und Hydrotherapien. Das Umfeld für eine solche Behandlung sollte die Ajune-Philosophie von Harmonie und Gleichgewicht widerspiegeln, eine sinnliche Reise zur inneren Ruhe.

Direkt von der Straße aus – im reichen Upper East Side Manhattan's gelegen – erhält der Kunde über die offene Glasfront eine Vorstellung von der andersartigen Kosmetikidee. Wände in warmtonigem Glasmosaik und Möbel in hellem Eschenholz mit moosgrüner Mosaikumrandung auf dem poliertem Betonboden schaffen mit dem Laden eine Art Vor-Bühne. Hier werden Spezialprodukte angeboten, die auf die kosmetische Behandlung abgestimmt sind. Geätzte Glaswände trennen den Laden vom Behandlungsbereich ab, sind sinnlicher Übergang. Auf dem Weg zu den Behandlungsräumen gleiten die Kunden durch den Raum des Flüsterns, ein langer Flur mit weißen Textilwänden, deren Falten an rieselndes Wasser erinnern soll. Der weiße Raum führt zu den Behandlungszimmern: ruhige Alkoven mit raumhoher Mosaikdusche und intimer Beleuchtung. Kerzenlicht, gewachste Oberflächen, weiche aromatische Düfte und beruhigende Klänge vervollständigen die Stimmung.

Ajune is one of the many day spas in the USA where patients can devote an entire day to beauty and a feeling of well-being, and at the same time escape from the stress of day-to-day life. But *Ajune* is far more: the plastic surgeon, Mauro Romita, and his dermatologist friend, Michael Albom, have joined forces to create a wellness setting that guarantees conditions that are ideal for purposeful follow-up treatments, which include medical treatments as well as beauty care. Under the direction of a registered nurse, the programme ranges from skin analysis to laser and hydro therapy. The setting for this type of treatment was supposed to reflect the Ajune philosophy of harmony and balance – a sensual journey toward inner peace. It is located in Manhattan's affluent Upper East Side. On entering directly from the street, customers get an inkling of the principles behind this totally different cosmetics idea through the open glass façade. The walls have been sheathed in glass mosaic tiles in warm tones. Furnishings in light coloured ash wood have been arranged on a polished concrete floor that is accented by a mossy green mosaic border, creating a sort of proscenium stage. The special products offered are selected specifically for each type of cosmetic treatment. Etched glass partitions separate the retail area from the treatment area, signalling a sensual transition. On their way towards the treatment rooms, patrons proceed through the "Hall of Whispers" – an elongated passage with softly pleated, white fabric walls permeated with the soft sound of trickling water. This white space leads to the treatment facilities: quiet alcoves with ceiling high, mosaic tiled showers, intimate lighting and softly aromatic fragrances. Candle light, hand waxed surfaces, wafting scents and calming sounds complete the mood.

FOR
FOR BEAUTY

AJUNE

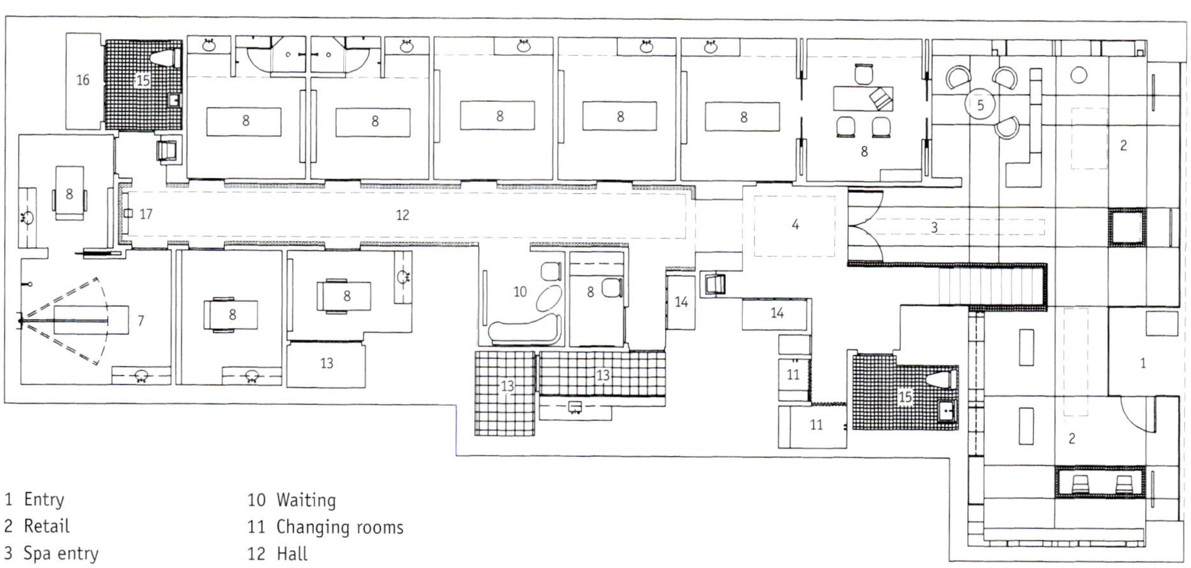

1 Entry
2 Retail
3 Spa entry
4 Foyer
5 Information/Retail
6 Patient information
7 Wet room
8 Treatment rooms
9 Make up/consulting
10 Waiting
11 Changing rooms
12 Hall
13 Storage
14 Closet
15 WC
16 Mechanical room
17 Water element

Project:
Ajune Medi-Spa,
New York/ USA

Design:
Robert D. Henry,
New York,

Area:
380 sqm,
13 Treatment rooms

Photographer:
Dan Bibb, New York

BrockmannundKnödler, Chemnitz

DESIGN
Petra Brockmann
mit Welonda, Darmstadt

BROCKMANNUNDKNØDLER

Friseure

Wellness im Stil eines gepflegten Hotels: Die Weite der ehemaligen Webstuhl-Fabrik faszinierte die beiden jungen Meister-Frisöre Petra Brockmann und Thomas Knödler als Ort für ihren exklusivsten Salon. Neben ihnen gibt es in der geplanten Kulturfabrik bereits ein Café und eine Werbeagentur. Das stimmungsvolle Areal und das angrenzende Parkgelände bereiten die von weither kommenden Kunden zwischen sieben und 70 Jahren auf das Konzept der Entspannung vor. Am Eingang über eine Industrietreppe angekommen überrascht eine gläserne Empfangstheke, orange hinterleuchtet. Darüber an der Wand sanft rieselndes Wasser in breitem gelben Rahmen. Äpfel und Leckereien auf der Theke versprechen Frische und Verwöhnung. Gleich neben dem ovalen Servicetrakt, in dem sich stilvolle Toiletten und die duftende Kaffeebar verbergen, fällt der Blick auf ein riesiges Gästebuch und auf raumhohe dünne weiße Stoffbahnen, die die einzelnen Sitzbereiche voneinander trennen. Keine üblichen Friseur-Hauben weit und breit, Wohlfühlen steht im Vordergrund. Die 3,50 Meter hohen schmalen Spiegel vor den Sitzplätzen dienen während der Beratung als beschreibbare Infowand. Und während die Meister beraten, holen sie geschickt Pflegeprodukte aus den quadratischen Schubladenwänden links und rechts des Eingangs und offerieren diese in kleinen gelochten Metallkörben. Herzstück des Salons aber ist der Warteplatz mit bequemen dunklen Eichenholzsesseln und roten Lederpolstern. An kleinen quadratischen Tischchen gibt es Getränke und Snacks, und das bis abends open end. Entspannender Blickfang ist eine raumhohe, gewölbte blauweiße Mosaikwand mit langsam rieselndem Osmose-Wasser, das die Raumluft verbessert und besonders in den Dämmerstunden wie eine mystische Feuerstelle aussieht. Direkt daneben führt eine schmale Stahltreppe hinauf in den Wellnessbereich für Sauerstoff- und Musiktherapie sowie Rücken-Massage. Es ist ein Salon der besonderen Art: Industrieflair mit Hotelcharakter in dunklem Eichenholz, in Rot und Weiß – in Szene gesetzt durch dramatische Lichtinseln, Düfte, leise Musik, perfekter Service.

Wellness in the style of a luxurious hotel: the spaciousness of a former loom factory fascinated the two young master hairdressers, Petra Brockmann and Thomas Knödler, as a potential venue for their highly exclusive salon.
In addition to them, the planned cultural factory already houses a café and an advertising agency. The atmosphere of the property and the surrounding park-like area prepare customers for the concept of relaxation. The customers, who range in age from seven to 70 and often come far away, arrive at the entrance via the industrial type staircase and are taken by surprise by the back lit reception desk. Behind it is a rippling water picture in a wide yellow frame. Apples and tempting tidbits evoke freshness and suggest that customers will be pampered and cosseted.
Next to the oval service area which divides the interior spatially, the eye is drawn to a gigantic guest book and ceiling high diaphanous sheets of white fabric which separate the individual seating areas. There are no hair dryers in evidence: the focus is simply on a feeling of well-being. During the consultation stage, the 3.5 metre high mirror serves as an information wall that can be written on. As needed, care products are taken out of drawers that are built into the walls to the left and right side of the entrance and offered to customers in perforated metal baskets. However, the heart of the salon is the waiting area with its comfortable oak armchairs and red leather upholstery. A narrow staircase immediately adjacent leads up to the wellness area, which is reserved for oxygen and music therapy as well as massage treatments.
A particularly striking effect – especially in the twilight hours – is produced by a curved blue and white mosaic wall with slowly trickling osmosis water, which improves the air quality of the interior and resembles a fireplace when it is illuminated. This is a truly unique type of salon: industrial flair coupled with hotel character, rendered in dark oak, red and white and theatrically highlighted by dramatic pools of light.

Gästebuch als Einladung

Guestbook as an invitation

Gläserne Empfangstheke mit rieselndem Wasser im Rahmen

Backlit glass reception counter with a ripling water picture in a yellow frame

Schmale raumhohe Spiegel als beschreibbare Infowände

Ceiling high mirrors serve as information wall that can be written on

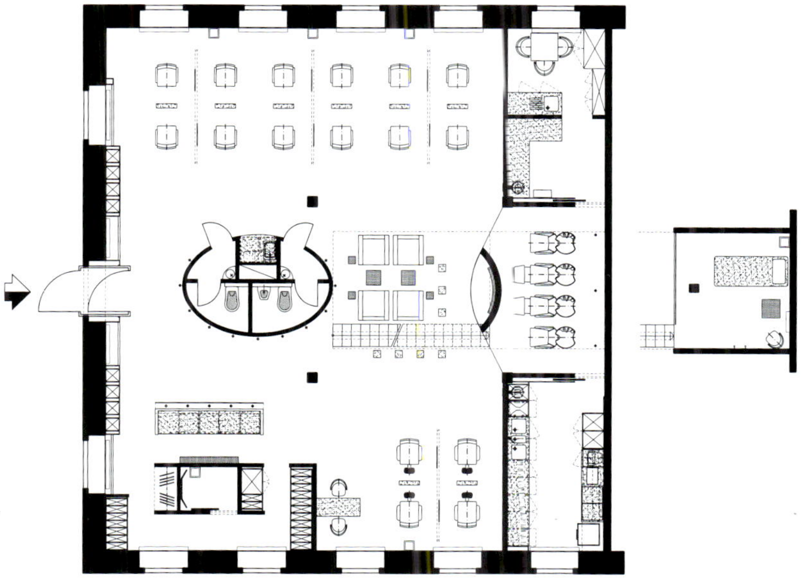

Project:
BrockmannundKnödler,
Chemnitz, Germany

Design:
Petra Brockmann mit
Welonda, Darmstadt

Realisation:
Welonda Einrichtungen,
Darmstadt

Area:
ca. 312 sqm

Photographer:
Ingrid Wenz-Gahler,
Frankfurt am Main

Läden / Shops

Aida Hairsalon
209 East 76th Street
USA-New York, N.Y.

Ajune Day-Spa
1294 Third Avenue
USA-New York, N.Y.10021
Tel. 001 212-628 0044
www.ajune.com

Anna Molinari-Blumarine
Old Bond Street 11A
GB London
Tel. 0044 20-7493 4872
Fax. 0044 20-7409 2807

Backoase
Bäckerei Bauernfeind-Jürgens
Hauptstr. 35
D-59755 Arnsberg-Neheim
Tel. 0049 2932-7909

Banana Music
Alameda Lorena, 1641
Cerqueira César
Sao Paulo – SP, Brazil
CEP 01424-002

Basiliou
Optician Shop
5 Erythrou Stavrou Street
GR-Athens-Maroussi

Bergman
Kaiserstr. 23
D-60311 Frankfurt am Main
Tel. 0049 69-2400 5840
Fax. 0049 69-2400 5844
www.bergman.de

Bread Shop
Jonathan Cohan
65 St. John's Wood High Street
GB-London NW8 7NL
Tel/Fax. 0044 20-7586 5311

BrockmannundKnödler, Friseure
Kulturfabrik Schönherr
Schönherrnstr. 8
D-09113 Chemnitz
Tel. 0049 371-45 90 48 07

Camper
125 Prince Street
(Manhattan-Soho)
USA-10012 New York
Tel. 001 212-358 1842
www.camper.es

Camper
Via Montenapoleone 6
I-28121 Milano
Tel. 0039 02-79 90 15
www.camper.es

Cirque de Soleil
Hotel Bellagio
3600 S, Las Vegas Blvd.
USA-Las Vegas, NV 89109
Tel. 001 702-693 71 11

Deerberg
Schuh-Versand OHG
Gabi und Stefan Deerberg
Heiligengeiststr. 27
Velgen
D-29582 Hanstedt
Tel. 0049 4131-40 23 23
www.deerberg.de

Fattoria Blu. Delikatessen
Enzo Cagol
Seestrasse 455 a
CH-8038 Zürich
Tel. 0041 1-488 64 44
Fax. 0041 1-488 64 65

Fila Sport.Life Store
Piazzetta Liberty 8
I-Milano
www.fila.com

Harriet Dorn
Women's Clothing Store
Edgemar Development
2435 Main Street
USA-Santa Monica,
CA 90405

Guitar Gallery
1504 East Buena Vista Drive,
Suite C-1
PO Box 22150
USA-Lake Buena Vista,
FL 32830-2150
Tel. 001 407-827 0118
Fax. 001 407-827 0119

Im Fürstenhof, Weinhandlung
Perkal & Partner ohG
Kaiserstr. 31–33
D-60329 Frankfurt am Main
Tel. 0049 69-23 44 13
Fax. 0049 69-23 40 70

Legrand Shoes
Grosse Bleichen 21
D-20354 Hamburg
Tel. 0049 40-3571 4173

LYNX Barbershop
17 Oxford Street
GB-London
19 Market Place
GB-Kingston-Upon-Thames

mademoiselle
I-Sorrento

Mandarina Duck
Piazza Lavani 1m/n
I-Bologna
Tel. 0039 051-22 26 03

Mandarina Duck
Rue Saint Honoré 219
F-Paris
Tel. 0033 1-4260 7620

me ISSEY MIYAKE
Matsuya Ginza
3-6-1 Ginza, Chuo-Ku
J-Tokyo

Microcenter Korasidis
Electronic Shops
9 Veikou Street
GR-Athens

Missoni Boutique
1009 Madison Avenue
USA-10021 New York, NY
Tel. 001 212-515 93 39

Nuon NV
Minervaweg 3
NL-3741 GR Baarn
Tel. 0031 35-629 41 41
Fax. 0031 35-543 11 05

Optique Niwaka
401 shimomaruya-cho
oikesagaru, kawaramachi-dori
nakagyoku
J-Kyoto
Tel/Fax. 0081 75-257 25 85

Perugina
Corso Vanucci 111
I-Perugia
Tel. 0039 075-573 66 77

Qiora Store and Spa
535 Madison Avenue
at 54th Street
USA-New York, N.Y. 1022
Tel. 001 212-527 9933
www.qiora.com

React
Sturegallerian 13
S-114 46 Stockholm
Tel. 0046 8-678 07 07
www.react.se

25 Records
Grosse Elbstrasse 148
D-22767 Hamburg
Tel. 0049 40-300 66 90
Fax. 0049 40-300 66 950
www.25records.de

Sony Style Store
Sony Center Berlin GmbH
Kemperplatz 1
D-10785 Berlin
Tel. 0049 30-2575 5777
Fax. 0049 30-2575 6767
www.sonycenter.de

SPAce.NK
127-131 Westbourne Grove
GB-London W2 4UP
Tel. 0044 20-7727 8002
www.spacenk.com

Studio W Cabelereiros Ltda
Av. Higienópolis, 674 loja 238
Sao Paulo – SP, Brazil
CEP 01238-000

Telfort Plaza
Grote Marktstraat 51–53
NL-Den Haag
Tel. 0031 62-600 04 44

The Klinik
Anna Forsling
65 Exmouth Market
GB-London EC1
Tel/Fax 0044 20-7837 3771
www.theklinik.com

Tritec AG
Holeestr. 145
CH-4054 Basel
Tel. 0041 61-307 99 33
Fax. 0041 61-307 99 39
www.tritec.ch

Via Spiga – Baroque Zen
Via Spiga 1
I-Milano
Tel. 0039 02-7639 7252
Fax. 0039 02-7639 0932

Watch2Watch
Karl Oliver
21 Heathmans Road
GB-London SW6 4TJ
Tel. 0044 20-7731 8231
Fax. 0044 20-7731 8286
www.watch2watch.com

Zebra Design Gallery, Glassware
Shop, Ze-Bar
Milan Cvjeticanin
Gosposka 4–10
SLO-61000 Ljubljana
Tel. 00 386 1-211 213
Fax. 00 386 1-125 02 42

Zero Lustrum Pukeberg
Nybrog 16
S-11439 Stockholm
Tel. 0046 8-545 850 02
Fax. 0046 8-545 850 09
www.pukeberg.se
www.lustrum.com

Architekten und Designer / Architects and Designers

The Leviathan
330 Second Treet N° 1
USA-Oakland, CA 94 607
Tel. 001 510-452 0775
Fax. 001 510-452 1175
www.aceland.com

Anamorphosis Architects
27 Mithymnis Street
GR-Athens 11 257
Tel. 0030 1-867 42 00
Fax. 0030 1-867 39 68
amorph@hol.gr

Anastassiadis Arquitetos
Rua Cerá, 124
Pacaembu
Sao Paulo – SP, Brazil
Tel. 0055 11-3661 7424
Fax. 0055 11-3662 2545
www.anastassiadis.com.br

Angélil-Graham-Pfenninger-Scholl
Architecture
Zypressenstr. 71
CH-8004 Zürich
Tel. 00411-2982020

Archi-Tectonics
Winka Dubbeldam
111 Mercer Street N° 2
USA-New York, NY 10 012
Tel. 001 212-226 0303
Fax. 001 212-219 3106
www.archi-tectonics.com

Architecture Research Office
ARO
Jenny Polak (marketing)
180 Varick Street, 10th Floor
USA-New York, N.Y. 10 014
Tel. 001 212-675 1870
Fax. 001 212-675 1645
www.aro.net

Volker Bender GmbH
Hertelsbrunnenring 13
D-67657 Kaiserslautern
Tel. 0049 631-341 63 0
Fax. 0049 631-341 63 99
www.bender-design.de

blockarchitecture
Graeme Williamson
83A Geffrye St.
GB-London E2 8HX
Tel. 0044 20-7729 9194
Fax. 0044 20-7729 9193

Cobalt Brand Development
David Thody
9 Tufton Street
GB-London SWIP 3Q8
Tel. 0044 20-7222 2882
Fax. 0044 20-7222 2442
www.cobalt.co.uk

Curiosity Inc.
Gwenael Nicolas
Hisaaki Hirawata
2-45-7 Honmachi
Shibuya-ku
J-Tokyo 151 0071
Tel. 0081 3-5333 8525
Fax. 0081 3-5371 1219
www.curiosity.co.jp

DC Design Company
Nymphenburgerstr. 58–60
D-80335 München
Tel. 0049 80-125 16 0
Fax. 0049 80-125 16 500

Droog Design
Gijs Bakker
Sarphatiekade 11
NL-1017 WV Amsterdam
Tel. 0031 20-6269 809
Fax. 0031 20-6388 828
www.droogdesign.nl

e15
Design und Distributions GmbH
Hospitalstr. 4
D-61440 Oberursel/Ts.
Tel. 0049 6171-97 95 50
Fax. 0049 6171-97 95 90
www.e15.com

ET Equipment Team GmbH
Agentur für Raum-inszenierung & Design
Postfach 11 28
D-33814 Leopoldshöhe
Tel. 0049 5202-98 03 0
Fax. 0049 5202-87 60
www.et-gmbh.de

Nenad Fabijanic
Prof. Architect
Arhitektonski Fakultet
Kacicéva 26
HR-10000 Zagreb (Croatia)
Tel./Fax. 0038 51-456 12 30

Rupert Gardner Design AB
Banérgatan 10
S-115 23 Stockholm
Tel. 0046 8-442 87 40
Fax. 0046 8-662 70 26
www.rupertgardnerdesign.se

Marti Guixé
Calabria 252, 2° 1a
E-Barcelona

Robert D. Henry
Architects
37 E. 18th St., 10th floor
USA-New York, N. Y. 10 003
Tel. 001 212-533 4145
Fax. 001 212-598 9028

Hisanobu Design Office
+ MOON BALANCE
456 Sasaya-cho,
Fuyachodori
Takeyamachi sagaru
Nakagoyu-ku
J-Kyoto 604 0983
Tel. 0081 75-221 64 03
Fax. 0081 75-221 64 30
vc3h-tjmr@asahi-net.or.jp

Jos de Vries Retail Company BV
Postfach 11 94
NL-3600 BD Maarssen
Tel. 0031 346-56 37 64
Fax. 0031 346-57 27 22
www.jdvpg.nl

Jump Studios Ltd.
Shaun Fernandes
35 Britannia row
GB-London N1 8QH
Tel. 0044 20-7688 0080
Fax. 0044 20-7288 1763

Jürg Landert
Gastronomie Konzepte
Consulting
Renggerstr. 60
CH-8038 Zürich
Tel. 0041 1-480 29 29
Fax. 0041 1-480 29 49
www.jlz.ch

Lorcan O'Herlihy Architects
5709 Mesmer Avenue
USA-Culver City CA 90 230
Tel. 001 310-398 0394
Fax. 001 310-398 2675
www.loharchitects.com

AMDL architetto
Michele de Lucchi
Via Pallavicino 31
I-20145 Milano
Tel. 0039 02-43 00 81
Fax. 0039 02-43 00 82 22
amdl@amdl.it

luxus
Moritz Müller Architekt
Ulrich Vollborn Design
Grosse Elbstrasse 164 A
D-22767 Hamburg
Tel. 0049 40-3861 3332
Fax. 0049 40-3861 1431
www.luxus.to

Shiro Miura
2 Nishihon-machi-Sakyo-ku
J-Kyoto 606 0826

Jordan Mozer & Associates, Ltd.
320 W. Ohio Street 7th floor
USA-Chicago III. 60610
Tel. 001 312-397 1133
Fax. 001 312-397 1233

NL Architects
Pieter Bannenberg
Van Hallstraat 294
NL-1051 HM Amsterdam
Tel. 0031 20-620 73 32
Fax. 0031 20-638 61 92
landmark@xs4all.nl

Fabio Novembre
Architetto
Via Mecenate 76
I-20138 Milano
Tel. 0039 02-504 104
Fax. 0039 02-502 375
www.novembre.it

Sandell Sandberg
Riddargatan 17 D II
S-11457 Stockholm
Tel. 0046 8-506 217 00
Fax. 0046 8-506 217 07
www.sandellsandberg.se

Studio d'architettura
Simone Micheli
Via Novelli 43
I-50135 Firenze
Tel. 0039 055-60 56 79
Fax. 0039 055-61 92 45
www.simonemicheli.com

The Formation Creative
Consultants Ltd.
Adrian Kilby
59 Charlotte Road
GB-London EC2A 3QW
Tel. 0044 20-7739 8198
Fax. 0044 20-7729 1950
www.theformation-cc.co.uk

Tromberend und Bathen
Hindenburgstr. 104
D-21335 Lüneburg
Tel. 0049 4131-39 11 12
Fax. 0049 4131-39 11 14

Matteo Thun
architecture, design,
communication
Via Appiani 9
I-20121 Milano
Tel. 0039 02-2900 0270
Fax. 0039 02-657 06 46
www.matteothun.com

20/20 Limited
20–23 Mandela Street
GB-London NW1 0DU
Tel. 0044 20-7383 7071
Fax. 0044 20-7383 7140
www.20.20.co.uk

Virgile and Stone Associates
25 Store Street South Crescent
GB-London WC1E 7BL
Tel. 0044 20-7323 3300
Fax. 0044 20-7323 5803
www.virgileandstone.com

Welonda
Design und Ladenbau
Berliner Allee 65
D-64274 Darmstadt
Tel. 0049 6151-34 27 60
Fax. 0049 6151-34 31 93
www.welonda.de

Pia Ziegler
Dipl.Ing. Arch. HdK
Neugutstrasse 15
CH-8002 Zürich
Tel./Fax. 0041 1-281 16 43

Bücher in der Verlagsanstalt Alexander Koch

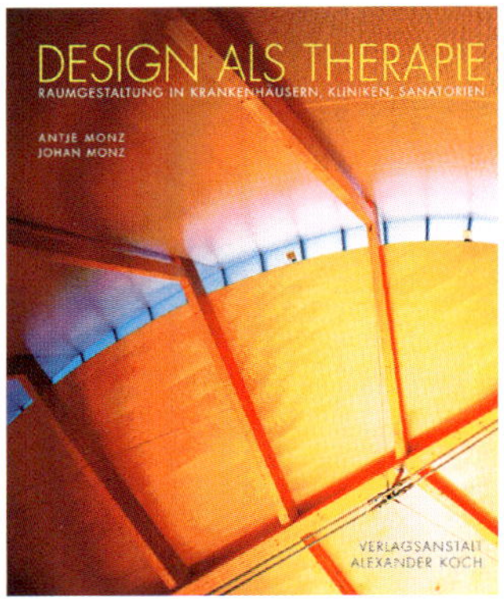

Design als Therapie
Raumgestaltung in Krankenhäusern, Kliniken, Sanatorien
Von Antje Monz und Johan Monz
176 Seiten, 388 Abbildungen, davon 272 in Farbe, Format 24,5 x 28,5 cm. Gebunden.
ISBN 3-87422-627-1

Eingang – Weg + Raum
Von Jürgen Knirsch
184 Seiten, 249 Fotos, davon 115 in Farbe, 171 Pläne/Zeichnungen. 24,5 x 28,5 cm. Gebunden
ISBN 3-87422-626-3

Hotels – Planen und Gestalten
Von Jürgen Knirsch
252 Seiten, 402 Abbildungen, davon 182 Pläne, Zeichnungen und 220 Fotos (132 in Farbe). Format 24,5 x 28,5 cm. Gebunden.
ISBN 3-87422-610-7

Messestand-Design
Temporäres Marketing- und Architekturereignis
Von Ingrid Wenz-Gahler
244 Seiten mit 552 z. Teil farbigen Fotos, Plänen und Zeichnungen, Format 24,5 x 28,5 cm. Gebunden.
ISBN 3-87422-622-0

Barrierefrei Bauen für Behinderte und Betagte
Hrsgg. von Axel Stemshorn
4. völlig überarbeitete und erweiterte Auflage.
512 Seiten, 864 Abbildungen,
Format 21,5 x 28,5 cm. Gebunden.
ISBN 3-87422-637-9

Arztpraxen
Gestaltete Räume für Arzt und Patient
Von Elmar Schossig – Sabine Damaschke – Bernadette Scheffer
200 Seiten, 373 Abbildungen,
Format 24,5 x 28,5 cm. Gebunden.
ISBN 3-87422-619-0

Wohnhauserweiterungen
Anbauten, Aufbauten, Ausbauten
Von Helmut Lerch
184 Seiten mit 210 Fotos, 246 Plänen und Zeichnungen, Format 24,5 x 28,5 cm. Gebunden.
ISBN 3-87422-642-5

Bausubstanz neu genutzt
Architektur individueller Arbeitsstätten
Von Helmut Lerch
168 Seiten, 235 Fotos, davon 65 farbig, 192 Pläne, davon 18 farbig, 3 Tabellen, Format 24,5 x 28,5 cm. Gebunden.
ISBN 3-87422-615-8

Mensch, Farbe, Raum
Grundlagen der Farbgestaltung
in Architektur, Design und Planung
Von Bettina Rodeck – Gerhard Meerwein –
Frank H. Mahnke
144 Seiten mit 207 Abbildungen, davon 78 Farb-Collagen, 80 Farbbilder, 36 Zeichnungen, Format 24,5 x 28,5 cm. Gebunden.
ISBN 3-87422-629-8

Büroräume Bürohäuser
Von Jürgen Knirsch
224 Seite, 236 Farbfotos, 220 Zeichnungen, Pläne und Diagramme, Format 24,5 x 28,5 cm. Gebunden.
ISBN 3-87422-643-3

Ladenplanung
Merchandising-Architektur
Strategien für Verkaufsräume: Gestaltungs-Grundlagen – Erlebnis-Inszenierungen – Kunden-leitweg-Planungen
Von Wilhelm Kreft
856 Seiten mit 1660 Fotos, Zeichnungen und Plänen.
Format 24,5 x 28,5 cm. Gebunden.
ISBN 3-87422-639-5

Café, Bar, Bistro
Design und Gastlichkeit
Von Ingrid Wenz-Gahler
192 Seiten mit 330 Farbfotos, Plänen. Text in deutsch und englisch, Format 24,5 x 28,5 cm. Gebunden.
ISBN 3-87422-638-7

Der Altbau
Renovieren, Restaurieren, Modernisieren
Von Otfried Rau und Ute Braune
360 Seiten, 650 Fotos, davon
33 farbig, 176 Zeichnungen,
Format 24,5 x 25,5 cm. Gebunden.
ISBN 3-87422-630-1

Architektur und Denkmal
Der Umgang mit bestehender Bausubstanz: Entwicklungen, Positionen, Projekte
Von Oskar Spital-Frenking
176 Seiten, 268 Fotos überwiegend in Farbe. 24,5 x 25,5 cm. Gebunden
ISBN 3-87422-640-9

Anzeige